2·6·79

GROUND UNDER OUR FEET

GROUND

UNDER OUR FEET

AN AUTOBIOGRAPHY

Richard T. *Ely*

ARNO PRESS

A New York Times Company

New York / 1977

Editorial Supervision: MARIE STARECK

———◆———

Reprint Edition 1977 by Arno Press Inc.

Reprinted from a copy in
  The Princeton University Library

THE ACADEMIC PROFESSION
ISBN for complete set: 0-405-10000-0
See last pages of this volume for titles.

Manufactured in the United States of America

———◆———

Library of Congress Cataloging in Publication Data

Ely, Richard Theodore, 1854-1943.
    Ground under our feet.

    (The Academic profession)
    Reprint of the 1938 ed. published by Macmillan, New
York.
    Bibliography: p.
    1. Ely, Richard Theodore, 1854-1943. 2. Economists
--United States--Biography. I. Title. II. Series.
[HB119.E5A3 1977]   330'.092'4 [B]   76-55184
ISBN 0-405-10011-6

GROUND UNDER OUR FEET

GROUND

UNDER OUR FEET

✿ ✿ ✿ ✿ ✿

AN AUTOBIOGRAPHY

by

Richard T. Ely

New York · 1938

✿THE MACMILLAN COMPANY✿

PRINTED IN THE UNITED STATES OF AMERICA
AMERICAN BOOK—STRATFORD PRESS, INC., NEW YORK

* * *

PREFACE

* * *

I WAS born before the Civil War. I have witnessed a panorama of events which has thrilled, saddened, inspired and ever kindled in me a burning desire to set the world right. I have been guided in my efforts by the philosophy that "the beginning and end of all is man." In my youth I was branded a "radical" for saying things which are today commonly accepted. This does not mean that the problems of the days of my youth have vanished. On the contrary, the conflicts raging today are essentially the same conflicts: between labor and capital, between government and industry; but they are being fought on a different plane. Technological advances have brought into view the possibility of abundance for all. Yet we do not have abundance for all. Therefore the battle rages between those who have and those who have not. Technological advances have resulted in a growing interdependence of human beings. Our economic relations are more and more closely interwoven, and more and more it is "one for all and all for one." Failure to act on this means disaster. If we apply ourselves intelligently and sanely to the problems of today we can look forward to a future worthy of man. If we unleash the forces of hatred, selfishness and brutality, we can look forward only to destruction.

Nearly half a century ago I made the following statement which is just as applicable today as when I first wrote it:

"The way which we must travel is long and weary, and yet it is one which affords delight in the prospect of progress. Looking into the future we may contemplate a society in which men shall work together for common purposes, and in which this wholesome co-operation shall take place largely through government, but through a government which has become less repressive and has developed its positive side."

This autobiography, itself, reveals a countless number of people to whom I am indebted for whatever I may have achieved in my lifetime. However, I must make special acknowledgment of a few whose contributions to this autobiography have been essential.

First of all among them is my sister, Miss Frances Mason Ely, who wrote *The Life and Letters of Richard T. Ely.* This manuscript, never intended for publication, was compiled with unusual skill and is based on a painstaking survey of letters and other records carefully preserved by my mother.

In the second place I must mention Professor Allan Nevins who holds a chair of history in Columbia University. This book was begun as a joint product with Professor Nevins. With the generous devotion of a true friend he withdrew as joint author, holding that my name alone should appear on the title page. Although not nominally an editor, in reality he has been an editor who has given me encouragement and helped me to express myself.

I cannot fail to express my obligation to my research associate, Miss Pearl Rosenthal, whose capacity for research and organization, whose literary skill and initiative have helped in countless ways to attain whatever excellence this work may have achieved. With untiring diligence she edited the manuscript and proofs, and prepared the index and chronological bibliography.

I must also mention Mr. A. S. Kenas, editor of *Summary & Sources,* who in a truly unselfish way has gone over the entire manuscript and has offered many invaluable suggestions.

It affords me pleasure to mention Dr. John H. Finley, Professor E. R. A. Seligman, Mr. William S. Kies and Mr. Robert H. Armstrong, who have read all or parts of the manuscript, and who have made helpful contributions. To these and to innumerable friends, of whom I have only mentioned a few, I express grateful appreciation.

Finally, I cannot fail to mention Dr. Josiah K. Lilly, whose generous contribution to the Ely Economic Foundation has made possible the completion of this work.

RICHARD T. ELY

COLUMBIA UNIVERSITY, NEW YORK
October 18, 1938

* * *

CONTENTS

* * *

IV.   Sowing the Seeds

V.   Reaping the Harvest

Appendices

* * *

ILLUSTRATIONS

* * *

GROUND UNDER OUR FEET

* * *

I

The Background of a Connecticut Yankee

* * *

THE HISTORY OF MY FOREFATHERS

WHO AM I? I am Richard T. Ely of the family of Old Lyme, Connecticut. I am the fifth Richard in direct line from the first Richard who settled there sometime between 1660 and 1670. There have been many Elys and many Richard Elys, who, like untold millions of human beings, have lived, married, had children, died, and been buried. Many of them stem from the first Ely family of Old Lyme and many have, at the end, returned to Old Lyme, where they have found a resting place in the beautiful Richard Ely cemetery. The heritage and traditions built up since 1660 have been a strong and inescapable influence in my life. I have wandered over the world and have lived in various parts of the United States and in other countries, but I am still a son of New England, a Connecticut Yankee.

Why should I write my autobiography? No individual is, in himself, of such importance that the world must be told the story of his life. But when significant social forces act through him, then there is adequate reason to tell the world about himself. Events which have taken place during my life would have taken place had I never lived. The conviction of my friends, that fully to understand a few of these events something should be known of my life, has prompted me to write this story.

1

Socrates' motto was "Know thyself." How difficult this is! Perfect self-knowledge is impossible, but I believe I may give a more comprehensive picture of myself if I examine the events of my life in the light of the history of my forefathers.

Three distinct settlements of the Elys were made in this country in the seventeenth century. The first was that of Nathaniel in Massachusetts in 1635, near the present city of Springfield. The second was that of Richard, on the banks of the Connecticut River at Lyme, shortly after 1660. The third was that of Joshua at Trenton, New Jersey, in 1685. The similarity of the coats of arms of these three indicates that they were branches of the same family. It is said that two relics of long ago, a tankard and a seal ring, also point to a common origin; but what that origin was has never been definitely determined. Various conflicting theories, each one involving romance, have been propounded by those who wished to believe in them. One theory holds that the tankard indicates great age. By a law which has been strictly enforced in England since the time of William and Mary, all sterling silver must have the "tower mark." The old tankard does not bear this or any other distinctive mark and therefore must antedate this time.[1] Both the tankard and the old seal ring bear the same coat of arms, the most significant feature of which is a triple fleur de lis. In ancient times the grant of the right to wear a fleur de lis on the family coat of arms appears to have been the highest mark of royal favor. It is alleged by some that our French ancestors were descended from a Huguenot who escaped the massacre of St. Bartholomew under the safe conduct of Charles IX of France, who gave him a pledge of safety—his own signet ring. It has been said that this story is curiously confirmed by a passage in *Ivanhoe*. Another tradition says that Charles presented the ring merely as a token of friendship to one of the ancestors of Richard Ely who was a high officer and a favorite of the King.

If either of these stories is true it must be that this Ely ancestor was a supporter of royalty. However, when Charles with his halberdiers and armed courtiers invaded the House of Commons in 1642, Richard aligned himself with the yeomanry and parliament. He was faithful not to the debased king, but to the law of the land.

This Richard was a Puritan, and in the year of the Restoration in England he felt obliged to renounce his home in Plymouth and come to the wilderness of the New World, so that he might be undisturbed in the free exercise of his religious faith. His arrival in Lyme about 1660 showed a sturdy adherence to principle which was well borne out in my father and the other Elys I have known. Another symbol of this trait is an old powder horn originally made and owned by Elihu Ely, great grandson of Richard Ely, who was born at Lyme, Connecticut, in 1735. It bears the inscription: "Made in Lyme, May 20th, year 1776, for the defence of Liberty. Liberty and no Slavery. Elihu Ely, owner." Elihu Ely was an officer of the Connecticut militia, took part in the battle of Saratoga, and was present at the surrender of Burgoyne in 1777. Both the powder horn and the sword he carried in these battles are now in the possession of Robert Erskine Ely, my cousin.

It is probable that the first Richard lived for a short time in Boston, with his son Richard. He was a widower and soon married a sister of Colonel Fenwick, the widow Cullick, who owned a tract of land in Lyme on which there was a debt of four hundred pounds. Richard Ely paid this debt, and when the land was transferred to him it caused him so much trouble that he found it necessary to take up his residence in Lyme. His estate consisted of three thousand acres of land, including what is still called "Ely's Ferry." In a few years the town of Lyme sold to his sons, Richard and William, one thousand three hundred acres adjoining their father's land, for two hun-

dred pounds, thus putting four thousand acres in the possession of the Elys of Lyme. Some of these lands are still in the
family.[2]

FREDONIA WAS NEW ENGLAND TRANSPLANTED

A strong attachment to the land is characteristic of nearly all
the Elys and of most New England families. New Englanders
like to own the land they live on and they cling to it as they do
to no other possession. This clinging to the land has had important economic consequences. It is the rule in any well-estab-
lished country that the net return on the capital invested in land
is low in proportion to the selling price and less than the return
of interest. Normally, one cannot borrow money to invest in
land and hope to repay it out of the income of the land. In
spite of this, we, in Connecticut, loved the land we owned and
would not let it go. I believe that this attitude, strongly im-
bedded in the "Connecticut Yankees," is a major explanation
for the remarkable lack of foreclosures in that state. In 1934, a
fellow economist and I visited Old Lyme and made a study of
foreclosures and land policies along the Connecticut River, beginning in Old Lyme at the mouth. We inquired of the various
town clerks, who were generally very intelligent women, about
the number of foreclosures, and our questions were answered
with puzzled looks: "Foreclosures? I don't remember. It seems
to me there was one three years ago." When we asked, "Any
distress sales of property?" the answer came quickly, "None."
At another town, the clerk could not recall; she thought that
perhaps there had been one four years ago. The replies were all
the same until we reached Middletown, a larger place, where
there were more foreclosures, but relatively few when compared
with those in Manhattan Island and other large urban centers.

The people of Connecticut pay their debts, and where I was

"Grandpa" Mason's House, Ripley, New York
Where Richard T. Ely Was Born

Second Richard Ely House, Old Lyme, Connecticut, 1700

brought up this creed was so applied that we looked upon a mortgage on a farm or a home as something of a stigma. The homes in the United States have been built more largely with the aid of building and loan associations than of any other agency. Generally speaking, they are still sound, but in some of the western states land booms have been followed by many failures. It has been reported that in Connecticut there has been only one failure of a building and loan association, and I have heard of the failure of only a few savings banks.[3]

Though my boyhood was spent in Fredonia, New York, life there was governed by the ideals and characteristics of Old Lyme, Connecticut. Fredonia was New England transplanted. My father and mother were married at her home in Ripley, New York, on March 2, 1853. Then they went to Southern Ohio where father was assistant engineer on the Sciota and Hocking Valley Railroad. The following winter, mother returned to her father's home in Ripley and there on April 13, 1854, I, Richard Theodore Ely, was born. Father came home to see me when I was about a month old. In the meanwhile, mother was suffering with the fever and ague which she had contracted in Ohio and she felt she could not return there. Father looked around Fredonia for a farm and in 1855 bought Deacon Seymour's farm which was one mile and a half northwest of Fredonia, toward the lake. We moved on April 3, 1856, and this was "home" for sixteen years.

The ideals and mode of living of the community in which I was brought up will be more readily understood if I briefly recount the history of Fredonia. Fredonia, New York, is pleasantly located between the hills of Chautauqua County and the shores of Lake Erie. The charms of its natural surroundings and its convenient situation upon one of the main highways between the east and the west have attracted a high class of intelligent and enterprising citizens.

Old records show that the land was first contracted for in 1803. The first three settlers were Thomas McClintock, Low Miniger, and David Eason. These three men in 1806 and 1807 sold out a large part of their holdings to Zattu Cushing and Hezekiah Barker and moved on to Westfield. Zattu Cushing, who became the first judge of Chautauqua County, reached Fredonia in February, 1805, coming from Oneida County with his wife and five children. They brought their household goods on two sleds, drawn by ox teams, and were three weeks making the journey. Between Buffalo and Silver Creek they nearly lost their lives traveling on the ice in a severe storm. They sheltered themselves as best they could behind the oxen and the sleds, and Judge Cushing blew on a horn until help came from the shore. They finally reached safety near Eighteen Mile Creek at one o'clock in the morning. Before daylight came, the ice was so badly broken that a later escape would have been impossible. Judge Cushing brought with him four cows, a barrel of salt, and a large quantity of apple seeds. For the remainder of the winter they lived in an unfinished house, with no door, no floor, and no chinking between the logs. For a floor, hemlock boughs were used to cover the bare earth.

As the land was cleared houses became larger and more rooms were added. When floors were put in they were made from split logs smoothed with an ax, doors were made the same way and held together with wooden pins—not a single nail was used. Many of our everyday appliances, such as matches, were unheard of then and life was necessarily plain and simple. Work required strength and patience; it was no small job to cut wood for buildings and fuel, and every man was an expert with an ax. Almost from infancy girls learned to sew, spin and weave, and a girl who reached her eighth birthday without having pieced a bed quilt was a family disgrace. The women made all the clothes for the family, spinning the yarn and weaving the cloth themselves. Little girls had to knit stockings and mittens as soon as they could hold the needles, and the shoes were usually made by the father of the family.[4] One of my earliest recollections is a pair of boots which Grandfather Mason made for me. They had a piece of red leather in front which was criss-crossed to form a diamond shape. When I first put them on I must have been wearing long pants for I remember sticking my pants into my boots as the farmers did and marching around the room to show off my beautiful new boots. I can recall, as if it were yesterday, the smiles of my father and mother.

Father was a civil engineer and did not know much about farming. But he believed that a farm was a good place to bring up children. He read the *Country Gentleman* and the agricultural columns of the *Tribune* to enable him to manage the farm efficiently. However, he always retained some fantastic notions about agriculture, such as the belief that crops grow while you sleep. We had all sorts of bad luck on the farm. Father cleared a fertile piece of ground on which to raise corn, but the crows ate the seeds and we had to go into buckwheat. We also lost one or two of our best cows. One, in rolling over, as cows sometimes do, could not regain her footing, and thus lost her life. Once, when we finally were successful in raising a tremendous crop of potatoes, we failed to get a good price for it.

The northern farm furnished a discipline of life which was invaluable. In many ways it was as strict as that of the German army, with which I came into contact years later. Although we had violent storms in western New York, it would never occur to me to look out of the window and say that on account of the blizzard I would leave the cows unfed or unmilked. As a child, I learned that there was work to be done and that was all there was about it. As a regular chore, I would go out to bring in chips for mother. This was not so hard as turning the old chain pump for water or working our old churn. How my little arms ached as I pushed the dasher up and down, up and down, up and down; it seemed the butter would never come. At harvest time, my brother George, who was younger than I, joined me in helping father. We were not strong enough to pitch hay on to the wagon or to pitch it from the wagon to the haymow. My father, however, pitched it both ways. When there was a stack of dishes to be wiped, I helped. Mother was one of the most rapid workers I have ever seen and I was just about able to keep up with her. In itself, this work was not disagreeable. What hurt me to the quick was to have one of the village boys see me at my task and call out, "Hello, Bridget!" This still rankles even after all these years. Every member in the family was expected to do his or her bit.

In the early years we had a servant only occasionally, but toward the last when mother began to teach painting at the Fredonia Academy our income was materially increased and we were able to have one regularly. However, all the time mother was teaching, often traveling a mile and a half to school and back again, she also managed to take care of the housework with the aid of but one girl. Her capacity was amazing and her store of energy seemed limitless.

Money was scarce and business was done largely by exchange. An old history says, "The first and only articles sent to market, for a number of years after the first settlement, were pot and pearl ashes, which were provisions of Nature to furnish means while the land was still being prepared for cultivation." [5] Montreal was the market and every settlement had its ashery. A later means of making money was stock-raising, and as there were no railways the stock had to be driven along the road to market. Traveling was done by horses or oxen hitched to lumber wagons in summer and by sleighs in winter.

The household was an economic unit capable of supplying its own needs. Although he was fairly prosperous, my Grandfather Mason probably never took in five hundred dollars in cash in any one year. His taxes probably never exceeded twenty-five dollars. Today, a man occupying the same position as my grandfather might have to pay about three hundred dollars in taxes. If my grandfather wanted to build a stable he engaged a couple of farm boys to help in the construction. One he may have paid fifty cents a day and perhaps he gave the other a calf. Those were the days of economic self-sufficiency and there was no reason to worry about money problems and bank failures. The interests of the community were more often centered in its churches and schools than in economic problems.

FREDONIA WAS A PROUD TOWN

The first school house was a log cabin which soon became too small to house the growing population since there were families with as many as twenty children. Soon a larger one of brick was put up; it is still standing and is now used as an apartment house. At first there was no "school tax," but instead a "rate bill," and a man was assessed not according to his property but according to the number of children he sent to school. In time the unfairness of this became apparent and the method of property taxation was established. There were no compulsory education laws and children stayed home to work when they were needed. Therefore, winter school was always much larger than the summer school, for the big girls and boys were not so much needed at home. Usually the winter teacher was a man and the summer teacher a woman, though once in a while a woman capable of enforcing discipline would teach the whole year. My mother was one of these women. When she was thirteen years old she was granted a teacher's certificate. She taught in district schools all around Ripley and was successful in gaining the love and admiration of her pupils. In one district where the pupils had rebelled and turned out the man teacher, the trustees came to mother and asked her to take the school and straighten things out. She asked the equal of men's wages, a higher wage than any women teachers were getting at the time. Their immediate response was one of surprise at her demands. Of course, they couldn't pay so much because she was a woman! She argued thus: "If I succeed where these men have failed, don't you think I should receive the same sum as those who failed?" Finally, they accepted her terms. At the start the students were wild and tried to torment her. Before long they became her ardent supporters. The following incident reveals her ability to handle people and explains why she succeeded where the men failed. When the students were coasting and she wanted them to return to the schoolroom she knew that by ringing the bell as a signal they would be tempted to stay a little longer. Instead, she put on her things and went out to join them, took a slide or two with them and then said, "Now for the school house." They came willingly.

The Fredonia Academy was the first institution of higher learning in Chautauqua County and was opened October 4, 1826, with a faculty of three instructors. There was recently discovered in the overhauling of papers, laid away a century ago, the original list of subscribers and subscriptions for the erection of the Fredonia Academy.

The academy was founded largely through contributions "in kind." The total value of the subscriptions amounted to $890, of which only $75 was pledged in cash. One subscriber contracted to give ten days of carpenter work, and one to do cabinet work valued at $30. Others offered $10 in labor and lumber and $20 in shoes; $40 "in some kind of property;" 3,000 feet of floor plank; 6,000 feet of clapboards; $3 in pork and 10 bushels in corn and rye; two hundredweight of beef and 2,000 feet of hemlock lumber; $10 "in sash;" $25 in "hats and shingles;" a cow "to be worth $15;" $15 in nails or glass, or in grain or cattle; two tons of hay. One subscriber gave "20 gallons of whiskey," which was a way of saying: "Be of good courage."[6]

The school had a very useful educational career before the time of extensive secondary school training, now provided throughout the state in the public high schools. Its curriculum carried various subjects beyond the range of ordinary schools and into the college realm. For many years Fredonia was the leading school town in Chautauqua County, but after the Civil War most villages put academic departments into their schools, and Fredonia seemed about to lose her supremacy. At the critical time Willard McKinstry, then editor of the Fredonia *Censor,* while looking over the session laws just received from the secretary of state for publication in the *Censor,* noticed an act providing for the establishment of four more state normal schools. Mr. McKinstry called a conference of about ten men to consider what steps should be taken toward getting a normal school for the village. After the New England fashion, they thought it best to call a public meeting. A call was sent out by one hundred and nineteen of the leading citizens and a meeting was held in Concert Hall, September 28, 1866. A prominent lawyer of the village was so eloquent and convincing that the state officers announced Fredonia as the location for the new normal school. Fredonia, alone, without even county help, offered to give the site and erect a suitable building. The cost to the village was set at one hundred thousand dollars, which was much greater than was at first expected. The total assessed valuation of the whole village was about a million dollars and the population a little under twenty-five hundred. But the taxpayers were proud of the educational status of Fredonia and willingly assumed the burden, selling 8 percent bonds to raise the necessary money. The financial ability of the trustees must have been of a high order, for the interest was always promptly paid and in twenty years the entire debt was discharged. Soon after its opening the academic department of the academy was incorporated in the normal school so that it was not merely a training school for teachers but also a general academic preparatory school. The Fredonia Normal School has always been considered one of the best in the state.

It has been said that Fredonia is a town of "firsts." Fredonia was the first town in the world where natural gas was used for illuminating purposes. The site of the original gas well, near the bridge over the Canadaway Creek, on West Main Street, is marked by a boulder and a bronze tablet erected by the D.A.R. The first organization of the Grange was effected at Fredonia. It was here that the name "Women's Christian Temperance Union" was first used. Miss Ellen Adams in her *Tales of Early Fredonia* writes that Fredonia had the first bathtub in Chautauqua County; Addison Crosby, who invented the first horseless carriage, also arranged the first bathroom in the Crosby house at Cordova. The tub was a cedar log from Ohio that was cut to a suitable length, chiseled out, and smoothed. The log was well oiled on the outside and rubbed till perfectly smooth inside. The water came from a well over which Addison Crosby had built a windmill. After the family left Cordova the tub was used for a watering trough for many years.[7]

One of the famous occasions in the history of Fredonia was the visit of General Lafayette on June 4, 1825, at the time of his good-will tour. He was received with great enthusiasm; the town was brightly decorated, music was furnished by a local band, and speeches were made in his honor. Ellen Adams, in her book on Fredonia, tells how the women of Fredonia wished to appear at their best when they bowed before the General. At that time a handsome Paisley shawl was owned by a generous woman who thought it would be a good idea to wear it

herself when she was presented to the General and then pass
it on to her friends. Evidently the shawl was very effective and
made an impression on the observant General, for afterward he
remarked, "Nowhere, even in the large cities, have I seen
handsomer shawls than those worn by the ladies of Fredonia."

THE CONNECTICUT YANKEES HAD A HARSH RELIGION

In the earliest days of the new settlement the founders of
Fredonia held meetings to give thanks to God for his protecting
care and to seek guidance in the everyday affairs of life. The
records of the Baptist Church show that when Judge Cushing
came in 1805 he and "five brethren and four sisters thought it
proper to meet on Lord's days to recommend the cause of
Christ and confirm each other in faith." In September, 1808,
articles of faith and a covenant were adopted and a council of
ministers met at Judge Cushing's home where the sixteen
"brethren and sisters" were examined and received into the
fellowship. In 1813, Judge Cushing was licensed to preach.
This Baptist Church was the second church organized in the
county, only the Presbyterian Church of Westfield being earlier;
but it is believed that the Fredonia Baptists were the first
to have a "meeting house," an old frame building which was
finished about 1822. The Presbyterian Church, organized September, 1810, was first founded as Congregational, but a few
years afterward adopted the Presbyterian form of government.
The Methodist Church was formed in 1811 and the first church
building, which is still standing, was turned into a barn when
the second church was built. The Trinity Episcopal Church was
organized in 1822 and was received in the New York State convention of the Protestant Church.[8]

In my childhood the relations between these churches were
far from cordial. Neighbors fought bitterly on matters of creed.

Religious beliefs were hotly argued over and all day visits were devoted to discussions of foreordination and predestination, immersion or sprinkling, infant baptism, eternal damnation, etc. Religious controversies were very much more violent in my childhood and early manhood than now and played a large role in my life. There were many preachers in the Ely family who were orthodox Congregationalists, except in western New York. It appears that since the Congregationalists and the Presbyterians had essentially the same faith at that time the orthodox Congregationalists agreed to give western New York to the Presbyterians. My father, an orthodox Presbyterian, claimed that the Presbyterians were not equally scrupulous, for they invaded the territory assigned to the Congregationalists. Far be it from me to enter into such a controversy; I mention it merely to suggest something of the nature of the Connecticut Yankees. Zebulah Ely is occasionally mentioned as a preacher, but the best known was Ezra Styles Ely of Philadelphia, who made something of a name for himself as a writer, and who was evidently prominent among the Presbyterians.

The religion of the people of Connecticut was a hard religion; the wrath of God as emphasized in the Old Testament predominated, and since the texts of sermons were generally taken from the Old rather than the New Testament we heard a great deal about an angry God. The future was dreaded as one of fire and brimstone, and the austere mode of living gave a discipline of life which had as its aim the building of character. My father took this very seriously and it helped to make his life rather a gloomy one. He was firm in his beliefs. His New England conscience was partly responsible for his quitting his last regular job as a civil engineer in railway construction. When he found that the job would have obliged him to work on the "Sabbath" he resigned, in spite of the fact that we needed his regular income. His New England conscience asserted itself in other ways which were financially injurious. My father would see a hay crop injured or even ruined by a rain on a Sabbath day, but he would not go to gather it as his neighbors did. Our farm would have made a good barley farm, but he would not raise barley on it because barley was chiefly used for the manufacture of beer.

On Sunday we were not allowed to play nor were we allowed to read anything but religious books. These were Sunday school books of fiction, extremely poor fiction, all patterned along the same line. Always the good were rewarded and the wicked punished. Every Sunday I went to Sunday school and recited several verses from the Bible. I look back on that experience without distress, and in fact with some satisfaction. After the recitation period there followed a long and dreary sermon and then a midday meal which we took with us from the farm and which we ate in or around the church in the afternoon. Gambling or anything approaching it was regarded as a terrible sin. I was not allowed to play marbles for "keeps" with the other boys and this shut me out of this sport, which the other boys would not play otherwise than for "keeps."

Those who know the religious history of New England will probably not be surprised that my father frowned upon the observance of Christmas. He thought that the customary celebration was in the direction of papacy and papacy was the "scarlet woman" in the Bible. But mother insisted that we should have the joys of Christmas and ultimately father's disapprobation waned, for my mother's wishes prevailed in this matter.

I remember one painful incident illustrating my father's nonconformist views. He felt that rich and poor alike should be welcome in the house of God and that there should be no distinction of dress between the rich and poor. Once he appeared in church in his farmer's overalls, much to the distress of the family.

Strongly did I wish to gratify my father and become a good Presbyterian. Conversion meant, however, a certain transformation by a mystical process. Faith was emphasized, and faith meant an acceptance of the Gospel in the light of this mystical transformation. Good works had nothing to do with it. Coupled with this was the old doctrine of infant damnation of the unbaptized, although this, even in my early childhood, was soft-pedaled. Try as I would I could not become converted, and I finally gave up the attempt to please my father in this particular. I always rejected the idea of a good God creating the human race and then tolerating arrangements which sent a large part of it to eternal torture. How is this compatible with the omnipotence of God and the all-embracing love that Christ taught? My last unsuccessful effort to become a good Presbyterian occurred when I was at Columbia College and attended the Fifth Avenue Presbyterian Church under Dr. John Hall. However, I gave that up. My Uncle Eugene Hough, with whom I was living and whose generosity made it possible for me to go to Columbia, was an ardent Universalist. This belief in universal salvation appealed to me strongly and for a short time, to the great distress of my father, I had a mind to become a Universalist preacher. This idea was short-lived, and in the course of my religious odyssey, I finally went over to the Protestant Episcopal Church which I thought offered a fuller and richer life.

One particularly strong New England trait, to a large degree an outgrowth of the rigid New England religion, was thrift. Those brought up in this religion were taught to think of the future and this habit of foregoing gratifications in the present and looking forward to the future was carried over into the economic sphere. Whenever I think of New England thrift I am reminded of a middle-aged New England spinster who was associate professor of Latin at the University of Wisconsin. In speaking of her relatives in Massachusetts, she said, almost in a whisper, "They save nothing!" It seemed to me that she was more horrified than she would have been had they broken all the Ten Commandments.

Another typical New England trait was sincerity. Things must not appear to be different from what they actually were. Since our means were limited my mother bought some plate silver. Father was greatly troubled because he felt that plate silver was ostentatious. He once told me about a Connecticut deacon who had the clapboards of his house planed on both sides. How absurd this seems to us now! Although Father would never have done that, he had a kind of sneaking admiration for this deacon who would not tolerate an appearance not based on reality. Mortification of the flesh was also an outstanding trait of the old New Englander; fleshly enjoyment was contrary to the asceticism of New England theology. For example, mirrors were frowned upon as administering to vanity. My father had a certain admiration for a New England deacon who could shave without the use of a mirror. Supposedly, looking into the mirror might cultivate vanity.

The Connecticut people, hard working and thrifty, with their strict consciences and harsh religion, with their high standards of sincerity and truth, with their intense devotion to the land, seem to many outside the State, and particularly in the South, to be hard and to lack in higher spiritual values. But when we observe the many evidences of the appreciation of beauty in the architecture and other art forms (Old Lyme is particularly noted as an art center), and when we see the warmth of affection in the typical family life, we become aware of another quality, quite different from the traditional hardness of the Connecticut Yankee, but no less real.

MY PARENTS

My attempt at self-analysis has given me a keen realization of the powerful influence of heredity. I shall, therefore, try to give the reader a picture of the family from which I sprang.

My father's mother was Irene Stetson. When she was very young, her father and mother died within a day of each other and she was adopted by her uncle, Amasa Stetson of Boston. He was worth more than half a million dollars, a sum sufficient to make him one of the wealthiest men of his time; and my grandmother was brought up with all the cultural advantages which money could buy. However, Amasa Stetson was a Unitarian, and a breach was opened between them when on a visit to relatives she was converted to orthodox Congregational teachings. On her return she tried to convert Uncle Amasa, fearing that he was doomed if he remained a Unitarian. The dissension between them caused her to leave home, and to add to his displeasure, she ultimately married my grandfather, a Presbyterian minister. Her uncle planned to disinherit her, but died suddenly without leaving a will. The fortune he left was so great that after the lawyer took his "pickings," which I am told were very large, and the widow received her third of the estate, there remained ten thousand dollars apiece for twenty-eight nieces and nephews.

My father's parents had been too poor to give him the advantages of a college education which he so desired, and which his father had obtained at Williams College. However, he did attend two academies of the New England type—one in Fredonia, and the other in Geneseo, where he received an education superior to that offered by most high schools today. It is remarkable, considering the effect which modern high school training has on the average boy, that he acquired the habit of reading Latin for pleasure. Once when he was riding on a train

Father and Mother

he left the book he was reading on the seat. Imagine the aston-
ishment of a stranger who curiously examined it, and found not
the expected novel, but a Latin work by one of the most difficult
authors, perhaps Juvenal. This fondness for the Latin classics
remained with him until the end of his life. In a letter dated
1899, and believed to be his last, he wrote: "I have been confined to the house for some weeks doing nothing hardly except
reading Curtius's *Life of Alexander,* [Latin, of course] which
is quite more lively than Caesar, which I have read through as
well as Curtius."

His thirst for knowledge was great and the disappointment
must have been keen when he was unable to go to college. In
writing to his mother on September 9, 1845, he said: "Now,
however good and desirable a thing a liberal education may be
(and who reads all hearts knows that I do thirst to know a little
more, to taste but a small draught from the ocean and eternity
of wisdom—pardon enthusiasm) yet there are certain bounds
which reason, justice, yea virtue, forbids to pass and though it
be necessary, I am willing to barely live along for the sake of
attending school if you are not able without involving yourself
in debt to pay my schooling and way and without subjecting
yourself to the trials incident to debt (worse than poverty) in
your feeble age I would rather, much rather, leave the study
for some occupation, though I should feel it sorely were I compelled to so do."

This love of learning was to be found in many New England
families and it was particularly marked in my father's family.
Many years ago when I was visiting Yale University, I took
lunch with President Hadley. He brought out a list of the
alumni; among them we found at least a hundred Elys, most
of whom had some sort of connection with our family.

I think it may fairly be said that my mother's family, although they were poorer in material goods than my father's,

were well loved and respected by their neighbors; no person in
the community was more highly regarded than my grandfather,
who was a farmer, a builder, and I know not what else besides.
My mother's family started in Massachusetts, stopped for a while
at Fort Ann in the Adirondacks, where my mother was born,
and then moved to Ripley in Chautauqua County. The widow
of my mother's uncle wrote to me about the trip to Chautauqua.
"I can well remember when our folks started for the 'far west'
(Chautauqua County), as it was regarded then. They were in a
big wagon—no cover. I can't tell you how many miles it was
from Fort Ann to Ripley, but I thought it was a long way, for
it was winter when we started in a sleigh, and we ended in a
wagon."

My father was an ardent wooer and it is said that once he
walked all the way from Fredonia to Ripley, some twenty-five
miles, to see his wife-to-be, and whenever he met anyone he
could not refrain from telling him that he was going to see
Harriet Mason. My mother and father built about them a home,
which though often poor in material things was rich in understanding and affection.

I was very fond of my Grandma and Grandpa Mason, and
many of the happiest days of my childhood were spent with
them. My earliest recollection is of a day when I was not quite
four years old. I remember swinging back and forth on a swing
which my father made for me in the kitchen and singing a
prayer: "Oh, God, please send my brother George and me a
baby sister." God answered my prayers and my sister Frances
was born.

Mother often drove the three of us to Ripley to see grandma
and grandpa. She counted up fifteen hundred miles that she
had driven Fannie, the horse, on these long trips. My love for
grandpa was so ardent that I never wanted to return home
from our visits to Ripley. Once I hid in the barn, hoping that I

Sister, Frances Mason Ely

Brother, George Stetson Ely

would not be taken back to Fredonia. My grandfather died August 9, 1861, and the following winter I spent at Grandma Mason's and went to school there. After her death a year later, I stayed with my Aunt Kittie and Uncle George, the last two left in the old home.

My mother's courage, unselfishness, and boundless love for all of us made home a very happy place. She was a woman of tremendous energy, ingenuity, and versatility. Physically, she was small and frail, and her health was never of the best. But nothing could stop her from using her great natural talents in every possible way. Whatever she did, whether it was raising flower seeds or making paper or wax flowers, she did better than anyone else in the community. She had natural talent as a painter, and without adequate training became one of the best artists in the history of Fredonia. Her paintings, often exhibited at the Chautauqua County fairs, took most of the prizes. She often withheld some of her paintings from the exhibits so that her pupils might carry off some of the awards. She sold many of her paintings and thereby helped George and me to go to college and my sister Frances to study music. If I have abundant energy I know that I have it rightfully from my mother. If I have kept a youthful spirit that, too, has come to me from both my parents. My mother was the type who never grew old. When she was an old woman young girls could talk to her about their love affairs as if she were one of them. My father, too, was loved by the young people. At his funeral a prominent attorney said that they spoke of him as "the old man with the young man's voice."

My father was a civil engineer and his proficiency in this field was well recognized by the members of our community. Poor as we were on the farm, I always felt that my father was a superior man, and that his superiority was appreciated by our neighbors. As a small lad it gave me satisfaction that the farmers of the neighborhood, in dividing the cheese from their cheese factory, always called on father to determine a fair division.

He was an enthusiastic student and by strict application, for which he had an extraordinary capacity, he learned much of many branches of science and literature. He was particularly noted for his library, which was far better than any other farmer's library and surpassed most of those in the village. From his early youth books were an integral part of his life. He could not do without them. Such a letter as the following, written in 1846, testifies to his interest in literature: "Send if you please, to me all the good poetry that you can get out of any papers that you may or can get hold of by Longfellow, Bryant, Dana, or Pierpont, and those of the 'upper ten thousand' will be acceptable. Even old pieces I would like when they are good, such as Campbell's, Goldsmith's, etc."

His interest in the natural sciences led Professor Charles Smith of the University of Wisconsin to observe "that the man of unusual power of mind differs greatly from ordinary mortals in what he sees with his eyes. Mr. Ely 'brought an eye for all he saw.' " Dr. Balthasar H. Meyer of the Interstate Commerce Commission tells of the time when he and my father were members of a party which took a short trip on Lake Mendota. My father was not only "unquestionably the most active man among us during the voyage, but he showed an intimate knowledge of nature. He told about such things as the grasses and pebbles in the water, the fishes, the nature of the bottom of the lake, how to make an estimate of the depth of the water, the relief of the land adjacent to the lake, and the trees in the forest. During a short stop he would not rest, but went ashore and examined the great boulders on the water's edge, appealing to both the captain and to a man near the beach for local information." Dr. Meyer appraised him as "the kind of an old man from whom a young man has very much to learn."

He was alive with a desire to correct the abuses he saw about him. Dr. Meyer recalls another occasion when my father attended a meeting of one of my economic seminars. The topic was the problems of rural society, and he expressed opinions which made a strong impression on everyone present. "He soon left the narrower field upon which we had concentrated our attention and took the position that unless our rural population, in common with all other classes, had something beyond material things to live for, our suggestions concerning their improvement would come to nothing." Then he concluded with these words: "Back of it all lies the man."

Above all, as this phrase indicates, my father was a humanitarian and a believer in social progress. Whatever might be our Fate in the Hereafter, it was our job to make the present world better—this was his philosophy. In our family prayers each morning he repeated a phrase the substance of which was that we could not be real Christians unless we contributed our part to the betterment of our fellow-men. Hamlet said, "The time is out of joint. Oh, cursed spite that ever I was born to set it right." My father was ever guided by a strong desire "to set it right." And I, too, even in boyhood, felt this same desire to "set the world on fire." Looking back on my father and the Elys who preceded him, I seem to have come honestly by this tendency to be a rebel. I recall certain incidents of my early youth which reveal this trait. We had a thirty acre meadow with many stones, which made use of the mowing machine difficult. Without saying anything to my father, I enlisted the services of my younger brother George and my sister Frances, hitched the old team of horses to the lumber wagon, cleared the stones, and piled them in one big heap. The last time I saw the old farm the pile of stones was still there. Furthermore, I was not pleased with the annual yield of hay. From the agricultural columns of Horace Greeley's *Tribune* I got the idea that it would be a good thing to sprinkle salt over the meadow. I collected old fish barrels which contained salt left after the fish had been taken out. The result was such a large hay crop that we could not get it all into the barn. My agricultural friends tell me that salt has no fertilizing quality; if this is true, the explanation must be that some remnants of the fish remained in the barrels.

A few years ago I came across an article by my father on the Chautauqua County jail, which he denounced as a disgrace to any civilized community. He wrote: "It certainly is worthy of grave consideration, whether the present method of congregating, herding together, criminals in the County jail, be not a fruitful cause, a promotion of crime. There are two objects for which prisons may be properly, defensibly used: The protection of society and the reformation of criminals. With respect to the first, I believe the jail furnishes only a slight and temporary relief, and as to the second, it fails, worse than fails; it works a contrary result." He asks a question which is still asked, "Will those having them directly in charge think of these things?"

It is to his credit that although he recognized the strength of the resistance to reform, this did not prevent him from taking the initial step, even if he knew he could never live to see it come to fulfillment. He often said, "Live as if you were going to die today and also live as though you were not going to die at all." It appears that this philosophy was adopted by other Elys. For example, my father's cousin Calvin Keeney of Le Roy, New York, a man of some note and means, planted an apple orchard on his farm in Michigan. When he was putting out his orchard, one of his neighbors came along and said jeeringly, "Keeney, do you expect to live forever?" Keeney answered, "If I do not live to gather the apples, someone else will."

My father was not one of those Yankees who went West and carved fortunes out of the natural resources and other opportunities so abundant in the pioneer state. He was not that kind of a Yankee. His New England conscience was too sensitive for the "rough and ready" work of the daring pioneers. He cared too much for reading, music, and the arts to concentrate on money making. How well I remember him leaning back in his rocking chair, his eyes closed, listening to my sister Frances play Beethoven. Beauty was sacred to him. On our thirty acre meadow we had several large beautiful elm trees. They reduced the fertility of the soil and lessened the yield of hay. Many farmers would have cut them down, but to him it would have been almost sacrilege to destroy their beauty.

My father defined his objects in life in a letter written in 1852. "My highest ambition with regard to myself is to have the heart to do good at all times, to all; to have the love of some virtuous intelligent Christian woman, to have the means and opportunity to study and read some, to live tolerably comfortably and to die at peace with God and all men."

One day, in the year 1899, he was reading his Bible, and as he looked up at a man who had just delivered vegetables to the door, the Bible slipped out of his hands—he was dead.

II

Feeling for the Ground

I GO TO DARTMOUTH AND AM SUSPENDED

WHEN I WAS SEVENTEEN I went to Mayville to teach in a country school and to decide where I would go to college the following year. I wrote to the folks at home, "I think teaching will be splendid"—but the bad cooking and other unpleasant physical details made me realize what a nice place home was. At the end of 1871, Father went to work on the Warren and Venango Railroad and since my brother George was helping him, I came home to care for the farm. I consulted with Dr. Homer Fuller, Principal of the Fredonia Academy, about the choice of a college. He was a Dartmouth man and did not have much information about any of the other colleges, so I decided on Dartmouth. I set out on August 20, 1872, armed with a letter of introduction from Dr. Cassety of the Fredonia Normal School and with fifty dollars in my pocket. Of that sum, thirty dollars came from the sale of a stall connected with the Presbyterian church which had housed our horse and buggy, and which we no longer needed after we moved to the village.

When I arrived at Hanover, I duly presented my letter of introduction to President Asa Dodge Smith. I was received with the kindly paternal air with which he greeted all the "boys," as he fondly called his undergraduates. He was particularly kind to me, and he generously granted me free tuition. At the time I characterized him as "the nicest fellow" I ever knew; later on,

I found that he had to pay seventy dollars out of his own pocket. I shall never cease to be grateful, for I do not know how I would have managed without his help.

Hanover was a place of about two thousand inhabitants. I wrote home that "part of the place looks pretty ancient but part is very pretty indeed. The college campus or 'village green' contains six acres and is surrounded by shade trees, large elms and maples, very pretty houses, and five or six college buildings." I roomed in a third floor, rather low half-story room, for which my room-mate and I paid twelve dollars and fifty cents apiece for the school year. I boarded in a club of about forty, paying three dollars and seventy-five cents a week. After three weeks, I wrote to Mother: "This staying away from home is about like getting used to being hung." But I did get used to it and managed to have a good time.

The Reverend Asa Smith had been head of a Presbyterian church in New York and his method of discipline was decidedly of the old school. When he became President of Dartmouth, he immediately restored the marking system, prescribed rules of conduct which were signed by faculty and students, distributed prizes for composition and history, and put back into the curriculum the full quota of dead languages of his day. But his paternal feelings for his "boys" outweighed the harshness of the discipline. On one occasion he suspended three sophomores for taking part in a "cane rush" and then wrote to their parents, to save them too severe a scolding, that he had chosen them for suspension because their physical and mental powers were superior, and therefore the measure would be more effective in maintaining discipline.

Once I was suspended for participating in a freshman strike. At the time it seemed tragic, but in retrospect it appears amusing. The situation was this: One of the rules which had been set by the trustees, and by which all students had agreed to abide, provided that we should attend three recitations a day. Our young tutor, Francis Brown, prescribed a fourth recitation in Greek. As a matter of conscience we believed that we should not attend this fourth class, and decided to cut it. After a short absence most of the students drifted back, but three of us, a classmate, Brooks, who afterwards attained distinction at the bar in Massachusetts, Dutton, and I, held out. Like the old Puritans we stood up for our rights. La Forest Dutton was a man who would have burned at the stake for his principles. He never came back, but went to Princeton and died there in 1875. Brooks and I finally capitulated on account of the distress of our parents. The faculty made it as easy as possible for us to sign a statement and thus to be reinstated.

President Smith found the college under the burden of a heavy debt and he started a campaign to raise one hundred thousand dollars through the churches. He succeeded in raising only a few hundred dollars, and was unable to effect the reforms he would have liked. The college library, for example, was a sad reflection of the poverty of Dartmouth at this time. The few volumes were poorly catalogued and contained a good deal of duplication. The library was unheated in spite of the severity of the winters, but this made little difference, since it was open only one hour twice a week. It was presided over by an undergraduate who received sixty dollars a year for his services. The dormitories were as inadequate as the library, and their bare discomfort and lack of plumbing were typical of those "horse and buggy days."

The alumni, dissatisfied with these conditions, requested that they be allowed to elect from their membership a certain number of the twelve trustees and thus be given a voice in the active management of the College. This move was prompted by the fact that most of the trustees were far past middle age and were not easily persuaded to consent to changes. President Smith, the trustees, and all of the faculty were strongly opposed to the proposal. They demonstrated this by promptly filling two vacancies on the board from within their own ranks and inviting the alumni to appoint an advisory board. The alumni stubbornly maintained their stand, and only at the end of a twenty years' battle did they gain their object. This change in the membership of the board of trustees had a remarkable effect in hastening the reforms and improvements which increased Dartmouth's popularity tremendously. If President Smith had been sufficiently open-minded, perhaps this would have come sooner. But even in my day, the alumni movement was paving the way for the immense popularity which Dartmouth enjoys today.

Athletics were actively participated in by a majority of the students. Football was particularly popular as a daily exercise and was played every afternoon except on Sundays and on days when it rained heavily. The game was a modification of English rugby, in which a spherical air-inflated ball was used. It was so organized that any number of students could participate. On entering college an equal number of students was assigned to the two literary societies, known as the Social and the Fraters, and on this basis the membership of the teams was decided. If any think it must have been an effeminate game because we used an air-inflated ball and no protective armor, they are greatly mistaken. Baseball, too, had been played for several years, and while I was there we had our first contest with an outside college, and won.

In 1872 and 1873 nearly every member of the student body became the victim of a boating mania. We bought a six-oared shell and entered a contest with twelve other colleges in their annual regatta in Southern waters. We wished to show them what the sturdy lads of the North, with muscles hardened in a vigorous climate, could do. One night in the fourth year of this sport a Connecticut River flood carried away the boathouses and boats, and this marked the end of shell-racing for the members of my class.

I GO TO COLUMBIA AND WIN THE FELLOWSHIP

At the end of 1872 my mother's sister, who lived in New York City, was left desolate by the loss of her only daughter, and urged me to come and live with her. In our straitened circumstances it was a great help to have a home offered to me. In addition, the prospect of attending Columbia College appealed to me. However, with the advent of the crisis of 1873, and the stoppage of all work on the railway with which my father was connected, I even thought of giving up college for a while and trying to get a teaching position. My parents would not hear of it, and since Columbia generously offered me free tuition, and my aunt and uncle offered me a home, I decided to go to Columbia. My uncle and aunt lived in rooms adjoining their photograph galleries at 487 Eighth Avenue; there was little place to study, and I had to sleep in one of the reception rooms for customers, but I was full of elation when I entered Columbia as a sophomore in 1873.

For nearly one hundred years Columbia College had found its home in the "limehouse" with the cupola on Park Place, completed in 1760. This had long been a delightful college site, but by 1850 commerce and business were beginning to crowd it; a plan for a new building was, therefore, conceived. Pending its construction, the college removed to what it regarded at the time as a temporary home, the old Deaf and Dumb Asylum between Madison and Fourth Avenues at Forty-eighth and Forty-ninth Streets. This old building with its columns and porticoes became a permanent site when the war interrupted other plans. It was to this building that I walked each day from my home many blocks away. One small block was sufficient to hold the entire university, including chapel, library, and even the president's home. President Barnard, who was appointed in 1864, had been connected with the deaf and dumb asylum years before. He was a veteran educator, having been graduated from Yale in 1828 and become Chancellor of the University of Mississippi. With his accession to the presidency, a new era in the history of Columbia was inaugurated. When he came there about one hundred and fifty students were enrolled in the college and the school of mines. We saw very little of President Barnard except at chapel exercises, where he seemed very dignified and venerable with his impressive white beard. Students saw so little of him that to them he appeared indifferent, and they in turn neither liked nor disliked him. I, and many others, supposed that President Barnard was satisfied with Columbia as it was. However, we were all aware that certain unfortunate conditions called for remedies.

One of the improvements which the Columbia of my day sorely required was adequate facilities for study. The library was open two or three hours a day; but the librarian, Mr. Betts, seemed to resent its use. He had what he considered a fine collection of books, which were meant to be looked at rather than read. After classes, when I went to the library to study, I would hardly begin, it seemed, when he would tell me it was time to close. Then when I tried to study in the classrooms, I would only get fairly started when the cleaning man came around and asked me to leave. This was one of the handicaps of students all the time I was at Columbia.

I later learned from Andrew D. White that President Barnard earnestly desired to remedy such shortcomings as these. He asked White, then recently chosen president of Cornell, to come to New York and make what we would now call a "sur-

Richard T. Ely: Junior at Columbia College, 1874

vey" of conditions at Columbia. At that time, Columbia laid aside each year a surplus of ninety thousand dollars. The trustees thought this was an admirable policy. Since the expenses were fully covered and each year there was a handsome margin, what more could be asked? Dr. White did not agree with this mercantile point of view. He told the trustees that they should be ashamed of themselves, for such a college surplus was a token of stagnation. He recommended that they should spend not only the ninety thousand dollars surplus, but another sum equal to it, and then appeal to the alumni to make up the deficit. His philosophy was, "We never made a friend at Cornell by doing something for him, but when he does something for us, he becomes our friend." Barnard, in adopting this policy, launched Columbia upon the tremendous growth which still continues.

It is my judgment that Columbia College, even at that time, was the equal of any college in the United States. It was definitely not on a university level—it was simply a college; but nearly every professor was an outstanding man. I realized, from the time I took my entrance examinations, that here was a faculty which "had the cussedest way of finding out what a fellow didn't know." Dr. Henry A. Short held the chair in Latin. He was an erudite scholar, but his instruction was not at all pedantic. He was a man of the world, and enhanced the value of his work by pointed observations on life. He would compare Latin literature with English literature in a way that illuminated both the Latin and the English. I got a great deal out of Dr. Short's courses, and feel I could not have gained more anywhere else.

Dr. Henry Drisler, who had edited both Greek and Latin lexicons, held the chair in Greek. He also was a fine scholar, but he stuck pretty close to the Greek and lacked the spirit and vivacity of Short. He was a kindly old man, and though many regarded him as rather dull, I felt a profound respect for him.

I recall him particularly in connection with one circumstance. In my last year, I decided to work for a fellowship, which was the highest honor the college awarded and carried five hundred dollars a year for three years. The three professors who examined me and in whose departments I undertook extra work were Short, Drisler, and Nairne. Drisler had a hard time to pull me through Greek, for I did not possess the fundamental grounding which some other students had gained at institutions like Phillips Exeter Academy. Drisler was very happy that he was able to pass me in Greek and give me the fellowship, even if it did stretch his conscience a little.

In addition to Drisler and Short, I recall Professor William Guy Peck who taught mathematics and astronomy. He had a broad face and a smile that came easily, and his manner was cordial. The mathematics that he gave us was typical textbook material, but he gave us more than mere mathematics. He put poetry into his course, and he imbued us with his own awe and wonder for the universe. After all, this was far more important than the mathematics and the astronomy which most students quickly forgot.

Although some graduates have written disparagingly of Professor Charles Murray Nairne, I think these comments are unwarranted. He was good in English literature and did a great deal to improve our English. Thoroughly versed in the Scotch "common sense" philosophy, he probably was as good a teacher of metaphysics as could be found. His teaching of the ideas of Sir William Hamilton, who had been his own instructor, impressed me and was part of the reason why I decided to go to Germany to study philosophy and find the "absolute truth."

It was my work in literature and philosophy under Nairne that gave me my fellowship. My essay on Oliver Goldsmith was adjudged the best in the graduating class and Professor Nairne was particularly pleased with it. There was great jubilation among my family when they learned at graduation that I had received the fellowship. On June 25, 1876, my mother wrote to my sister the following account of the joyful event: **2044579**

"In the first place, throw up your hat and clap your hands, for the dear boy has got the Fellowship. He did not know for a certainty until it was announced—though he was pretty well assured of it; but to go farther back, he delivered his speech and there was but one or two whose delivery was as good as his, clear and strong and no straining for effects. He was quite surrounded with bouquets—when the President began the announcing of the prizes, Richie's soon came on. The President spoke of the extreme difficulty in getting it and gave him great honor for his success. When it was announced the class gave cheer after cheer, stamping and clapping, I mean, and then when he went up again, cheering, and when he came down they made the house ring and everyone it seems to me grasped his hand as he passed on to his seat. It was delightful to see their interest in him. He took the second German prize and when that was announced, they cheered again. They felt that he had done well and expressed it nobly. One young man, a very wealthy one, Eugene Seligman, came into the box and was introduced to us. Another one that George had met said to him, 'You are proud of your brother today and justly so.' "

During one term, we had economics once a week and we read Mrs. Fawcett's *Political Economy for Beginners*. From this we were assigned a lesson on which our teacher asked us to answer a series of printed questions. The course seems ridiculous when we compare it with the attention which economics receives in Columbia College today, but the neglect of the subject was in accordance with the narrow view of education then generally held. It is easy to understand why, at this period, I planned to study philosophy instead of economics, for under the circumstances, economics made little impression on me.

Most of my fellow-students were rich young New Yorkers. In reading the autobiography of Michael Pupin, who was the second man to take the fellowship in sciences, as I was the second to take it in letters, I was reminded of my own experiences. He was a poor boy from the Balkans, and I was a poor farm boy from western New York. He noticed that his classmates never asked him to contribute funds to athletic events, and I had the same experience. Our rich classmates invited us poorer ones to social functions and made us feel as if we were one of them. Eugene Seligman thought of competing for the fellowship. I feel certain that he could have taken it away from me, but he felt that I needed it, and therefore he generously stood aside. When I returned from Germany and was tramping the streets of New York looking for a job, it was this same Eugene Seligman who made me a loan which happily I was soon able to repay. Friendship with such classmates as Seligman helped to make the years I spent at Columbia among the happiest in my life.

I SAIL TO GERMANY IN QUEST OF THE TRUTH

After winning my fellowship at Columbia in 1876, it was considered a matter of course that I should go abroad to study, preferably to Germany. Philosophy was my major at that time. My problem was to find out who were the outstanding German philosophers and where in Germany they were to be found. Incredible as it may seem, I could not find on the Columbia faculty a single man who could tell me anything definite about German universities. One day I went to hear a lecture by Professor Martin of New York University on the philosophy of Herbert Spencer. I talked with him afterwards and he suggested that the man who knew most about Germany was Noah Porter, President of Yale University. I made my way to New Haven and then to President Porter's house. I arrived during the middle of the day and President Porter was entertaining a large dinner gathering. He greeted me on the steps of his house and gave me a long finger for a handshake. He suggested a philosopher by the name of Ulrici, who was at the University of Halle.

With this meager information, but with an earnest desire to justify the honor which Columbia had bestowed on me, I sailed on the *Pomerania*, May 24, 1877, and arrived in Hamburg on June 7th. I stayed in Hamburg only one day and tried to see as much of it as possible. What first impressed me was the low cost of living in Germany. I wrote home— "Why, the cheapest thing a man can do here is to live!" I marveled at the fact that "a pleasant room with three windows, together with breakfast, costs three marks, about seventy-five cents." In the evening of my first day in Germany, I went to what I preferred to describe as a "German concert" rather than a *Bier Garten* or *Halle*. The music was fine, and the price of admission about four cents. I was also delighted with the "many splendid walks and drives and parks in Hamburg." Before I had a chance to notice much else I left Hamburg for Kiel.

I remained in Kiel until September and lived with a German family so that I might learn to speak German as quickly as possible. I learned the language easily, and began to feel encouraged about myself when I talked with a German "who would not believe me when I told him that I had been in Germany only a little over six weeks." Kiel was an important military post and one of the first things I noticed was the "soldiers one sees everywhere." I wrote: "I am sure I couldn't say how many thousand soldiers there are here. You know that the Germans as a rule are obliged to serve three years. . . . I wonder what 'Young America' would think of such laws." The attitude in Germany toward dueling was also new to me. I related in a letter the story of the "son of one of the richest men in Kiel who lost his life in a duel. Nothing was done about it, and in the papers it was noticed as a sad incident. They consider the scars which they carry on their faces, and some have many, as marks of honor."

All this was interesting and I quickly became adjusted to German customs. But my immediate purpose in coming had been to see Ulrici, whom Dr. Porter of Yale had recommended and to whom he had given me a letter of introduction. After spending the summer at Kiel, I already felt misgivings regarding the advice he had given me. Among my German friends, I had not found anyone who had even heard of Ulrici. I was determined to stick the thing out. Finally I heard that I could find him in Halle in September. I left Kiel and went to Halle, hoping to begin my serious studies at the university there. The first thing I did was to see Ulrici. I found that he lived on the second floor of what we would call an apartment house. He came out to greet me on a small terrace, attired in a long black gown. We talked for a while and he told me that he had retired, but that he had a Shakespearean museum and would be glad to have me come and see it. That was the last thing I heard him say and I never saw Ulrici after that day.

I was fortunate in meeting Simon N. Patten, who had been in Germany for some time. He had attended Northwestern University where he had been regarded as a gawky, rural mannered fellow, with the peculiar idea (in the eyes of his fellow students) of taking his own intellectual development seriously. His craving for intellectual stimulus was not appeased at Northwestern. He persuaded his father to allow him to join his friends, Edmund J. James and Joseph French Johnson, at the University of Halle. It was here that I first met him. My first impression of Patten was that of a man overflowing with kindness. He was eager to help and I owed a great deal to him at

this time of my life. It was through him that I met Professor
Conrad. He introduced me into the cultured family of Frau
Pastor Lange, and it was my good fortune to live in this family
while I attended the university. Frau Lange's daughter Mar-
garethe had become engaged to Dr. James, and afterwards came
to this country and became his wife. The Germans in the city
used to predict that Dr. James would never come back to fetch
his fiancee, or even send for her. I would not venture to assert
that no German girl has ever been left disconsolate by an
American student or that American girls would not have similar tales to tell to German girls. However, Dr. James did come
back. And their marriage was one of the most ideally happy
ones I have ever seen. I soon became very happily settled with
the Lange family and I wrote to Mother on November 12,
1877:

"I have now settled upon what lectures I will take and will
accordingly report. I have history of philosophy five times a
week by Professor Haym, philosophical exercises two hours a
week by the same—logic and introduction into philosophy four
times a week, by the same. Exercises in Kant's *Critique of Pure
Reason*, twice a week by Dr. Thiele; a *privat docent*—physi-
ology of the sense, twice a week by Professor Dr. Berunstein;
Greek—Sophocles' *Electra*, twice a week by Professor Dr. Kiel;
exercises in Latin disputation, once a week by the same, he
speaks Latin very readily. Modern history, beginning with the
Reformation, three times a week by Professor Droysen; exercises in political economy, two hours a week by Professor Conrad. About Pompeii, once a week by Professor Heydemain;
dancing lessons, four hours a week; that is twenty-four hours a
week. . . . My principal study is philosophy including psychology
and my two auxiliaries, political economy and history. . . ."

The professors whom I knew best were Haym and Conrad.
I wrote that "of all the professors in Halle, I like Conrad the

best." Conrad was chiefly interested in problems of agrarian policy and agricultural statistics. His writings reflected a practical point of view and he seemed to be uninfluenced by the dogma of any particular school. Although he was not a great original thinker he was a splendid teacher. At his lectures and in his seminar he assembled and stimulated a large number of distinguished students, many of whom were Americans. He was very fond of us and never missed an opportunity to say a pleasant word or boost us.

Haym, too, was a splendid lecturer and teacher. He was one of the few German professors who held Round Table discussions at his own home. In his classes he used the old plan of dictating two or three hundred words which we took down verbatim for discussion. Goethe had once ridiculed this method, but I learned a good deal of the history of philosophy from it. Although not a great original thinker, in presenting the ideas of others he could not have been surpassed. Haym never told us what his own thoughts were, but he very ably presented what others thought. His apparent skepticism did a great deal to influence me to abandon my youthful idealistic purpose of seeking the absolute truth.

Originally I had come to Germany to find the absolute truth, and I thought that the Scotch philosophy of Sir William Hamilton was a good approach to this goal. But as time went on I got farther and farther away from philosophy. I saw that if I was ever to be a great philosopher and make a really worthy contribution, I needed preparation which would take far more money and time than I had. Slowly I began to abandon the idea of making philosophy my major. While this process of discarding my original ambition was going on, a new and attractive goal was suggested to me. One of my fellow-classmates at Columbia, David Calman, had gone straight to Heidelberg to study. He, and other friends in Heidelberg, sent enthusiastic reports from that university about the admirable work done there in economics and political science, and they were equally enthusiastic about the beauties of the place.

I finally decided that if I did possess any speculative capacity, I would have ample room for exercising it in economics, where I could keep my feet on the ground and at the same time make a beginning without as lengthy a preparation as would have been necessary in philosophy.

I FIND MY MASTER IN KARL KNIES AT HEIDELBERG

I left Halle on the 23rd of April, and on the way to Heidelberg stopped a few days at Mainz. I saw the city thoroughly, made a little trip on the Rhine, and spent one day in Wiesbaden, "the handsomest place I have so far seen in Germany." Reaching Heidelberg on the last day of April, 1878, I reported home that I was "once more settled down and so pleasantly that I feel more at home than before in Germany."

One spring morning I called upon my major professor, Karl Knies. He greeted me pleasantly, perhaps I had better say benevolently, for he was a kind-hearted man. After a brief preliminary discussion, he asked me to name my minors, it being understood, of course, that economics was my major. I told him my first minor was *Staatsrecht,* which was given at Heidelberg by Professor Bluntschli. (*Staatsrecht* can best be translated as "political science.") My second minor was philosophy. I had come to Heidelberg from Prussia, where those who took their Ph.D.'s must have philosophy at least as a second minor. I recall the puzzled look on Professor Knies's friendly face when I offered this subject as a second minor. He said that he did not believe that I could take philosophy as a second minor because I was in the faculty of political science and law, and the combination was impossible. I recall, as if it were yesterday, how

Professor Knies then went to a high cupboard in his office, which was part of his home, and how the good professor took down from it the statutes of the University of Heidelberg. These confirmed his position. So here was I, who had begun with a major in philosophy, not allowed to choose it even as a second minor.

Each day I studied and listened to lectures until five o'clock and then walked until seven or eight. The walks were beautiful. One day "I made quite a walk with another American. We went to Heilbrun with the cars and then walked along the Neckar for about twenty miles. More lovely scenery it was difficult to imagine."

One of the events I shall always remember is related to my mother in the following letter written on August 7, 1878:

"My dear Mother. . . . Yesterday was an important day in its way, for Heidelberg, that is to say, *Schlossbeleughtung,* an illumination of the castle took place. Last evening the entire castle was illuminated with chemical lights. I shall have to describe it to you, more minutely. The corps-students, at whose expense the affair took place had a dinner at a place some distance up the Neckar and sailed down in the evening on rafts, arriving at Heidelberg at about nine. In the meantime the one who had charge of the illumination had everything prepared to set off the chemicals by electricity. As soon then as the students came opposite the castle they sent up a great number of rockets as a signal and in the next instant the old castle, not before visible to the spectators, who were on the other side of the river, burst into view, an immense mass of flames. You have no idea of the grandeur of the spectacle. Generally one has no idea of the size of the castle, because it is so difficult to take it in at one view, but during the illumination the old pile of ruins stood out by itself in the darkness, several hundred feet above us, and the flames making the most exquisite reflections in the waters of the Neckar. It lasted several minutes, after which the *alte Brücke,* the old bridge, was illuminated. Besides this the students on the rafts had some very fine fireworks. I was with Mark Twain and some Americans; Mr. Clemens said it was the finest sight he had ever seen."

At Heidelberg there was a delightful atmosphere. I met people from all parts of the world and learned to take what I called a "cosmopolitan view of things in general." I found that "all the good in the world is not confined to the United States."

I was pleased by "how nice these German professors are to the students. They are very different from American professors in this respect. It is that which makes studying in Germany such a pleasure to every real student. You learn here, and only here, how to do independent, real scientific work."

There were two men at the university who were my heroes. One was Professor Karl Knies, my major professor; the other, Professor Johann K. Bluntschli, who had charge of my minor, *Staatsrecht.* When I think of Professor Bluntschli, I recall first of all his beautiful home, on the outer walls of which were painted inspiring quotations. I do not know how modern architects would regard the old Bluntschli home, but to me it was very attractive. Bluntschli was about seventy years old when I listened to him, perhaps a little older. Nevertheless, he was in the fullness of his powers and I feel I learned a great deal from him. I think of him as a benevolent old gentleman, although he was a good deal younger than I am now. He was jolly, full of smiles and laughter, and doing what was in his power to promote peace and prosperity at home and abroad. We learned his code of international law and we followed, to some extent, what is called the case system of looking up pertinent documents. What rank his work on international law has now, I do not know, but to me it appeared very significant.

It is Knies, however, whom I am glad to acknowledge, more

than any other one man, as *My Master*. He was a man of somewhat more than medium height, broad-shouldered and sturdy.
He wore a full beard which was, as I recall it, reddish and a
little parted in the middle of his chin. Somehow he reminds
me of a dangerous anarchist. Why, I do not know, unless it may
be that he resembled some anarchist I once saw. Actually he
was a progressive economist, with a proper respect for existing
institutions, which he did not want to abolish but rather to improve by evolutionary processes. He was not a man to whom
one could get very close in personal relations. I am inclined to
think he was a lonely man, because he could never find words
in which to express the warmth of his heart. He was awkward
in his manners and in his writing. Once in the library at Heidelberg I came across one of his books which had been decorated
by scribbled margin comments. In the margin, beside a sentence which ran some two pages in length, a despondent student had written, "oh, weh-oh, weh!!!"

My memory of Knies is that of a sad man carrying on his
shoulders a heavy weight. He felt that he had not received the
credit due him for his original work and his leadership in modern economics. Knies conceived of economics as belonging
neither to the natural nor to the mental sciences, but to the
group of historical disciplines which have for their object the
study of man in society in terms of its historical growth. This
conception had widespread influence; together with Roscher and
Hildebrand he was credited with the founding of the historical
school of economic thought. He felt that Professor Roscher did
not fully acknowledge his contribution, and I believe he was
right in this.

Above all, he was very sympathetic to the aspirations of the
workingman, and spoke of his privations and excessive toil in
a way that would have stirred the ire of the Old Guard of the
United States. Knies wished not only for Germany to have

Karl Knies. Heidelberg 1889.

peace and prosperity; he wanted these things for all nations. One incident brings this out. He was a specialist on money; one of the best known of his works is *Welt Geld*. He deeply regretted that Bismarck had made the mark a trifle less in value than the shilling, because he thought that international money was a benefit and tended to promote international peace and prosperity, which he had so much at heart. Bismarck, on the other hand, deliberately acted to make the mark different in value from the shilling, because his aspirations were wholly nationalistic.

I recall also with very warm feeling the humanitarianism of Bluntschli. A favorite phrase of his which always impressed me as vital and significant was *menschenwürdiges Dasein*, "an existence worthy of human beings." There was a decided difference in point of view between General von Moltke, the gifted general who led Prussia and Germany to victory against the French, and Bluntschli. Von Moltke did not like the pacifist views of Bluntschli at all. He wrote an open letter to him in which he used the memorable words: "What you want is only a dream, and at that, not even a beautiful dream." Unfortunately, the forces which represented von Moltke's ideas were, in the end, strong enough to outweigh the idealistic desires for peace of men like Bluntschli and Knies. Living in Germany, I could not fail to be impressed by the militarism I saw. I wrote:

"With the Germans war is a very highly developed science. That is the whole of it. It was as much a matter of science as a game of chess. The Germans were ready for war, the French were not. The Germans knew what they were doing every time they made a move, the French did not. You have no idea of the high state of development of military science, especially organization here. Everything goes like the most perfect clock work. I am writing at 9 P.M. and now the Germans have an army of 400,000; by tomorrow at 12 M, I suppose they could have

1,000,000 men in the field, perhaps more. Every man's name is registered, who is able to serve. The government officers know just where he is and can put their hands upon him at a minute's notice; every man's orders are already made out, that is, every one has his order to report himself at such a company, in such a regiment immediately, or upon so many hours' notice and it only remains to distribute the orders. Thus the entire military force of Germany, which in an extremity includes every able bodied male, is ready to begin action at any time. . . ."

While I was observing the movement of German affairs in general, and attitudes and personalities of professors and public figures of importance, I was also diligently preparing for the examination for my Ph.D. degree. On the morning of the appointed day, I put on my swallow tail, kid gloves, and tall hat, and appeared for my examination. It took place in a large room at a long table; I was placed at the head of the table and around me on both sides were gathered the professors who might ask me any questions they wished. Up to this point the ordeal was exactly like those I have experienced in American universities. There was one difference, however. In the corner of the room was a little table on which were placed cake and wine provided for the pleasure of the professors during the recess. I was asked if I did not care to join them. I had already learned that the candidate must refuse this invitation. I do not know what would have happened if I had replied in the affirmative. In the history of Heidelberg, nobody has ever replied in the affirmative. So there I sat, anxious and worried, while my professors were having a jolly time with the refreshments.

After what seemed like an unending period, the examination was resumed. When it was finally completed, I did not know whether I had passed or failed. The following morning, according to custom, I called on the Oberpedell (this may be translated "the Head Janitor"). Personally I thought I had passed but with a low *Predicat*. It was not merely a question of passing, but of several different grades. One could obtain the graduate degree but without honors; or one could obtain it *multa cum laude, insigni cum laude,* or *summa cum laude.* When the head janitor told me I had passed and received a *summa* I began to run as fast as I could. I did not stop until I reached, at the top of the hill, the rooms occupied by one of my friends to whom I told the good news. The following night, another candidate, who had also been successful, and I, gave a reception for our friends, a *Kneipe.* What happened at this *Kneipe* I do not recall clearly, and perhaps it is just as well that I do not recollect.

I was very happy to be able to write home about the good news; I knew what joy the glad tidings would bring to my family. My brief note was a gross understatement of the elation I felt. "You will doubtless be pleased to learn that I was successful yesterday in passing my doctor's examination, a celebration of Frankie's [my sister] birthday. Please don't forget that I am hereafter to be addressed as Dr. Ely."

I AM THRILLED BY THE BEAUTY OF THE ALPS

My degree earned, I set out for Switzerland, for a vacation, to learn French, and to see what the University of Geneva had to offer. I traveled all through Switzerland, and was repaid by more beauty than I had ever before seen. In Geneva I lived in a pension where I met students from all parts of the world. This gave me an insight into world affairs which I often wished that my most distinguished student, Woodrow Wilson, could have had before he was plunged into world affairs.

The University of Geneva was a letdown after the German universities. A man by the name of Dameth gave economics, but his course was so elementary that it reminded me of what

I had learned at Columbia under Professor Nairne. Its real value was that it helped to improve my French. I also took a course in French literature given by a Frenchman who had become a Swiss. This was a splendid course and in itself equal to the sort of thing the German universities gave.

After five pleasant but not very profitable months in Switzerland, I decided to return to Germany for the third year of my fellowship. I planned to go to Berlin to continue studying, and at the same time to teach private pupils, write for a number of papers, and "spend much time in listening to the proceedings of the Reichstag." On my trip north from Switzerland to Germany, in company with a party of friends, I made a long excursion in the Jura Mountains, starting at half past four in the morning and not returning until about midnight. We went to the head of the Lake of Neuchatel and from there westward to the Jura Mountains. We could see the Lake of Neuchatel, the Lake of Geneva, the plain lying between them, the Mont Blanc chain, and the mountains of the Bernese Oberland. I wrote home that I wished my descriptive powers were of a sufficiently high order to picture the beauties of the scenes I saw. However, another experience made such a vivid impression on me that I used whatever powers I did have to express my enthusiasm over the "finest view I ever had of the Alps." In a letter I wrote:

"It was from the Chaumont, a mountain three thousand five hundred feet high, directly back of Neuchatel. It was a most rare view, such as not one traveler out of five hundred enjoys. It was at sunset and the atmosphere was exceptionally clear. The mountain peaks were entirely free from clouds; also an exception. I saw in its full glory the entire Alpine chain from the Sentis to Mount Blanc. The long range of lofty mountains, the ice and snow covered peaks reaching up into the very heavens until they seemed to belong no more to this world, the glow of the setting sun lending a certain warmth even to the cold and passionless grandeur of the scene, all made upon my mind an ineffaceable impression. The mind seemed to expand and mount upwards, leaving far behind the earth and the things of earth. Yes, the ancient Greeks, with their fine appreciation of the grand and sublime, did well to make Olympus the dwelling place of the chief of the gods, Jupiter, the father of gods and men, whose movements shook the earth to its foundation and whose thunderbolts struck terror into all living creatures."

On my return from Switzerland to Berlin I went through the Black Forest, the highest point of which was the Feldberg. "From the Feldberg, I descended directly into the Hölenthal, 'Valley of Hell.' Whatever is particularly wild and irregular in nature, the Germans like to connect with the Devil . . . the way led through field and forest and was hard enough to find, as it had become perfectly dark. I suppose the Black Forest is safe enough now, but it is not pleasant to wander through a wild region, far from any public highway alone and late at night, meeting now and then strange looking people, having the appearance of being capable of anything. At one place, I knocked several times before receiving any answer and then, instead of one of them coming to the door as you would expect from civilized Christian people, they let out a great dog at me. As good fortune would have it, two men happened to be returning very late from their work just at this minute and saved me from what might have been an unpleasant experience. After receiving my directions, I started again on my way and reached my destination without any further adventures. The last part of the journey was a steep descent through a thick forest. I could not see my hand before my face and had to feel my way along. The road happened to be pretty good for, as I saw the next morning, by stepping too far to one side, I might have made the descent with unpleasant rapidity. You will have an idea of the descent from its name, Holensteig, the 'Climb of Hell.' "

After this I went through Freiburg and Strassburg on my way to Berlin. I saw the cathedrals in both places and thought that in Strassburg was the "grandest one I ever saw." I stopped a short time at Heidelberg, an afternoon at Frankfort, and spent "two nights and a day in Eisenach. Eisenach is one of the most charming places I was ever in. It is surrounded by beautiful forests, which alone would make it a delightful place for me. I love a fine forest. In wandering about in one, I feel happy. I experience the cares and vexations of the world no more. I am peaceful and tranquil.

"At such times I can appreciate what Rousseau exclaimed after he had escaped from the multitude to his lonely retreat; 'O Nature, O my Mother, here I am alone with you, here am I happy!' . . . the principal point of interest in Eisenach is naturally the beautifully situated Wartburg, celebrated as the residence of Luther for some time. It is there that he threw his ink-bottle at the devil. Nothing more of the spot is to be seen, however, as tourists have broken off the plastering and carried it away as memories. The lawlessness of the English and American tourists—for it is needless to say that they did it; a Frenchman or German wouldn't dream of such a thing—is something astounding. My next stopping place was Weimar, celebrated, during the latter part of the last century and the first part of this, as the residence of Germany's greatest authors: Wieland, Herder, Schiller, and Goethe. . . ."

I stopped next at Halle, and at last reached Berlin. I had not been in Berlin twenty-four hours before the city began to seem familiar to me. I attributed this gift of becoming easily acquainted to my powers of endurance as a walker. I immediately recognized that Berlin offered splendid opportunities for a student. I described them in a letter:

"The galleries, for one thing, are large and magnificent. They are arranged so that one can follow the development of art from the earliest times, through all the great schools up to the present. . . .

"For my work on German politics, I shall have great advantages. Professor Gneist, member of the German Parliament (Reichstag) and a distinguished professor of politics, reads lectures this winter on German and Prussian constitutional law."

I followed my plan of teaching private pupils and attending the Reichstag. I found that "the speaking in Prussian Parliament is nothing extraordinary—the Germans are not natural orators." I became a member of the Royal Statistical Bureau, of which Dr. Ernst Engel was director. Many German students did regular statistical work, serving the bureau without compensation. I intended to stay only one year in Berlin and, since I did not want to be a professional statistician, I could not become a regular apprentice. I did gain, however, the privilege of attending the Round Table and the lectures given by Director Engel and Professor Adolf Wagner. I became acquainted with Dr. Engel's law of consumption, and I believe I was the first one to call attention to it in this country. This I did in my *Introduction to Political Economy* published in 1889. I received a good training in method from Engel's lectures, and I shall always remember one remark he made in speaking about the balance of trade. He said, "Anyone who draws any general conclusions as to prosperity or the reverse merely from a favorable or unfavorable balance of trade has not grasped the first fundamental principle of economics."

I SELL MY FIRST ARTICLE

Toward the end of my year in Berlin my money began to run out. Although from time to time I received help from my artist-

mother, who gave me more than she should have given, I had
to do what I could to defray my own expenses. I cannot but
recall the friendly attitude of the University of Berlin and especially of Professor Wagner. I was allowed to post on the bulletin board of the university my offer to instruct students in the
English language. I had several students and this helped somewhat to meet expenses. I also wrote articles for the New York
Evening Post and other papers. In November, 1879, I received
$5.79 from the *Evening Post* for an article on Germany and
Russia. There was nothing remarkable about it except that it
was the first money I ever received for a production of my pen.
I had also written an article on "American Colleges and German Universities," and sent it to *Harpers Monthly*. This article
served to get me out of a very tight spot. One day I had left in
my pocket, if I recall correctly, the total sum of three pfennigs,
about three-quarters of a cent. What was I to do? At the University of Halle, another fellow-student and American was
Marcus Hitch, who afterwards became a lawyer in Chicago. I
put on my hat and made my way to my friend's home about a
mile away. When I got there, I said, "Marcus, I am dead broke,
I have come to you for a loan." He replied, "I was just putting
on my hat to come to you." He, too, had reached the end of his
resources. I then returned to my room, trying to think of what
to do next. What friend did I have in Berlin who could help
me out in the present emergency? When I arrived at my room,
I found a letter from Harper and Brothers, London, with twelve
pounds sterling in it, in payment for my article "American
Colleges and German Universities." I was delighted with this
amount. Twelve pounds sterling was equal to two hundred and
fifty marks, which was about fifty dollars in New York at that
time. My spirits rose and I made my way to my friend Hitch
to tell him the good news. When I did, he replied that he had

just received a remittance from home and was about to visit me to tell me of it and also to help out.

My contacts with German higher education had convinced me of its superiority over American, and led me to investigate the underlying causes. It was evident that students entered the German universities with thorough backgrounds in mathematics, history and literature, languages, etc. I was particularly impressed with their linguistic accomplishments. On one occasion a number of people were invited to a party. After coming together it was found that one of the guests did not speak German well—so they all spoke French during that evening. In no city in the United States would that be possible. One of the reasons, undoubtedly, is that our schools are so poor. In the American college I found that so frequently there was very little to build on. In later years how often I quoted from the Bible or from Shakespeare only to meet the blank looks on students' faces. I often asked myself, "What can we assume in the way of knowledge?"

In the United States, the German universities had been taken as models in a sort of blind attempt to imitate them. What misled so many American educators and presidents of American universities was that apparently all the work in a German university was elective. They erred seriously in imagining that they were turning American colleges into German universities by making studies elective and optional. The nature of the German universities and the differences between them and the American colleges were understood by very few people at the time, and I felt compelled to point these out in my article.

The German university was a professional school, a place where a young man prepared to earn his "bread and butter." It was not a school to develop in a general way intellectual powers or to give students universal culture. Each student had in mind

an examination which was to admit him to a means of livelihood and he pursued only the studies required for passing it,
and pursued them no farther than was demanded. The freedom
in German universities was the freedom given to men selecting
their own professions. Public authorities minutely prescribed
requirements for these examinations. In this way they controlled
the university courses.

The American college, as it used to be, had a closer resem-
blance to a German gymnasium than to a German university.
In the gymnasium there was little if any election of studies;
courses were rigidly prescribed and severe discipline was maintained, and the students received a very thorough training in
preparation for university work. Many thought that Harvard
College was becoming like a German University when the elective system was introduced and elaborated under the late President Eliot. Before this, Harvard had been somewhat like the
German gymnasium. Under the elective system it was neither
like the gymnasium nor like the German university. I, for my
part, think that the history of Harvard College under Eliot was
in some respects a disservice to American education. He shunted
us off on the wrong track. In this article I concluded that "what
is necessary, then, as regards our professional schools is for the
state by proper legislation to raise the standard of requirements
and so assist the colleges and universities in giving us an able
and properly educated set of professional men as in Germany."

In spite of my limited resources, I enjoyed the German manner of living, and my enthusiasm often overflowed in letters.
In one I wrote:

"In America we would undoubtedly be healthier and handsomer if we knew how to live. If we could ever learn that when
God gave us a faculty for enjoyment, pleasure and means of
gratifying it, He meant we should enjoy ourselves, that we
honored Him not only in church-going and long prayers, but

also in laughing, jumping, dancing and being happy in this world! So long as we continue above all people in the world, to neglect this truth in our lives, we will continue to suffer for it."

While I was in Berlin, I had one opportunity to compare British and German diplomacy. The great Berlin Congress, following the war between Russia and Turkey, took place at the time when Bismarck was at the height of his power. The English were represented at the Congress by Beaconsfield (Disraeli). Great as Bismarck was, he was not the equal of Beaconsfield or the English in the field of diplomacy. I recall one or two instances of significance, trifling as they may seem at a glance. The most fashionable hotel in Berlin at that time was the Kaiserhof. Beaconsfield engaged forty-eight rooms at the Kaiserhof. As compared with the interests involved, the expense was simply nothing, not equivalent to an American dime. Yet what an impression it made on the Germans! They spoke of it with awe. *"Acht und vierzig Zimmer hat Beaconsfield in dem Kaiserhof genommen!"* This gave, as I could clearly perceive, an impression of the wealth and power of the English. Then I recall another incident. At the conference table, Bismarck, who drank strong wine and smoked strong cigars, passed a cigar around to Beaconsfield who put it in his mouth and smoked it. He said afterwards, "I would have smoked it even if it killed me." How clever! He might have said, "Your Excellency, I do not smoke such strong cigars, thank you." But Beaconsfield showed good psychology in cultivating and maintaining a favorable atmosphere (*Stimmung*) in which to accomplish his aims.

When the smoke of battle was cleared away, and the spoils had been divided, it seemed to me, as a young observer, that England had carried away the lion's share of the spoils. The Germans recognized that the English have always done this.

No diplomacy has been the equal of that of England. The English diplomats represent a combination of superior brains, the best available training in whatever history has to afford, coupled with lifelong experience.

I FIND AN INVALUABLE FRIEND IN ANDREW D. WHITE

What meant more to me than anything else during my year in Berlin was the friendship of Andrew D. White, President of Cornell, who was on a leave of absence and was acting as our American minister in Germany. I had occasion to write to him in order to secure a ticket of admission to the German parliament. His reply was very cordial. He wrote, "I shall be very glad to be of use to you in the matter suggested in your letter, especially if you are the Mr. Ely of whom Dr. Barnard wrote me." It was gratifying to know that President Barnard had written of me favorably, and I readily accepted his invitation to visit him at the legation.

I am only one of a vast number whom Dr. White helped on the way and I find it hard to avoid superlatives in speaking of him. In the prefatory note to my *French and German Socialism in Modern Times,* my first book, published while I was still in the twenties and two years after my appointment to the Johns Hopkins University, I used these words:

"The publication of this volume is due to the friendly counsel of the Honorable Andrew D. White, President of Cornell University; a gentleman tireless in his efforts to encourage young men, and alive to every opportunity to speak fitting words of hope and cheer. Like many of the younger scholars of our country, I am indebted to him more than I can say."

Evidently he took a great fancy to me, and I was always welcome at the legation. I often wondered at this, as there were

certainly other American students who did not have the same
accessibility to Dr. White. Why this was so I cannot fully explain. What is it that leads one man to feel a strong affection
for another? I was a poor and struggling young student, awkward and diffident, and it is not modesty which makes me say
I was singularly lacking in charm. But of charm, Andrew D.
White had enough for himself and for me, with some to spare.
What did we talk about? Perhaps I should rather say, what did
he talk about? He was a rare and gifted speaker and I was glad
to listen to him. We spoke a great deal about Cornell University, about its founding, about its early days, and especially
about his relations to Ezra Cornell. I was interested in his psychology and the way he worked cleverly with Ezra Cornell and
with Mr. Sage, a benefactor, and one of the trustees of Cornell
University. Andrew D. White, himself, was a man of wealth
and this gave him a great advantage in securing gifts for Cornell. When a president can say to others, "I give so much, you
join with me," he has a very great advantage, especially if he
is clever in handling men.

We spoke about the conflict between science and religion,
and his views at the time seemed radical. I do not think they
would be so regarded now. At any rate he was a religious man
in the truest sense of the word. The story is told in his autobiography and other writings. I think especially of the slanders
and malignity in the "holier than thou" attitude of those who
are the opponents of progress.

Especially interesting to me as a Columbia College graduate
and Fellow was what he told me about his conversations with
President Barnard of Columbia, and the influence which he had
on Barnard in urging that the surplus funds be spent to enlarge
the college. President Butler even today applies this philosophy,
and as a result of it Columbia has spent far more than its current income and had made friends by appealing to the alumni

and others to give millions of dollars for the resources of Columbia.

The only explanation I can give for his special interest in me was the new ideas I had in relation to economics. He had been brought up in the old dogmatic English school of economic thought which believed that the absolute truth had been discovered and that there was little for subsequent writers and students to do except to learn this truth. Those who believed were considered orthodox, and those who questioned were unorthodox. They held that free trade was the only sound policy whether regarded from the point of view of ethics or economics. Those who were advocates of protectionism were, at the best, muddle-headed, and if they were not muddle-headed, they were dishonest and corrupt. They were predatory malefactors advocating policies to promote their own selfish interests at the expense of the country. After all, as one of the professorial advocates of free trade said, the all-sufficient answer to the protectionist was "Thou shalt not steal."

This orthodox dogmatism was characterized by an absolutism of theory that was particularly obnoxious to the German school of thought by which I was so strongly impressed. Karl Knies said that absolutism takes two forms, namely, perpetualism which implies that a policy holds good for all times, and cosmopolitanism which holds that any one policy can be applied to all lands. He believed that perpetualism was a worse form of absolutism in theory than cosmopolitanism. It is a more serious error to suppose that the same policy is applicable to all times than to suppose that it is applicable to all lands. Imbued with this philosophy I felt contempt for the dogmatic English economics, which was uncompromising in its opposition to protection. From Knies and others I was learning a fundamentally scientific approach in which relativity and evolution played a large role. Here was Andrew D. White, who had been educated at Yale College and who was a prominent Republican, as sincere and honest in his convictions as any man I ever met—and here was I, a young fellow, full of enthusiasm, telling Dr. White that free trade was not an absolute truth. Though free trade might be a good policy at some times, at other times a protective tariff was called for. He was greatly pleased to hear me voice these views.

Andrew D. White was a very wise man and I learned from him a fine way of looking at the world. He said I must not make the mistakes so many of his friends were making. They were carrying on research, writing and rewriting books, revising and re-revising. They wanted to make their work so perfect that they would have the last word. In many cases they tinkered away at their writing too long and then fell into their graves with nothing accomplished. It was Dr. White's idea that you should get your ideas down on paper, out of your system and into the printed word. Write what you have to say and do not be so conceited as to think that you can write a perfect book. Of course you are going to make mistakes; someone will come along and correct your mistakes; then you can rewrite the book. I recognized this as good counsel and I followed it. Some may say that I followed it too unreservedly, but, at any rate, I transformed my various ideas into numerous books and articles. They have been criticized, and justly so. Perhaps, if I wanted to review them now I would be one of the severest critics. But I believe that in writing them I have served, even if in small measure, as a clarifying influence on economic thought.

MY WRITING CAREER BEGINS

Andrew D. White did more than give me good advice. He asked me to make a study of the administration of the city of Berlin. He had an excellent reputation in Germany; he was the

kind of man that the Germans liked to see as our representative, a scholar and a gentleman, not a politician, like so many
of our other representatives who were a mortification to educated Americans living in Germany at that time. Armed with
letters from Dr. White, I began my study of the administration
of the city of Berlin. An introduction from the American Minister would have counted for something in any case, but coming
from Andrew D. White, everything was thrown open to me. I
was very welcome when I went to the mayor's office and to the
other offices asking for materials. As a memento of this work,
I have now in my possession a budget of the city of Berlin with
corrections made in ink. What a beautiful budget it was! Clear
as a crystal!

My first-hand investigation and the information I got from
reports and other secondary sources revealed Berlin as a model
city. A great many responded to my comments on the excellence
of the administration of Berlin by saying, "It is because the
King of Prussia is able to govern the city." How far from the
truth this was! The administration was a thorn in the side of
the King of Prussia because in many ways it was democratically
governed, and the Kaiser never was able to control the administration.

The man who at that time was said to have more influence
in the city council than anyone else was Rudolph Virchow, who
had made a great reputation for himself in the field of medicine. As a young physician he was sent in 1847 to make a study
of a typhoid fever epidemic in Upper Silesia. The impressions
gained in this experience were a determining factor in the development of his political views. He became an enemy of feudalism, a faithful supporter of liberalism and democracy, and a
staunch opponent of the Bismarckian policy of the eighteen
sixties. It has been said of him that "essentially a humanitarian,
progressive liberal of independent and courageous character, he

typifies the highest conception of public service." I often heard it told that when members of the city council met, and someone would look around and remark that Virchow was missing, then they would all wait for him to arrive before proceeding with business. It is to their credit that they recognized a man of ability and looked for leadership to him.

To understand government in Berlin in my day one should compare it with an American state university. The city council corresponded in a rough way to the board of regents of the University of Wisconsin. It was their duty to call a man as mayor. When I first went to Germany and after I was in Hamburg a day, I happened to pick up a newspaper in which I found an advertisement of a German city for a mayor. All candidates were asked to send in applications with their qualifications which were required to be very high. Von Vorchenbeck was mayor in my time. He had made a success as a mayor of Breslau, so they called him to Berlin. The office was regarded as a permanent one in the same way as the presidency of a university is here regarded as permanent. As a matter of fact the tenure is somewhat better. In an advertisement of another city for a mayor the tenure was mentioned as twelve years. If the man was not re-elected after his period of office, he was retired on a pension. The employees under the mayor were highly qualified men and were appointed a good deal as members of a University faculty are. They usually started young and worked their way up, if as they went on they demonstrated their fitness. A great deal was done to encourage excellence in the civil service, such as the bestowal of orders of various sorts, which were highly prized. The result was that the civil service was stimulated to win social distinction.

One of the admirable things about the city of Berlin was the large number of citizens who held what were called honor offices, *Ehrenämter*. They received no salary, but they were active in schools and charities among other things. No American city at that time had so many private citizens participating in municipal government and I felt that in this respect there was a good deal for us in America to learn.

I recall an experience with the personal income tax which revealed the efficiency of German civil service. German tax officials at that time determined the amount of the tax from indications of a person's income rather than by direct questions. One day they called on me in my room, looked around a bit, asked me a few questions, and then left. Later I was asked to pay a tax on an assumed income of three thousand marks. They were very competent in their judgment, for this is just about what I should have had as an American student in Berlin. However, my fellowship money had by this time nearly run out, and I had no steady income. I went with the bill to the tax office and told them I could not pay it as I was only in Berlin as an American student temporarily. They then cancelled the amount they had demanded from me for my income tax. The entire affair left a pleasant impression on me. I felt I was dealing with men who knew what they were talking about and who were gentlemen.

At that time, under Bismarck, it was proposed that Prussia should purchase its privately owned railways which also extended into other states. The theory appeared to have been adopted in Prussia that the way to control the privately owned railways was to parallel them with publicly owned railways, a theory which also received attention in this country. It did not work out well. German civil service was high-grade, and the publicly owned railways in Germany were very well managed. But if the publicly owned Prussian railways were operated at their best and as if they had been privately owned, it would have bankrupted the privately owned railways.

The subject received much discussion in the Reichstag and

it was concluded that railways should either be privately owned and regulated by the State or owned altogether by the State. The alternative chosen was that of public ownership. In addition to the economic reasons for this there were also military reasons which played a large, although not an exclusive, role in bringing about this change in policy. It was desired that it should be possible to have men march into one end of a railway station and out at the other end fully equipped and prepared in case of war. This is exactly what happened in the World War.

Andrew D. White now asked me to make a report upon the purchase of the private railways for our department of state. Again, I had access to all the important sources of information and I gathered a great deal of material, some of which was very rare, and is now in the library of the University of Wisconsin. I thought at the time that Andrew D. White was trying to avail himself of the services of his young friend in the interests of his country. Afterwards I had to take a more modest view of my own superiority for this particular task. Members of the legation were irritated because he had asked me instead of them to report to the department of state.

It was this report, however, which served to get me started on my way and later helped me to get a teaching post at the Johns Hopkins.

* * *

III

Finding the Ground

* * *

I RETURN TO AMERICA AND SEE A CRISIS IN THE LABOR MOVEMENT

IN THE SUMMER OF 1880, I left Germany, spent a short time in England, and then sailed from Liverpool. I landed in New York on a hot and disagreeable midsummer day. As I walked through the streets of New York, my heart sank within me. The city was dirty and ill-kept, the pavements poor, and there were evidences of graft and incompetence on every hand. Is this my America? I asked myself. I thought of the clean, beautiful streets of Berlin and Liverpool, and the painful contrast made me want to take the next boat back to Europe. This was a momentary impulse. I knew I could not leave my parents and the land in which my ancestors had lived for more than two hundred years. This was my home and I vowed to do whatever was in my power to bring about better conditions. My youthful ambitions were high. A year of fruitless search for a suitable job ended happily, in a position at the Johns Hopkins. But before I tell the story of the Johns Hopkins, I want to recount my impression of what was happening in the United States, and to tell what I wanted to do about it.

Lord Morley has truly observed that "great economic and social forces flow with a tidal sweep over communities that are only half conscious of that which is befalling them." While there can be no doubt about this, it is equally true that in looking back over past history we often find at least an imperfect consciousness of the true nature of existing crises. On my return from Germany, after an absence of three years, I became aware that our country was experiencing a crisis in which the potentialities for good or for evil were great beyond precedent. This was a time when either optimism or pessimism was easy, but both were dangerous. There was enough that was alarming to excite one to vigorous action; there was enough that was promising to encourage the brightest hopes.

When we look through American history, we find frequent turning points—many genuine crises. All important social movements have their crises; in the last quarter of the nineteenth century the American people witnessed a crisis in the labor movement. It was marked by a deep stirring of the masses—not a local stirring, not merely a national stirring, but an international, world-wide stirring of the masses. The manner of producing material goods was examined critically and pronounced faulty. The distribution of these goods among the various members of the social organism was also critically examined and pronounced iniquitous. Proposals were made for new modes of production and distribution of economic goods. The masses desired changes, not merely in surface phenomena, but in the very foundations of the social order.

What was the labor movement of the nineteenth century? What is the labor movement we are experiencing today? These questions bring us to the heart of things. They may be answered in the same way. The labor movement, in its broadest terms, is the effort of men to live the life of men. It is the systematic, organized struggle of the masses to attain, primarily, more leisure and larger economic resources. The end and purpose of all is the true growth of mankind; namely, the full and harmonious development in each individual of all human faculties—the faculties of working, perceiving, knowing, loving

—the development, in short, of whatever capabilities of good there may be in us. And this development of human powers in the individual is not to be entirely for self, but it is to be for the sake of their beneficent use in the service of one's fellows in a Christian civilization. It is for self and for others; it is the realization of the ethical aim expressed in that command which contains the secret of all true progress, "Thou shalt love thy neighbor as thyself." It is directed against oppression in every form, because oppression carries with it the idea that persons or classes live not to fulfill a destiny of their own, but primarily, and chiefly, for the sake of the welfare of other persons or classes. Men's interests are inextricably intertwined, and we shall never become truly prosperous so long as any class of the population is materially and morally wretched. As a social body, we can no more be in a sound condition while we have a sub-merged element, than a man can be whose arms or legs are suffering a foul and corrupting disease. Whether we will or not, we must, in a manner, rejoice together and suffer together. The true significance of the labor movement lies in this. It is an effort to bring to pass the idea of human development which has animated sages, prophets, and poets of all ages; the idea that a time must come when warfare of all kinds shall cease, and when a peaceful organization of society will find a place within its framework for the best growth of each personality, and shall abolish all servitude, in which one "but subserves another's gain."

In the last half of the nineteenth century, movements for the organization of labor became world-wide in character, and the workers in different lands, to an increasing extent, were strik-ing in concert. For example, workingmen in Belgium, learning of a strike in England, refused to accept offers of employment in that country. They came to this country for employment, and when they found that here they were expected to take the place of strikers, they returned to Belgium, with money furnished them by their fellow-workers in America. A great strike of dock-laborers would break out in London and be carried to successful completion with the aid of contributions received from Australian workingmen, living on the other side of the globe. In our American Pittsburgh, representatives of six nations met and formed a union of glass workers designed to embrace everyone engaged in that industry in the entire world. In 1893, the American Federation of Labor extended an invitation to organized workingmen everywhere to hold a world's congress of labor in Chicago. This circular was addressed to "Wage-workers of all countries! Comrades, recognizing the identity of interests of the wage-workers of the world, the great bond of interest and sympathy which should prevail in the hearts and minds of all toilers. . . ." It stated, further, that the object of the congress was "to formulate and discuss the very many questions affecting our interests, to give a greater impetus to the cause of progress and civilization, and to make known to the world by our unalterable determination that we insist upon being larger sharers in the world's progress."

This emphasis on the international solidarity of labor was significant, for prior to 1882 the American labor movement had not been in any sense an expression of a particular class movement and had shown no revolutionary tendencies. It had been restricted to skilled workmen who saw that collective bargaining was a far more successful method of exerting pressure on employers than individual bargaining. Each trade union handled its own employers, and although the social solidarity of labor was not denied, the idea was not actively put into practice. It was not until the unskilled group was drawn into labor organizations that the labor movement began to assume the nature of a class movement. This occurred during the depression of 1884–85 when wage reductions and unemployment affected the unskilled and semi-skilled to a larger degree than the skilled. American labor organizations had never experienced such a rush to organize as that in the latter part of 1885 and during 1886. The high point was reached in the autumn of 1886 when the combined membership of labor organizations approached the million mark.[9]

The most prominent of these organizations was the Knights of Labor. Large sections of the oppressed laboring masses gathered together under its banners and heralded it as their champion. Their leaders, many of whom I knew personally, including their President, Terence V. Powderly, were men of high personal character who felt that they were serving humanity. They were willing to make all sorts of sacrifices to accomplish this purpose. The social philosophy of the Knights of Labor, particularly, appealed to me, for their avowed purposes were, in many ways, excellent. They did not emphasize class war; in fact, in certain instances they would admit teachers, preachers, other intellectuals, and even employers. Several of my students were allowed to join the Knights of Labor to understand the working of the labor movement from the inside.

Their power, which was somewhat over-rated at the time, was not so great, as it was significant of the development of a new phase in employer-employee relationships. As a result of the Gould railway strike of March, 1885, directed by the Knights of Labor, Gould declared that he would arbitrate all labor difficulties. Thus, for the first time, a powerful capitalist was compelled to yield to a labor organization and recognize its potential force.

In the beginning I had hopes that the Knights of Labor would do a great deal to bring about peace and prosperity for the country. Alas! my hopes were not well founded. The order grew rapidly and it was not possible to keep control of the great and growing mass of its members. Political movements, nation-wide boycotts, sympathetic strikes, and general strikes became the order of the day. The strike which proved most disastrous to the interests of labor was the nation-wide strike for the eight-hour day declared for May 1, 1886. The initiative in this strike was taken by the trade unionists while the general officers of the Knights adopted an attitude of hostility. However, in the ranks of labor the proposed strike found ready response. Early in the strike occurred the bomb explosion and consequent riots in the Haymarket Square of Chicago. The event was attributed to anarchists, and thus served to connect the activities of labor groups with those of such anarchist groups as the International Workmen's Association. This association, which included the Chicago anarchists, had worked out a system of thought and action. It was characterized by extreme combativeness, by the ease with which minor disputes grew into widespread strikes, by a reluctance to enter into agreements with employers, and by ready resort to violence. The period of police terrorism in Chicago which followed the Haymarket riot showed the labor movement what it might expect from the public and government if it combined violence with a revolutionary purpose. Although the bomb outrage was attributed to the anarchists, and not generally to the strikers for the eight-hour day, it did materially reduce the sympathy of the public and served to intimidate many strikers.

By July 1, 1886, the membership of the order had diminished to 510,351. This retrogression was the result of a number of circumstances. In part it was due to natural loss of enthusiasm by a mass of people who had suddenly been set in motion without experience. In some measure it was a result of the aforementioned disastrous disputes. This so-called upheaval of the eighties offered a practical test of the rival claims of the Knights and the trade unionists. Samuel Gompers, whom I knew personally, and who for most of his life was president of the

American Federation of Labor, believed in craft unionism and held strongly that employers should not belong to any of their unions. He had a better understanding and grasp of the situation than the leaders of the Knights had. He realized that the time was not ripe for industrial unionism and all that went with it. This issue of structure, that is, the conflict between "craft autonomists" and the "one big union" or industrial union advocates, has remained the outstanding factional issue in the labor movement.

The most immediate cause for the downfall of the Knights, however, was the organization of employers. Employers organized sectionally, nationally, and internationally. We began to have an organization of capital which embraced within the scope of its activity many nations. Even the idea of a world trust—an exclusive world combination of capitalists—was proposed. In small localities in the United States, where the power of the Knights was especially great, all the employers, regardless of industry, united to defeat the Knights. In large manufacturing centers, however, the organization generally included only the employers of one industry. To attain their end these associations made liberal use of the lockout, the blacklist, and armed guards and detectives. The determined attack and stubborn resistance of the employers' associations after the strike of May, 1886, and the obvious incompetence displayed by the labor leaders, caused a turn in the tide of the labor movement.

In spite of all this activity, which I have merely sketched, the general public actually knew very little about the various aspects of the labor movement. A reading of the press of that time will reveal an exaggeration of facts and figures which unduly magnified the power of labor organizations. This dramatic exaggeration of the forces of labor, and of the Knights in particular, made it impossible for the ordinary man to get a clear conception of the labor movement. He was unaware even of the

elementary differences between socialism and anarchism. There
were a great many trees all around, but no one could see the
forest for the trees. I plunged in and tried to make a road
through the trees and to get a glimpse of the forest. In writing
the *Labor Movement in America* I thought I was doing something very remarkable and making a real contribution to human
affairs. Looking back over the many years since the book appeared, I do not feel particularly proud of it and sometimes I
feel inclined to disavow it. But, after all, it is my child, and
there it stands and will stand indefinitely. At the time I was
full of enthusiasm and was fired with the thought that I was
fulfilling a mission. I expected a good deal of opposition, if not
persecution, on account of the position that I was taking in
regard to organized labor and to the labor movement in general. However, I felt that I had a mission that I must fulfill; in
the words of St. Paul, as I wrote to my mother at the time,
"Woe is me if I preach not this gospel!"

I MAKE A PLEA TO THE CHURCHES

The struggle between the organized forces of labor and capital which manifested itself in this spectacular crisis of the
eighties indicated a conflict which was deep and which would
probably be prolonged. A crisis means an opportunity and I
saw in this special crisis an unprecedented, unparalleled opportunity for the church to direct the conflicting forces into such
fruitful channels that they might have become powerful for the
"good of man and the glory of God." I extended the following
plea to the church in my book *Social Aspects of Christianity:*
"The Church must gain leadership. This does not mean that
clergymen, as such, should be recognized as preeminently social leaders of the time, but that the Spirit of Christ should be
infused into the social movement under consideration and the

social forces which are producing this upheaval should become mighty ethical forces."

I made an appeal for "a profound revival of religion, not in any narrow or technical sense, but in the broadest, largest, fullest, and most complete sense, a great religious awakening which shall shake things, going down into the depths of men's lives and modifying their character. This religious reform must infuse a religious spirit into every department of political life." [10]

The all important question of the period was, "Do these conflicting forces promise peaceful revolution, or one of violence and bloodshed, a beneficent or a maleficent revolution?" The answer I gave in *Social Aspects of Christianity* was, "That depends upon their religious character." In estimating the true import of the social crisis of any period in our history we must not fail to inquire into religious movements. Religion is a social cement, a social tie. It is strange that when some have called attention to the importance of religion as a social force, men, in the name of science, have denounced them and ridiculed them for so doing. Yet it is hard to think of anything more unscientific than any philosophy of society which neglects a consideration of the role played in its evolution by religion. The attempt to neglect this role is more than unscientific; it is absurd. While the social ties are many in kind, religion is the only force which has sufficient power to unite individuals into a society. It is a necessary element in the social organism, if its members are to work harmoniously together.

What of the religious movements during this critical period? After the publication of my *Social Aspects of Christianity* I was asked by someone what I meant by the title. To the individual making the inquiry, salvation was merely an individual process. And so it was with many. The power of Christianity for the moral life of the individual was recognized; but the power of

Christianity for the intellectual, scientific or political life of nations in a revolutionary age, or for the industrial life of that generation, was a problem of the day. I have always held that the mission of Christianity, like the mission of the Jews as revealed in the Old Testament, was the salvation of the individual in a community. The entire duty of man is summed up by Christ in two commandments, the first of which inculcates love to God, and the second, love to one's neighbor, "and the one is said to be like unto the other." Nothing is more difficult, nothing requires more divine grace than the constant manifestation of love to our fellows in all our daily acts; in our selling, buying, getting gain. People still want to substitute all sorts of beliefs and observances in the place of this, for it implies a totally different purpose from that which animates this world. It is when men attempt to regulate their lives seven days in the week by the Golden Rule that they begin to perceive that they cannot serve God and mammon; for the ruling motive of the one—egotism, selfishness, is the opposite of the ruling motive of the other—altruism, devotion to others, consecration of heart, soul, and intellect to the service of others. Men are still quite willing to make long prayers on Sunday, if on week days they may devour widows' houses; or, as the Reverend Mark Guy Pearse said at Chautauqua, "They are ready to offer their prayers and their praise on Sunday, if on Monday they may go into the market place and skin their fellows and sell their hides."

Our theological seminaries have learned professors to teach their students, the future clergy, how to obey the First Commandment, and the various branches of learning taught are called theology. But we find in them few to teach us how to fulfill the Second Commandment, and in 1880 no one. This is the function of social science, the science of human happiness. It is in this duty to love and serve our fellows that I find the most convincing proof of the divinity of Christ. "Let us see your love for God in your manifest love for man." This is the message of Christ; this, I regard as the grand distinctive feature of Christianity, this exaltation of humanity. When you accept this you find in the command to love your neighbor as yourself, a sure, firm basis, a standing ground from which you can clearly develop an ethical system and determine the relations which ought to exist between the church and the world.

It has been said that the church is a representative of Christ whose Kingdom was not of the earth. True, but the higher has the basis in the lower life, and the administration of the church's earthly stewardship determines its attainment of the higher responsibilities. That Christianity which is not a living force in matters of temporal concern is certainly a defective Christianity. When we inquire into the consequences of the notion that Christianity has chiefly to do with another world and not with the establishment of righteous relations and the development of character in this world, we shall find an explanation for the aberrations of the church. During the critical eighteen nineties the church certainly neglected the enforcements of our duties with respect to temporal concerns and as a result we found among the elements of the social movements a spirit of resistance to Christianity. In many cases, this resistance, passing into open attack, culminated in the revilings uttered by men like the Chicago anarchists and John Most, who said the church was bad, thoroughly bad, a bulwark of privilege; in Europe, of dynasties; here, of plutocrats. As a result of observation and reflection, I was forced to the conclusion that there was a clear alienation of thinking wage-workers from the church. The following sentences, from a Chicago labor paper, written by men inclined to be comparatively conservative, and who resisted all proposals of violence and anarchy, express a view which was generally held:

"On Thursday evening, the Reverend C. F. Goss addressed

a meeting called under the auspices of the Brotherhood of Car-
penters. In order to get an expression of opinion from his
audience, he asked who had ceased to sympathize with the
churches to hold up their hands. It is needless to say the number
of hands that were uplifted caused a pang of regret to the
speaker.

"A question that we would like to propound to the ministers
of Chicago is—'Have the working classes fallen away from the
churches, or have the churches fallen away from the working
classes?' We know hundreds and thousands of workingmen
who have the utmost respect, admiration and even love for the
pure and simple teaching of the gospel, and the beneficent and
exalted character of Jesus Christ, and yet they scarcely ever put
their feet inside the church that 'is called' His. Not because
they love the church less, but because they love their self-respect
more. They realize that there is no place in the average Chicago
church for the poor man unless it is in the position of janitor,
certainly not in the cushioned pews surrounded by individuals
who not only regard poverty as a disgrace, but by their vulgar
display endeavor to perpetually remind the poor man of his
poverty— While there are noble and notable exceptions, it must
be confessed that but a few of the average Chicago preachers
go out of their way to 'preach the gospel to the poor';—of
course, 'good' people who are 'rich' establish mission schools
for the 'bad' people who are 'poor'; and they succeed in bringing within the fold occasionally a few women and children who
are not sufficiently intelligent to realize that a mission school is
a sort of religious souphouse, where the gospel is distributed
as charity."

"Heaven," said another writer of this class, is "a dream invented by robbers to distract the attention of the victims of
their brigandage."

An article in Most's paper, the *Freiheit,* concludes with the exclamation: "Religion, authority, and state are all carved out of the same piece of wood. To the devil with them all!" And the Pittsburgh manifesto of the Working People's Associations contains this sentence: "The church finally seeks to make complete idiots out of the masses, and to make them forego the paradise on earth by promising them a fictitious heaven." [11]

In all my strivings to reform conditions, I have tried to be constructive rather than destructive. I was, and still am, a firm believer in the institution of American democracy. I felt, and I still feel, that we must work through these fundamental institutions, even though they are not free from evils. Even though the people were justified in condemning the coldness and indifference of the churches to suffering humanity, I felt that if the germs of better things in the church were taken hold of and developed they might be powerful institutions in directing the social forces which were in action. If this was so, I felt that through them we must seek our social salvation. Therefore, in many articles and addresses, I attempted to expound the thesis that Christianity is primarily concerned with this world, and it is the mission of Christianity to bring to pass here a kingdom of righteousness. In my writings and my addresses I also attempted to answer the question, "What will constitute a kingdom of righteousness?" What must we strive to accomplish in social reform? The answer I gave then still applies today.

"First of all, we must seek a better utilization of productive forces. This implies, negatively, that we should reduce the waste of the competitive system to its lowest possible terms; positively, that we should endeavor to secure a steady production, employing all available capital and labor power; furthermore, the full utilization of inventions and discoveries, by a removal of the friction which often renders improvement so difficult. Positively this implies, also, that production should be carried on under wholesome conditions.

"We must so mend our distribution of wealth that we shall avoid present extremes, and bring about widely diffused comfort, making frugal comfort for all an aim. Distribution must be so shaped, if practicable, that all shall have assured incomes, but that no one who is personally qualified to render service shall enjoy an income without personal exertion. In the third place, there must be abundant public provision of opportunities, for the development of our faculties, including educational facilities and the large use of natural resources for purposes of recreation." [12]

My attempts to influence the churches were not confined to my writings alone. I used every means within my reach to awaken the conscience of the churches to an appreciation of their obligations, the obligations resting upon them to do their part in bringing about a social order in harmony with the principles of Christianity. I spoke in churches very frequently. I addressed religious gatherings of all sorts, like the Epworth League, St. Andrews Brotherhood, etc. Among my friends and supporters were a great many men prominent in the churches, and also, I am sure, a great many among Jewish rabbis. I was associated with men like Bishop Potter, Bishop Brooks, and Bishop Huntington, and others in the Church Social Union and in the Christian Social Union. From Archbishop Ireland of St. Paul, too, I received encouragement and support in my struggles. Some of the younger men, particularly the Right Reverend Msgr. John A. Ryan, D.D., supported me.

I also knew Cardinal Gibbons, one of the greatest of all American cardinals, and I worked shoulder to shoulder with him at one time in averting a strike of street-car employees in Baltimore. At the time of the threatened strike the working day was seventeen hours. The conductors and drivers, for those were the days of the horse-driven cars, hardly knew their own children. A bill was introduced for a twelve-hour day. It was bitterly fought by the railway interests who said they knew of technical reasons why this bill, if passed, would not work. I fought as strongly as I could for the passage of this legislation. More effective, perhaps, than all I could do was the work of Cardinal Gibbons, who wrote, at this crucial time, a strong article on behalf of the street-car employees. Happily, the bill was passed, the strike averted, and somehow or other the street-car owners were able to adjust themselves technically to the new bill.

I TEACH AT CHAUTAUQUA

It was largely through Chautauqua that I was able to exercise my greatest influence. No one can understand the history of this country and the forces which have been shaping it for the last half century without some comprehension of the important work of that splendid institution that was, and is, Chautauqua. For many years, Chautauqua was a popular gathering place for the uneducated, as well as the educated. The "common people" flocked eagerly to listen to the talks which were given there. There were among the speakers men like William Jennings Bryan and Sam Jones, the preacher. These men commanded vast audiences which listened with rapt attention to what might be called a variety of evangelism. These two orators, however, were not typical of the men who came to address the great gatherings in the amphitheater. Bryan, of course, was a very great orator, and I do not think that Chautauqua needs to make any apology for him. Sam Jones, however, was on a lower plane. At times he was dignified, but at other times he acted a little like Billy Sunday, although he never quite got down to his level. Bishop Vincent brought men like Sam Jones to Chautauqua because he knew that their homely philosophy held a strong appeal to a wide intellectually untrained audience. Although Dr. Herbert B. Adams and I were too sophisticated to appreciate the homely wisdom of Sam Jones' lectures, Bishop Vincent realized that they had a universal appeal. Once his son, George Vincent, said to us: "You two boys don't bring in enough money to pay your salaries. It is men like Sam Jones who make it possible to engage you to do the kind of work which you are doing." The Vincents made Chautauqua stand for lifelong education for the many, not just for the few. In this lay its greatness.

Among those who were customarily invited to Chautauqua were to be found a number of the most distinguished men of the time. They were great thinkers as well as fine speakers. Having the gift of utterance, which scholars generally lack, they were ideally suited to extend the cultural influence of Chautauqua. I recall most clearly Professor Mahaffy, the Greek scholar from Trinity College, Dublin, a most polished gentleman. Men like Phillips Brooks, Washington Gladden, and President Eliot were among those who high-lighted the parade of outstanding educators who helped make Chautauqua what it was. It was almost as fascinating for an observer to study the audience, representing as it did, a cross-section of American life, as it was to listen to the speakers. Men in their shirt-sleeves, others in their Sunday best, all listened quietly, intently, their upturned faces plainly revealing their emotions. They were often profoundly moved by the discourses they heard, they were always interested. Nowhere else could they, farmers and laborers, get the solid mental food they were being fed so liberally here.

Superficial observers saw only the great crowds gathered together. Some Americans felt a certain degree of contemptuous tolerance for what they saw on the surface. But much more significance is to be attached to what is not obviously seen. If some men in our country did not see the importance of the service that Chautauqua was rendering the people, there were great men in other countries who did. Ambassador Bryce was one such person. He became familiar with Chautauqua and its work while on a visit to America. So great was his admiration for the place that he characterized it as one of the most wonderful things he had seen in America.

In 1884, I was invited by Bishop John H. Vincent, the founder, to teach in the summer school and to participate in the work of Chautauqua. For the next seven years, which were significant in many ways, I remained at this great institution. I was joined here by my senior at the Johns Hopkins University, Professor H. B. Adams, who, I believe, remained as long as I did. My students were mostly college graduates, and my courses were on a university level. For a number of years I also conducted a correspondence course, but I was not a popular lecturer. Seldom could I gather a big crowd together and when I could, they did not know what I was talking about. This is not said in disparagement of the crowd but of myself. There were many good scholars among those who came to learn, but it is only a rare few who can hold a crowd by their personal magnetism and give them a great message. If, as many believe, I had a message, I had to convey it to the world through my writings and my students rather than through my lectures.

It was for the Chautauqua Literary and Scientific Circle that I wrote the first edition of my *Outlines,* under the title *Introduction to Political Economy.* In this first edition of the *Outlines* there is to be found the general philosophy and principles that have shaped all future editions, including that of 1937. This book had a very wide circulation. I have been told by one of the publishers for Chautauqua, that they sold as many as two hundred thousand copies of this edition. You could hardly find a hamlet anywhere of any size where somebody had not read this book and where it had not been discussed. To illustrate, in Madison, Wisconsin, we used to buy our milk from a station maintained by the university. Here one could go and buy milk on the "cash and carry" plan. One day, the man who served us caught my name and asked: "Are you Richard T. Ely, the Richard T. Ely who wrote the *Introduction to Political Economy?* Why! I read your book years ago in the Chautauqua course!"

Instances such as the above were innumerable. They reveal the wide ramifications of the influence of Chautauqua, that is, of the real Chautauqua. It is desirable to distinguish clearly between Chautauqua, New York, and the roving Chautauquas established throughout the country. These were just money-making affairs and had no more real connection with the actual Chautauqua than a similarity of name. Their activities are to be deplored since they created an unfortunate amount of confusion as to the merits of Chautauqua. There was no way that this could have been checked. The name, Chautauqua, geographical designation, could not be copyrighted. Chautauqua was the greatest movement this country has ever seen for adult education. I was in a position during those seven years, not only to contribute to this movement, but to observe what an uplifting and vitalizing influence it had through the length and breadth of the land.

Another touching illustration comes to mind. One day, driving down from Chautauqua with my wife to the home of my parents in Fredonia, New York, we stopped at a place near Brockton. For some reason which I do not at this moment recall—it may have been for a glass of water or merely to rest—we stopped on our journey at the home of an old lady. In the course of a pleasant conversation with our hostess, she ushered us across the hall into the parlor. There, on the wall, we saw a certificate awarded to her after completion of the course in the Chautauqua Literary and Scientific Circle. It seemed to brighten the entire room, just as the excellent four year course it represented probably had brightened the life of its owner.

These certificates might have been found in many an isolated home during that period. They were awarded to those who successfully completed the four year course in the Chautauqua Literary and Scientific Circle. Chautauqua never awarded degrees, and those "highbrows" who have spoken contemptuously of the "degrees" conferred by Chautauqua merely reveal their ignorance of the true facts.

If I have been fortunate enough to contribute anything fundamental to further the splendid ideals of Chautauqua, it has been returned to me tenfold by the opportunities afforded me there to meet some of the truly great men of the day. Among these were men who were my students. I believe it was through the correspondence course that I first made the acquaintance of both Charles J. Bullock and David Kinley. These men have been loyal friends. Their respective careers, each fine in its own way, have been a joy to me. Charles J. Bullock has become a full professor at Harvard. David Kinley went with me to Wisconsin and later became president of the University of Illinois.

Among the comparatively few business men who were my students, I recall particularly one prominent Wall Street banker. His enrollment in my correspondence course was in a sense ironical but typical. The small town banker would have thought it absurd to take a course in banking with a professor whom he would have called a mere "theorist." But this financier took his work very seriously, he wanted to learn more, he was open to suggestion, and we had some very interesting correspondence which, I believe, was mutually profitable.

It was, however, among my colleagues that I found a man whose friendship I valued most highly. He was Dr. William Rainey Harper, then professor of Yale University, and afterwards president of the University of Chicago. That university was then simply a proposal. We spoke about it often. I doubt if there is anyone living who knows more about his early ideas for the development of the university than I do. He always hoped that I would go with him to Chicago, but it turned out otherwise. Dr. Harper was especially eager to continue his research work. He said, more than once, that if it came to a choice between his research and the presidency of the university, he would give up the presidency; but that too turned out otherwise. One would have to be a superman to carry the heavy load of administrative work involved in the presidency of a university and at the same time keep up his research and writings. Dr. Harper's greatness lies, therefore, in that he was the first president of the University of Chicago. For nobly fulfilling his functions in that office, great praise and honor have justly been accorded him.

What a character this learned scholar was! What a wonderful man! At the age of fourteen, he was graduated from Muskingum College. A few years later, while still under twenty, he eloped with the daughter of the president of his alma mater. One night he went to the president's home, raised a ladder to the second story, helped his future wife down and off they went to be married. Having known Dr. and Mrs. Harper for many years, having spent many pleasant days with them either at their home or ours, I know that they never regretted that youthful venture. Theirs was, indeed, a happy marriage. How could it have been otherwise when an attractive young girl, still in her teens, marries a Peter Pan? He was a Peter Pan who never grew up; to the last he was a boy and delighted to indulge in boyish pranks. The spirit of boyhood was always a part of him. Once when Dr. Harper, Mrs. Harper, my wife and I went to the World's Fair in 1893, this spirit manifested itself. He acted in a way that would now delight my little boy, Billy, six years old, who would regard him as an ideal playmate. Although Mrs. Harper appeared to be a little disturbed by his boyishness, I was filled with admiration for this man in whom youth seemed to be eternally embodied. How grand it would be if more of us old duffers were like him!

For seven years, Dr. Harper and I ate our meals at the same table in the friendly Hotel Athenaeum. This hotel had very generously made arrangements to help college boys work their way through school. They were given various jobs in the hotel, for example, most of the waiters at the hotel were of this group. The boy who waited on us was a very dignified Yale student. My wife and I were somewhat troubled, at one point, about the problem of tipping; should we or should we not leave a tip? Towards the end of the season the student-waiters gave a concert. Their songs relieved us of any doubts on this score. I recall a few scattered lines from one of these improvised tunes:

> The Hotel Athenaeum sets a good meal now and then
> Yet I think I can distinguish between a rooster and a hen
> And my jaws refuse to masticate the cock that used to crow
> When Columbus found America four hundred years ago.

Then, tapping their pockets, they sang the refrain—"Here's where the good tip goes."

The group at our table at the hotel was a jolly crowd. Once Harper made a suggestion that was typical of his flair for gaiety. He proposed that instead of eating the full course dinner according to the menu, we should begin with the dessert and end with the soup. This we proceeded to do. During one of these backward sessions, I recall that George E. Vincent, son of Bishop Vincent, passed by and grinned at this exhibition of "his freaks" as he smilingly called us.

The name of George Vincent must be added to the list of those for whose friendship I am ever grateful to Chautauqua. At that time he was just getting on his feet. His father was training him to take charge of Chautauqua. My wife and I often talked with his mother about him and his future. With what maternal love and solicitude Mrs. Vincent watched his development, step by step. The day finally came when he did take charge of Chautauqua. He continued to guide its development according to the traditional philosophy that Chautauqua must "be kept in close and sympathetic connection with the great currents of national life. It must be a center from which the larger and more significant movements may gain strength and intelligent support." This was only the beginning of a great career. He continued to grow, going from one responsible post to another—president of the University of Minnesota, president of the Rockefeller Foundation, etc. His career, highly gratifying to his friends, must have afforded great and lasting satisfaction to his mother and father. The greatest compliment I can pay him is to say that he pretty nearly fills his father's shoes. To have even approached the stature of his father would have made him a remarkable man, and he has almost attained that height himself.

I have reserved for the last my impressions of Bishop John H. Vincent, just as one always keeps to the end that which is most highly treasured. Yes, I treasure my association with Bishop Vincent. Although he towered above most persons that he met, he was always humble. It makes me feel humble when I think that this man, who was so much my superior, looked up to me in various ways and even took my advice. I recall once that he denounced monopolies in a lecture he gave before a great audience gathered in the amphitheater. To some extent, he was right, just as to some extent Senator Borah is right today. However, I suggested that he should make a distinction between private and public monopolies. I told him that public monopolies were often a great blessing and usually worked to the interests of the people. Thereafter, whenever he lectured against monopolies, he always made it clear that he was opposing private monopolies.

Although he was a man of learning and light, he felt that his lack of a modern university education deprived him of something which his associates had. Be that as it may, it certainly did not deprive him of a keen perception of the value of education. He firmly believed that education must and should begin at the cradle and not end until the grave.

Bishop Vincent was a courageous man and a loyal friend. Always seeking new truths, he was not afraid to support them. He believed in me and he gave me the opportunity to preach the gospel that the beginning and end of all economics is man, and that economics must be subservient to the ethics of Christianity.

I PREACH SOCIAL SOLIDARITY

Many of my books were especially influential in the field of religion. Bishop Vincent was largely responsible for the use of my *Social Law of Service* by the Epworth League, the youth organization of his own church. Because I am convinced, today more than ever, that this book contains much that is wise, because I humbly believe it to be one of the few inspired things I have ever done, I am profoundly grateful that its contents were made available to at least a portion of the youth of this country. I like to think that this work, particularly my views on social solidarity, had some influence on the thought and actions of those who read it. I believed that "To upbuild human character in men you must establish for them right social relations. On the other hand, we fulfill our own mission and develop our own true individuality, not in isolation, but in society, and by bringing ourselves in body and mind into harmony with the laws of social solidarity. . . . Social solidarity means the oneness of human interests; it signifies the dependence of man upon man, both in good things and in evil things. Social solidarity means that our true welfare is not an individual matter purely, but likewise a social affair; our weal is common weal; we thrive only in a commonwealth; our exaltation is the exaltation of our fellows, their elevation is our enlargement. Social solidarity implies not only fellowship in interests and responsibilities, but that unity in nature which is brought before us by the expression, 'human brotherhood.' Social solidarity signifies not only that man needs association with his fellow-men, but that he shares with them their sins and their sufferings. Our sin is sin for others; their sin is our sin. There is no such thing, either as purely individual sin, or a purely individual righteousness." [13]

Bishop Vincent also introduced some of my books in the Methodist reading courses, courses marked out for those who were preparing for the ministry. These books remained a part of that course for a great number of years, although I do not know precisely how many. I do know that a few years ago, most of the Methodist ministers of middle age would probably have been found to have read these books and to have been influenced by them to some degree.

Social Aspects of Christianity, particularly, reached a very wide audience. In it I listed the following subjects which I thought should be taken up by the church because they were all religious subjects:

"1. Child labor—a growing evil—diminishing in other countries, increasing in this, removing children from home at a tender age, ruining them morally, dwarfing them physically and mentally.

"2. The labor of women under conditions which imperil the family. These are the facts about child labor, and the number of women wage-earners as gathered by my friend, Dr. E. W. Bemis, and published in his article on 'Workingmen in the United States,' in the American edition of the *Encyclopaedia Britannica:*—

" 'The number of males over sixteen engaged in manufacturing in 1880 was 2,019,035, an increase in ten years of 24.97 percent. The number of females over fifteen was 531,639, an increase in the same time of 64.2 percent; and of children 181,-921, an increase of 58.79 percent. . . . The employment of women in all gainful occupations is increased fifty percent faster than the population, or than the employment of men, and the same is true to a still greater extent of the employment of children, save in the very few states which have stringent factory laws and make any genuine effort to enforce them.'

" 'To show the effect of good laws properly enforced, it may be mentioned that in Massachusetts, the banner state of the Union in labor legislation, although still behind England, it has been found possible to diminish child-labor by seventy percent.'

"3. Sunday labor, an increasing evil, against which working-men throughout the length and breadth of the land are crying out bitterly. Their papers abound in complaint. A mass meeting has been held in Chicago to agitate against Sunday slavery. What an opportunity for the church! And remember, that the spirit of the fourth commandment means that a man should have one day in seven free, if he cannot by any possibility (street-car employees, e.g.) have Sunday. The spirit of the institution of Sunday has in too many instances departed, and it has been forgotten that Sunday has been made for man. Some people talk as if in Sunday observances they were conferring a favor on God. Sunday is to too many merely an arbitrary matter, just as if God had commanded us in entering a room always to enter with the left foot foremost. Thus, we have actually had controversies as to whether we should observe Saturday or Sunday, as if it made the slightest difference. So frivolous have become many things with which at least some Christians concern themselves. 'The letter killeth, but the spirit giveth life.' There are also those who imagine that, if it is really necessary for them to work their employees on Sunday, they do not break the fourth commandment in compelling them to work Sunday, and also on all other days of the week. It is one of the best features of the programme of the American Sabbath Union that they contemplate agitation for a six-day law, which shall make it illegal to contract for more than six days' work in seven. Such a law ought to be accompanied with adequate provisions against subterfuges and with severe penalties for disobedience. It is thoroughly Christian in spirit. It will also test the sincerity of those who claim that Sunday work is a necessity.

"4. Playgrounds and other provision for healthful play and recreation in cities—an antidote to the saloon and other forms of sin.

"5. Removal of children from parents who have ceased to perform the duties of parents. Homes, real homes should be found for these.

"6. Public corruption, about which let us have something precise and definite. The moral iniquity of city councilmen, who accept street-car passes, or writers for the press, or legislators and judges who accept railroad passes, might profitably be treated under this head.

"7. Saturday half-holidays, a great moral reform which has been accomplished in England, where men work but fifty-four hours a week. N.B. England, with short hours, is of all countries most dreaded in international competition. Some of you will point to New York, but I say the experiment has never been honestly tried in New York. Furthermore, it must be borne in mind that it is not enough merely to assist in securing leisure. It is necessary to show people how to use leisure. This, like other things, must be taught by precept and example.

"8. A juster distribution of wealth. Under this head a refutation of those ridiculous persons who would have us believe that wage-earners now receive nine-tenths of all the wealth produced—quackery and jugglery which must delight Satan.

"9. A manly contest against the deadly optimism of the day which aims to retard improvement and to blind to actual dangers. After careful thought and observation, I believe the social consequences of optimism even more disastrous than those of pessimism, though both are bad enough. Less spread-eagleism in America, more repentance for national sins, e.g., the most corrupt city governments to be found in the civilized world." [14]

Today, half a century after these words were first written, they seem matter of fact. They have lost some of their meaning. It is unfortunate that they have not lost more of their meaning. If today these words were completely meaningless then the book would have completely fulfilled its purpose.

THERE HAS BEEN HEAT, BUT NOT ENOUGH LIGHT

Today I ask myself the question: "How much nearer are we to the goal of a righteous social order?" What have been the fruits of so much energy expended and so many immeasurable sacrifices? Some even ask, "Can we accomplish the ends which we have in view and will the effort which we put forward to accomplish these ends meet with a return commensurate with the exertions involved?" These great movements in which I played a role have swept over the world with force enough to have accomplished great things, if only the tremendous energy and devotion had been wisely expended. There was heat, but not enough light. So it has been through all the ages. Think of the children's crusade of the Middle Ages. What a splendid thing it was! The Christian world was aroused, and the display of courage, and the enthusiasm on the part of the children and others was magnificent. Yet what a tragedy it was, because all this feverish activity was not guided by a unified practical principle, a light to guide the way.

What confusion there had been on the part of the Protestant churches! How often has it happened that one particular economic doctrine has been advocated by the church and has been claimed as the only expression for applied Christianity. Once I was asked to speak before a great gathering of Methodists in Evanston, Illinois. It was their belief that every Christian must attach himself to the theory of the single tax. Because I was conscious of my own integrity, I could not see my way clear to advocate the single tax. For this reason, they thought that I must have lost my way; they suspected me of selling out to the interests, especially the real estate interests. The advocates of the single tax said, "Here we have applied Christianity. Follow Henry George in his eloquent and moving plea for a new and better social order." Yet it seemed to me that the natural rights doctrine of Henry George was thoroughly unscientific, a belated revival of the social philosophy of the eighteenth century. I believed that the economics underlying Henry George's pleas was unsound. My experience had shown me that his idea of unearned increment worked untold injury. Therefore, I was accused of forsaking my earlier faith because I could not attach myself to a movement which I felt was producing harm and retarding social progress. This attitude was typical of the conditions I saw in the Protestant church during my whole life. The various factions of the church have seized on this or some other particular proposal for social reform as a panacea and have said to its followers: "If you are a Christian, you must adhere to this panacea." These diverse groups, with diverse methods of solving their common problems, each would say: "I am the economic Christ, I am the Way, follow me." In so many cases, it was a false Christ who would arise, mislead the multitude, and cause endless destruction.

As I look about me I discover wise guidance in various religious groups. One is in the Jew's Mosaic legislation. I think we must say that Moses was one of the greatest statesmen of all time. He had a clear perception of the economic problems in the primitive economic society of Israel, many of which are still with us today. Moses clearly perceived the evils of indebtedness and he accordingly provided for the liquidation of debts from time to time to keep the economy of Israel sound, and prosperity widespread. In the year of Jubilee, debts were to be canceled and people were to be given an opportunity to start over. He also believed that where debts were incurred to relieve personal distress, interest should not be taken. In the Mosaic law, land was not to be regarded as a commodity, for the final ownership was God's. "The land shall not be sold forever, for the land is mine." It was to be used by the earthly owner for home and subsistence. Speculation in land, buying and selling for gain, was absolutely inconsistent with the spirit of the legislation. If poverty necessitated it, temporary possession could be given with widely extended rights of redemption. Although these ideas are sound in principle, they were never carried out. In modern complex society they could not be carried out any more than in primitive Israel. But, if we cannot apply these laws to the letter, we must aim at the spirit for which they stand. It will require our best brains, with all good will and we must remember that "the letter [of the law] killeth, the spirit giveth life."

When I turn to the Catholic Church I find encouragement in the Encyclicals of Leo XIII and Pope Pius XI. I, as a Protestant, do not find anything but sound economics in these products of the wise old Vatican, especially those sections dealing with the relations between labor and capital and between man and land. In answer to my request, the Right Reverend Msgr. John A. Ryan, D.D., has written a summary of these two Encyclicals which appears in the Appendix.

Many Protestants, too, strove mightily to bring about a better social order. We in America may be proud of the heroic figures who coupled zeal with intelligence in pointing out the evils in our social system, exposing them fearlessly when it involved sacrifice on their part. In the latter part of the nineteenth and the early part of the twentieth century, there was a certain splendid flowering of the various religious organizations. Bishop Vincent was a fearless leader of the Methodist Episcopal Church. Noteworthy is the statement of the social creed of the church adopted by the general conference of the Methodist Episcopal Church in May, 1908 (see Appendix). Washington Gladden, pastor of the Congregational Church in Columbus, Ohio, was a man of the highest type, who proclaimed the social gospel of righteousness and fought for what he believed to be the truth in a way that reminded many of us of Martin Luther of old. He pointed his finger at a mighty evildoer and said, "Thou art the man," just as the prophet Nathan said to King David. Shailer Mathews and Phillips Brooks must not be forgotten when we think of the flowering of the churches. To go back a little farther, we cannot fail to remember William Booth and the Salvation Army, which still continues its good work, and which has gained the admiration of Christians and Jews. I also have praise for the Church Social Union, of which I was, for some time, secretary.

In spite of these praiseworthy movements, I cannot fail to discover a certain confusion and lack of unity among the Protestants. Perhaps this is due to the splitting of Christians into many religious organizations. Perhaps here we find an argument for the efforts being made to unite Christians. The merit of the

Encyclicals of the Catholic Church is that they stand for the whole body of Roman Catholics. This gives them a wide and spacious house in which to move about; it is a house with metes and bounds, and not with the whole wide world to roam about in; the Ten Commandments still hold.

IDEAS GOVERN THE WORLD

In considering its influence in achieving the desired reforms we must realize that the church may only affect the social order through the mind and will of those who come under its influence. The activities of the churches must be part of a larger program of education to be participated in by many agencies.

"Nothing can exceed in importance the improvement of education, taking education in the largest sense of the word. Aristotle, over two thousand years ago, perceived the truth which our Washington uttered so forcefully, that education should be adapted to the conditions of each country, and particularly that in democratic countries, education should prepare and equip the young for democratic institutions. 'In proportion as the structure of a government gives force to public opinion, it is essential that public opinion should be enlightened.' These are the words of Washington. But there never was so much need for education as at the present time, because society never before was so complex, and social problems have never before been so difficult of solution. We who live in democratic countries call each citizen sovereign, and we should see to it that each citizen has an education befitting a sovereign. If we are wise, we will prepare ourselves as carefully for civil life as Germany trains her sons for war, begrudging no expense, no expenditure of time designed to accomplish our purpose." [15]

I have always been an idealist in the philosophical sense, firm in my belief that ideas govern the world. I have always believed that the mind of man must be posited as a free creative force, the direction of which is determined by education.

The history of ideas is the history of man. Ideas distinguish man from all lower animals, and all that is significant in human history may be traced back to ideas. From time to time, in the history of mankind, an idea of such tremendous import has found acceptance in the minds and hearts of men that it has been followed by a new era in the progress of the human race. The idea of Jehovah, which found acceptance among the ancient Hebrews, was one of these germinal ideas, which made the world ever thereafter a different world. That idea has been molding human history ever since it was first clearly received and promulgated. The idea of itself, from the time of its reception up to the present, has been growing larger and more elevated and refined. It has undergone a perpetual process of purification, and has been one of the great psychical forces which give shape to human history. Christianity came into the world as the outcome of another grand idea, and since its reception the world has been a new world. Its mighty significance has been recognized in dating all events with reference to the founder of that religion. Everything which happens is either before Christ or after Christ. Altogether apart from any peculiar belief in the mission and person of Christ, this could not be otherwise. Passing on down the stream of human history, we come to still another idea which has made the world different from what it was before, and is thus giving direction to human history. This is the idea of evolution, the general acceptance of which we must recognize as the distinguishing characteristic of nineteenth-century thought.

In the twentieth century the idea of liberty in a democracy, for which the people of England and America have stood pre-eminently, has been shaping our history. If this idea of liberty is to survive, it must be based on universal love and human brotherhood. These ideas, and these alone, can save the world. Unless they come to fruition our modern nations, in spite of their material triumphs, will go the way of the great empires of the past.

"MEN, NOT BRICKS AND MORTAR" AT THE JOHNS HOPKINS UNIVERSITY

It cannot be too often stated that education must play a vital part in keeping alive our democracy and in adapting our fundamental institutions to the attainment of an ideal state. Education is a slow and costly process, but men with foresight and a keen appreciation of our need have given generously of their time, energy, and wealth to further this great unifying force.

Johns Hopkins was one of these. A wealthy Baltimore business man who had accumulated a large estate, he had never married and when he grew old he did not know how he would divide his wealth. The story goes that a remark made by a friend influenced his decision. This man told him, "There are two things which are sure to live: a university—for there will always be youth to learn; and a hospital—for there will always be suffering to relieve." Therefore he divided seven million dollars between a hospital and a university, both of which were to carry his name. We are here concerned only with the three and one half million dollars which made possible the Johns Hopkins University. The use of this fund was to be guided solely by the judgment of the board of trustees. Very wisely, this board summoned Presidents Eliot of Harvard, White of Cornell, Angell of Michigan, Porter of Yale, McCash of Princeton, and Barnard of Columbia, and asked them to suggest for president a man who would be capable of conceiving and guiding the development of the university-to-be.[16] Unanimously these men named Daniel Coit Gilman, then president of the newly organized University of California. In the course of a varied career he had already served as librarian at Yale, and as secretary and money-raiser for the Sheffield Scientific School. On October 24, 1874, he received a letter from Reverdy Johnson, Jr., chairman of the board of trustees, in charge of the founding of the Johns Hopkins University, inviting him to act as president of the embryo university. Daniel Gilman promptly answered the letter in these words: "As I read that this munificent gift is free from any phase of political and ecclesiastical interference and is to be administered according to the judgment of the trustees; when I think of the immense fund at your control; when I think of the relations of Baltimore to the other great cities of the East and especially of the relations which the university should have to the recovering states of the South, I am almost ready to say that my services are at your disposal." Thus, Daniel Coit Gilman, at the ripe maturity of forty-four years, offered his great spiritual and intellectual wealth for the founding of a university which was destined to "naturalize in America the idea of a true university." [17]

To his mind there were six requisites which must be fulfilled before the university could be launched; an idea, capital to make the idea feasible, a definite plan, an able staff of coadjutors, books and apparatus, and students. The capital was at his command. He already had some very definite ideas. He spent one year in Europe to see what they were doing in their universities, to clarify his ideas, and perhaps to modify them. The system in the German universities appealed to him, but the new university was not to be an imitation of anything. He "did not undertake to establish a German university, nor an English, but an American, based on and applied to the existing institutions of our country." He wanted it to be able to offer training of a higher order than that given at the existing colleges and universities. He wanted it to be a haven for those who had a genuine interest in research. As a result, the Johns Hopkins University was an innovation in American educational history. For the first time in an American university, the graduate and professional schools constituted the center of its activities, and the undergraduate school was but an appendage. In February, 1876, in his inaugural address, he made known to the world the ideals of the new university. He interpreted the significance of the worldwide discussion regarding the aims, methods, deficiencies, and possibilities of education in the following way: "It is a reaching out for a better state of society than now exists; it is a dim but an indelible impression of the value of learning; it is a craving for intellectual and moral growth; it is a longing to interpret the laws of creation; it means a wish for less misery among the poor, less ignorance in the schools, less bigotry in the temples, less sufferings in the hospital, less fraud in business, less folly in politics; it means more study of nature, more love of art, more lessons from history, more security in property, more health in cities, more virtue in the country, more wisdom in legislation, more intelligence, more happiness, more religion." These words reflected a plan for his own life; they became a plan of life for the university. He believed that its purpose should be "not so much to impart knowledge to the pupils, as to whet the appetite, exhibit methods, develop powers, strengthen judgment and invigorate the intellectual and moral forces; to prepare for the service of society a class of students who will be wise, thoughtful, and progressive guides in whatever department of work or thought they may be engaged; to impart a knowledge of principles rather than of methods." It was to stand for the doctrine that "religion claims to interpret the word of God, and science to reveal the laws of God; the interpreters may blunder, but truths are immutable, eternal, and never in conflict." The motto of the Johns Hopkins University became, "The truth shall make you free." [18]

Although he had large plans and high ideals and always seemed to be looking a long way ahead, he was never impractical or dreamy. His mind was steadily fixed on what could be done with the available means. The use of the funds was guided by one principle: "Men, not bricks and mortar." Gilman believed that the glory of a university should rest on the character of its teachers and scholars and not on their number, nor on the buildings for their use. He boldly made the announcement that the "best men who could be found would be first appointed without respect to the place from which they came, the college wherein they were trained, or the religious body to which they belonged." He wanted to give them salaries high enough to put them completely at their ease and relieve them of common cares.

Each of his six full professors received five thousand dollars a year. This was very high, especially in Baltimore, where living costs were lower than in most large cities. Some of the men in Yale, at this time, had salaries of not more than half this amount, and very few at Harvard had salaries as high as this. Although the finances of the Johns Hopkins suffered a severe shock in the failure of the Baltimore and Ohio Railroad, upon the dividends of which it so largely depended, Gilman stuck firmly to his belief that he should put all his money in men and give them every possible aid in their teaching and research. Furthermore, he wanted to give them only students far enough advanced to keep his teaching staff stimulated to the highest point. As a means of attracting to the university students of unusual ability, he established twenty fellowships to be held from periods of one to three years. Before this, fellowships and scholarships had not been used to any great extent in the United States, and their success at the Johns Hopkins was an important factor in causing their widespread employment in many of our universities. He believed that productive research was an indispensable part of the activities of a professorial body, and in order to facilitate and encourage the research activities of the faculty, he promptly began the publication of the *American Journal of Mathematics*, the *American Journal of Philology*, and the *American Chemical Journal*.

In his choice of men, President Gilman showed rare talent. He gathered about him a group of six men whom he made full professors. They were not only eminent scholars, investigators, and teachers, but able advisers. They differed widely in temperament, methods, and origin, and it was this very diversity which helped to give Johns Hopkins that intense and picturesque vitality which was so marked during its early years. "They were men actively at work, not mere rehearsers of knowledge garnered in some forgotten past and poured out soullessly to deaden the souls of the unfortunate." [19]

In addition to these six full professors, Gilman gathered together a group of young men, lecturers and assistants, of whom I was one. He always gave the impression to others that we younger men belonged in the same category as the full professors, that we were merely young and were going to arrive presently. He rejoiced in our success; he was delighted to get the first appreciative newspaper clipping, to obtain the first copy of a new book. And he never hesitated to give his men the pleasure which he knew his praise carried. I can think of many instances when Gilman's praise meant more to me than any small increase in salary would have meant. One day as I walked through the corridor near Gilman's office, I noticed on the bulletin board a clipping in praise of something I had written. I knew Gilman had put it there, and you can imagine the thrill I got out of it. He would often praise the younger members of the faculty to the students. Once, in talking to one of my students, he said, "It is remarkable how that young fellow Ely wants to get down to fundamentals and succeeds in doing it."

He knew this remark would get back to me. This is the sort of man Gilman was.

Another personal incident brings to mind the words: "Give him scope!" These words are an admirable summation of Dr. Gilman's attitude toward the members of his faculty. At one time, a group in New York City was talking about turning Cooper Union into a research school and making me director. They said that this was the kind of school that Peter Cooper really wanted. Although nothing came of this, President Gilman at the time said to me, "If I am consulted, I shall recommend you and say, 'Dr. Ely is a mature and competent man, give him scope!'" This idea of giving a man scope was fundamental with him. He believed that compulsion had no place in research and his only inflexible rule was, "Do your best work." The result was an atmosphere of eager, unforced work.

The following incident illustrates the extent to which academic freedom prevailed. I made an address before the alumni association of the law department of the University of Maryland on oyster legislation. The speaker before me had been John K. Cowen, President of the Baltimore and Ohio Railway. The assurance with which he had presented his economic knowledge, speaking like a pope, was irritating. I seized my opportunity to speak and made what I fear was a savage attack on Mr. Cowen. Later on Mr. Cowen retaliated; he launched into a bitter attack on me and said that so long as Professor Ely was at the Johns Hopkins University, he would never send any of his sons there. I learned of this from my colleague, Professor H. B. Adams, but President Gilman had never said a word to me about it, in spite of the fact that the episode must have irritated him considerably. He held firm to his belief that academic freedom must prevail.

Physically, the Johns Hopkins University was a very modest institution. It consisted of a number of private houses on

Howard Street, which was barely a respectable part of the city. Some rooms were enlarged, some torn down, and some additions were gradually built in the immediate neighborhood. We had no campus, no football, no baseball. This did not satisfy the Baltimorians because they did not have anything to show the visitors. Once, while my wife was riding in a trolley-car, she overheard a conversation between two ladies as they passed the university building. One of them said, "What is this we are passing?" The other replied, "I don't know. I think it must be a piano factory." This cut to the quick those Baltimorians who wanted something physically impressive to show visitors.

At a library party held one gusty September evening in a cozy cottage on the coast of Maine there gathered a group of Johns Hopkins men and their friends dressed to represent books. Dr. Gilman appeared in faultless evening dress, with only a copy of his annual report in his hand. The whole library of wits was baffled. Long after all the other grotesquely costumed characters had been guessed, that picturesque white-haired figure with the university report remained as inscrutable as ever. It was a young girl from New York who cried at last, "I have got you—you're 'Progress and Poverty' by Henry George." It matters little that her clever guess was wrong—that Dr. Gilman meant to impersonate the Book of Daniel. She had compressed into a neat phrase the popular understanding of Johns Hopkins. But the public was less impressed with its progress than its poverty. It is true that there was no outward magnificence. Some of the buildings were even ugly, but each one fitted its use, and there was a good supply of everything needed for actual work. What any student needed and the university did not have was instantly bought, even if it meant running into debt. One observer, after a tour through Johns Hopkins, aptly remarked, "They have millions for genuine research, but not one cent for show." [20]

Gilman was not interested in buildings. He was interested in men, "not bricks and mortar." It took great courage to await the recognition which attends the achievement of a vital but not superficially showy result. Daniel Gilman had the courage, and his achievement was genuine and vital. There was a certain atmosphere there that could not be found elsewhere and it still lingers on. I recall that several years after I went to Wisconsin, President Charles Kendall Adams spent some time at the Johns Hopkins. He returned full of enthusiasm, and he said, "They have got it, they have got it!" What was that "it" they had in my day in such large measure and which they still have? It was the spirit of youth. Johns Hopkins was headed by older men who had this spirit themselves. It was an inspiring atmosphere in which research and love of unfolding truth were richly fertilized.

ALBERT SHAW AND JOHN FINLEY WERE MY STUDENTS

I was twenty-seven when I joined the faculty at the Johns Hopkins and most of my students were about my age. They were warm-hearted and affectionate young men, and ties were formed which have lasted a lifetime. It is a source of great satisfaction to see that so many of my students have been successful and have had significant influence on world affairs. I like to think that I contributed, in some small way, particularly to the careers of three of my ablest students, Albert Shaw, John H. Finley, and Woodrow Wilson.

I recall, as if it were yesterday, looking up from the desk in my little office to see a tall dark young man standing in the doorway. To me it appeared that he was almost as tall as the door. He said immediately, "I am Albert Shaw. I am editor of a country newspaper in Iowa, writing articles on the silver question, strikes, boycotts, etc., but I know nothing about these things, and I have come down to learn about them." There is no doubt in my mind that at that time he was writing better articles than any other country editor in Iowa, but he alone knew that he didn't know. It recalled to me the story of Socrates, which I had read at Columbia College. The oracle had said that Socrates was the wisest man in all Greece. Socrates, being a very modest man, was much perplexed; he could not understand why the oracle had spoken thus. Being a religious man, however, he had to accept what the oracle said. So he scratched his head and slept on the matter for two or three nights. Then he said, "I have it! All these Greek philosophers know nothing, but I alone know that I know nothing, and that is why I am the wisest man in all Greece." Here I had another Socrates who has become a great journalist—to my mind, one of the greatest journalists in the United States. I gave him and Woodrow Wilson their examinations for the Ph.D. degree at the same time. I had been lecturing on French and German socialism and one of the questions I put was: "Give a succinct account of German socialism." It was a joy to read the answers of these two men; in style and substance they were worthy of the *Atlantic Monthly*. It so happened that Dr. Shaw's first position was with the Minneapolis *Tribune,* upon which he entered a week after taking his degree. Something, possibly an attempt on the Emperor's life, had happened which turned the attention of the world to German socialism. As soon as he entered the office, the proprietor said, "Do you suppose you could write an editorial on German socialism?" Shaw replied that he would see what he could do. So he sat down and reproduced the answer to the question as he had given it to me the preceding week. The chief was delighted with it, and also highly pleased to think that he had on his staff a writer who could produce such work just on tap, as it were.

Shaw has always been a keen observer and he set for himself

an exacting pace which he was able to keep up. Cyrus Northrup, president of the University of Minnesota, once said that the articles by Shaw were like streaks of light on the editorial page. One of his first efforts was a monograph on the co-operative coopers who were making barrels for the great flour mills of Minneapolis. This was published in the first volume of the publications of the American Economic Association and was a joy to me, for it was not only a good economic monograph, it was literature. It attracted wide attention and found a large sale which helped to replenish our almost empty treasury. He wrote other monographs which made an impression, and he soon gained recognition. Ultimately he acquired and edited for many years the *Review of Reviews,* one of the best periodicals of its kind that the country has ever had.

When John H. Finley came to us he was a poor boy, the son of a farmer. He and his brother Robert had gone to Knox College in Galesburg, Illinois. They hired a room there, and together prepared the food which they brought from their farm. Later Finley became president of Knox College. As I think of my former students, I am impressed by what heredity does. Environment counts, but heredity is fate. I could not fail to see that there was good blood in the Finleys, although it was much later that I learned that a Finley, a brother of a grandfather or of a great-grandfather, was once president of Princeton College. Finley impressed all who met him on account of his fine character, as well as his mental qualifications. Everyone knew he was a man who could be relied upon. And the solidity of his character was flavored by a charming sense of humor.

While Dr. Finley and his brother were students, I was writing articles twice a week for the Baltimore *Sun.* These were called, "Problems of the Day," and were afterward published in book form. At that time, I had no stenographer and wrote out the articles in my own hand. Unhappily, they could not read my handwriting at the *Sun* office. Dr. Finley and his brother were the only ones who could read it. I had a class from nine to ten, and one from one to two. Between these two classes I wrote my articles. As I would write, Dr. Finley, who has a beautiful hand, and Robert, who had a clear hand, would copy what I wrote. Then one or the other would rush the article down to the offices of the *Sun,* to appear the next morning. One day my wife came in while this was going on and laughingly said: "I see you are copying my husband's articles." Dr. Finley replied, "We do not call this copying, we call this interpretation." Dr. Finley has often since, in his own inimitable way, called attention to this amusing situation at my expense. One day at the Town Hall Club he told the story to a large group with this adornment: "One time when we were copying the manuscript, a gust of wind came along and blew one page of Dr. Ely's work out of the window and on to the sidewalk. A Chinese laundryman, coming along at this moment, picked up the paper and after turning it around several times, finally exclaimed, 'Ah! a letter from home!' "

Dr. Finley had a varied career. He was associated for a time with charity groups in Baltimore. Later, he was with a fine group in New York which had as its aim the improvements of the charitable institutions there. After this he became president of the College of the City of New York, and when he was installed, I listened proudly to the fine tribute paid him by Grover Cleveland. He had already been professor at Princeton. Then he became chancellor of the University of the State of New York. Finally, Mr. Ochs, publisher of the New York *Times,* called him to an editorship on that paper. Mr. Ochs did this because he had so much confidence in his sound judgment. Now, at seventy-three, he has become editor-in-chief of the New York

Times. In the course of these various changes, which sometimes disturbed me a little, he has at last a position he would prefer to any other in the United States.

I WAS WOODROW WILSON'S TEACHER

Woodrow Wilson's coming to the Johns Hopkins University in the autumn of 1883 is an ever-memorable event. We, in the faculty, and his fellow-students were most favorably impressed with Wilson as soon as we saw him. He had a forceful and handsome face, and a fine figure. He had not been with us long before we knew that we had in Wilson an unusual man. There could be no question that he had a brilliant future.

It cannot be said that we at the Johns Hopkins molded Wilson, because he developed from within according to his own innate ideas. He was Scotch Presbyterian and he had been influenced by the environment of his father's home in Virginia; he was a Virginian of the Virginians always. He was proud of his Scotch-Presbyterian heritage, and well he might have been for the Scotch Presbyterians had always produced leaders of a high order, upright, hard working, and intellectually distinguished. After graduating from Princeton College in the class of 1879, he studied law at the University of Virginia under Judge Minor, one of the greatest law teachers of that time. Woodrow Wilson felt a keen admiration for the stern discipline Judge Minor was able to exercise over his students. I remember his once saying that if Judge Minor ordered an examination for three in the morning every student would be on time. Wilson had himself in large measure that quality he so much admired in Judge Minor. Following graduation, he opened a law office in Atlanta, Georgia. But after one year of practice, he felt dissatisfied with the prospects. I doubt if a larger measure of financial success would have changed his

course. His heart was not in the law. His year of experience with
the crude actualities of practice had disillusioned him. He wrote,
"Here the chief end of man is certainly to make money, and
money cannot be made except by the most vulgar methods."

He wanted to become an author and a professor. I am inclined to think that he always had, at the back of his head,
thoughts of a political career. In a letter written in February,
1885, he expresses this in his own words: "I have a strong in-
stinct of leadership, an unmistakable oratorical temperament,
and the keenest possible delight in affairs; . . . I have a passion
for interpreting great thoughts to the world; I should be complete if I could inspire a great movement of opinion, if I could
read the experiences of the past into the practical life of the
men of today and so communicate the thought to the minds of
the great mass of the people as to impel them to great political
achievements." [21]

Indeed, he did have the gift of utterance to an unusual degree. His teachers at the Johns Hopkins soon discerned this.
Like many other graduate students, Wilson lectured in outlying
towns to supplement his income. One day he gave a lecture at
Towsontown, in which he spoke of socialists as being "long-
haired and wild-eyed." When I met him the next day, I asked
him, "Why did you refer to socialists as being 'long-haired and
wild-eyed'? I am no more a socialist than you are, but I've never
seen one who followed your description." Wilson answered,
"If you say such things you make people believe you are a conservative, and then you can go ahead and do progressive
things." Wilson's speeches were always very convincing, even
if they were not absolutely sincere. One hundred years from
now, schoolboys will be reciting extracts from Wilson's
speeches, which at times reached the very highest level. He believed that one should present the knowledge he acquired with
power and beauty of style. He studied and practiced public

speaking. There was always a fitness in whatever he said at any public gathering. Soon after I came to Madison, there was a gathering in my honor. I fear I was somewhat awkward, gauche, in my remarks. Wilson was called upon. He made a beautiful and fitting address. When I think of the contrast, I cannot, even now, help feeling mortified.

Also he could speak beautifully and say nothing, if he wished. I recall another occasion when he spoke before a gathering of graduate teachers at Madison. I was moved deeply by what he said. On my way home I tried to recall the substance of the talk and could not remember anything. Perhaps he felt that he had no message to give, and therefore, he delivered a perfect speech.

Just as he was a master of style in his speech, so he was in his writings. His belief that economics and political science should be written as literature set an example for his fellow-students and his associates. How far do most of us fall short of this ideal! In his dissertation for his Ph.D. degree, *Congressional Government,* he aimed to carry out the ideas of the English cabinet system of which he was an ardent champion. When the manuscript was handed to me for examination my eyes were giving me a little trouble. I took the paper home and gave it to my wife, saying to her, "Will you please read this aloud to me?" She thought I was giving her something that would be a frightful bore, and indeed most doctoral theses are. But she did not complain and set about her task. As she read, she became so interested that she was reluctant to stop.

Wilson's major was not economics, but political science. The salient feature of the work at Johns Hopkins was the seminar method, exemplified particularly by Professor H. B. Adams' history seminar, where an attempt was made to apply to the social sciences the laboratory methods used in the natural sciences. Whether we were economists or historians we all belonged to this seminar. Professors, fellows, and students were all brought together in one room, on the wall of which was the motto taken from Edward W. Freeman: "History is past politics, politics present history." Woodrow Wilson was a brilliant member of Dr. Adams' historical seminar. At first he was critical of Adams as well as of me. He thought Adams skipped lightly over too many subjects. He said of me that I was a "hard worker," "a conscientious student," but that Schönberg's *Handbuch* was my economic bible, and that I needed an impulse from outside to get started. The reason for this impression is incomprehensible to me. Certainly I never had an economic bible because I was too much of a born rebel and a skeptic. At that time Schönberg's *Handbuch,* written by a group of the best German economists, was the best textbook for graduate students. I also used German texts in order to help graduate students master that language, proficiency in which was required for the Ph.D. degree. If I did have any bible it would be found in the books and lectures of Professor Karl Knies.

I did not have Wilson's gift for utterance and my lectures were not the polished, finished productions that would have aroused his enthusiasm. His standards of style were so high that when he tested his own professors by them he found them "weak and slatternly" in the presentation of their material. If Adams and I had given polished lectures like the French professors in our field, he might have thought more of us, but we would not have accomplished so much.

The method I was following had proved most fruitful with the students who studied under me. I wished to trouble my students, to raise questions in their minds, and to have them solve problems in their own way. To use an expression from Socrates, my job was to act as "midwife" to get ideas in my students growing and if possible to help bring them to birth.

Scholastic honors meant nothing to Wilson. Before he came to Johns Hopkins he had had considerable experience with col-

leges and universities. He dreaded the rigid adherence to standardized curricula. What he wanted was to master the subjects
he was interested in. He determined to settle the matter with
Dr. Adams. Adams received his confidences sympathetically and
gave him full permission to go on with his "constitutional"
studies. He promised Wilson all the aid and encouragement he
could give to further his independent pursuits. Adams' response
to Wilson's request was in accordance with the philosophy of
study which was applied in the seminar. Wilson, of course, was
elated. Later he admitted that he had expected too much of
Adams and myself. He reached the conclusion that "everything
of progress comes from one's private reading—not from lectures."

One day I called into my office Mr. Wilson and another
Southern student, Mr. Burr J. Ramage. I laid before them a
plan for a book on the history of American economic thought
we three were to write. I can well remember the smile that
lighted up Wilson's face and the satisfaction that he took in
this idea. He went to work and wrote out in his own hand an
eighty-page account of the Ricardian economists, the manuscript
of which I still have and treasure as a precious possession. Mr.
Ramage also wrote as much in his own hand. I was to work on
pamphlet literature of economic significance which appeared in
our early history. I thought it would be easy to gather what
material was needed for the kind of study that we proposed to
make. However, the work did not go as fast as I had anticipated.
I wrote a letter to the New York *Nation* speaking about the
project and soliciting co-operation in securing the desired literature. I had little response and soon found it was a far more
difficult task to gather this literature than I supposed. Another
cause for suspending the project was that before we made much
more than a beginning we separated. Mr. Ramage went south
and died there many years ago. Mr. Wilson went to Bryn Mawr,

then to Wesleyan, and at last to Princeton. Our separation and
his absorption in public duties terminated the project, although
in no formal way was it ever abandoned. In the later years of
his life, after he became Governor and then President, it would
have been folly to ask him to go on with the undertaking. His
contribution, however, was a creditable performance. It expressed what were then somewhat new and modern ideas in
this country, namely, an appreciation of the evolution of thought
and the relativity of economic doctrines. It is a thorough and
objective study of the works of Vethake, Wayland, Tucker,
Bowen, Amasa Walker, and Francis A. Walker. Included in the
manuscript is a discussion of "Notes on Political Economy by a
Southern Planter." Of the economists in this group, he seemed
to admire Walker most. It is a careful, factual study and reflects little of the personality of Woodrow Wilson, the man.

Wilson was not interested in economics as much as in political science, although he was a good economics student. I was
somewhat uncertain as to his deep interest in the project in spite
of the fact that he had so eagerly gone into it. I was very much
gratified to learn from Mr. Ray Stannard Baker that the notes,
memoranda and letters left by Mr. Wilson indicate that he attached great importance to our plan. In a letter written to Professor R. Heath Dabney of the University of Virginia he spoke
about the project. "I am wading through innumerable American textbooks written by writers of the orthodox Ricardian
school [Perry, Bowen, Wayland, Vethake], for the purpose of
writing, with as profound an air of erudite criticism and infal-
lible insight as I can by any means counterfeit, about one-third
of the projected treatise. I am to get full credit as joint author
of the volume—but the question that is worrying me at present
is—will it be creditable?" My feeling of uncertainty concerning
his deep interest in our project may possibly be attributed to
the fact that Wilson was not of a demonstrative nature.

In one particular connection, however, I did feel that Wilson responded favorably to my teaching. When I returned from Germany in about 1880 I brought back with me the idea that the problem in our age is not one of legislation but fundamentally one of administration. In the early days of the Johns Hopkins University I gave a course on administration in which I brought out the idea that in matters of administration the United States lags far behind other countries with which we would like to rank. I felt that our weakness had been due to reliance on mere legislation. When I talked about the importance of administration, I felt that I struck a spark and kindled a fire in Wilson.

Another time, however, when I was lecturing on the labor movement he showed evident displeasure with my views. He seemed to change his attitude toward labor after he got into politics, years later. It was at a banquet to which a number of us who were attending the annual meeting of the American Economic Association were invited, that I heard Wilson give a decidedly progressive if not radical labor speech, for the first time. Professor Davis R. Dewey, sitting beside me, who had been one of my students in the Johns Hopkins University, nudged me in the side and whispered, "That's where some of us were twenty years ago." It would be conceited to say that he caught up with me. It would be cynical to say that politics made the difference. But who can tell? So often I find that the seed which is sown, and apparently rotted in the ground may at last sprout and bring forth fruit. Some seeds have a lasting quality.

In my contacts with him over a period of several years, he was calm and restrained. We at the Johns Hopkins University were a group of scholars working together. You could not forget what you were there for. When you walked through the halls you might be hailed with something like, "Well, Wilson,

how are you coming on with your 'Congressional Government'?"
We were a warm-hearted group of young men who became
deeply attached and showed marks of affection for each other,
as young men are apt to do, in such ways as putting one's arm
over the shoulder of a fellow-student or even a member of the
faculty. I never saw Wilson do this. If he had any deep affection for his associates I never saw any manifestations of it.

In spite of his customary restraint, he was capable of using
strong language and becoming indignant. So far as I can recall
he revealed to me only twice what might be called his "pet
peeves." He did once when he was talking about President
Thomas of Bryn Mawr, whom he did not like. Another time,
when speaking about progressive schools, he used swear words,
I would not say like a Mississippi pirate, but at any rate, strong
enough. He would not send his daughters to progressive schools,
so called. They went to Goucher College in Baltimore, because
he wanted them to have sound fundamental training without too many frills. I think he was right in this. He also wanted
them to have contacts with the South, with its culture and
refinement.

He had a strong admiration for my wife, who was a Southern
woman of a high type. She was as good a talker as he, and I
knew when he came to visit us he came more to see her than
to see me. I recall one of these visits shortly after his election
to the presidency of Princeton. I had recently returned from
California, where I had purchased an imported Chinese chair
with the expert aid of the wife of my former student, Carl
Plehn. The chair was of the knockdown type and we had just
put it together when Wilson and Van Hise walked in. The first
person to sit in it was Woodrow Wilson. As he had just been
made president of Princeton, my wife laughingly remarked that
she would henceforth call it the "president's chair," little thinking that he would some day be President of the United States.

Generally, Wilson was a gallant with the ladies. As one of the members of the round table once said, "He certainly knows how to handle himself with the ladies." I recall one conversation in my home in Madison. He was talking about the Northern ladies. He said, "I can never be with a lovely woman without telling her how beautiful I think she is." Then he added, stammering, "This seems to startle the ladies in the North, but they seem to like it."

Wilson held tenaciously to his own ideas and went his own way. Dr. H. B. Adams was a humanitarian and was eager to do his part to make the world a better place to live in. For example, he had especially at heart the improvement of the civil service and wanted to help toward the establishment of a training school for the civil service in Washington which was to correspond to the schools at West Point and Annapolis. I am sure this interested Wilson and met with his approval. However, there was before Congress at that time the Blair bill, which provided for the distribution of a certain amount of money among the states, in proportion to the degree of illiteracy in each. The purpose was to help the South, which had fallen so far behind the rest of the country with respect to its public schools. Adams put his best efforts into encouraging the passage of this bill, which interested him profoundly. Wilson actively opposed the bill because of his "states rights" sentiment. He wanted the Southern states to work out their own salvation and not to become dependent on the federal government. No one, of course, and least of all Adams, disputed Wilson's right to go his own way.

We saw manifested in Wilson as a graduate student a certain exaggerated individualism. I believe that in this characteristic individualism we find an explanation for many of his actions. Eventually one had to dot every "i" and cross every "t" according to Wilson's notions if he was to be a friend. An illustration of this is afforded by his relationship with Thomas Nelson Page. Wilson appointed Page, a fellow Virginian, who had attained well-merited distinction in literature, as minister to Italy. He later broke with him because some of his ideas about the World War and the peace were different from Wilson's own. I am positive that Page never voiced publicly any disapprobation of what Wilson wanted. But in private conversation, he advanced notions which Wilson did not approve and thus caused the breach between them.

Wilson's excessive individualism had a most important effect on the history of the world. This determination to go his own way was undoubtedly strengthened by the adulation he received in Europe after the war. He was looked upon as a "god," and peasant women knelt down before him in worship. Had he been of a large and generous nature he would have taken with him to Paris men like Elihu Root and Taft. We might have had a better treaty and it might have gone through the Senate without any formidable opposition. We might have had a league which would have enforced peace and which would have given the generation after the war a far happier history. He did not feel that he needed the help of others, especially Republicans, and subconsciously, at least, he wanted the glory for himself. This was unfortunate. Although Wilson had a knowledge of history, and although he had traveled more or less extensively, to the end of his days he remained parochial-minded. He did not know the world—least of all, the European world. He could not understand that a country like Austria-Hungary was not an artificial creation but an outgrowth of economic forces. After I received my Ph.D. degree at the University of Heidelberg, I lived for some six months in a pension in Geneva. There I met students from all parts of the world, especially a great many Greeks. This gave me an insight into world affairs which I often wished that Wilson could have had before he was plunged into them. What was especially illuminating to me was the situation in the Balkans. Wilson had advocated self-determination of nationalities. I recall one fellow-student and boarder at this pension, whose native home was a small village in the Balkans. There were seven different nationalities to be found in that one place, he told me, and not one nationality would speak to the other. What possibility was there of self-determination here?

Wilson's excessive individualism resulted in an inability to co-operate with others at times when co-operation was essential to the achievement of his goals. During the World War I was chairman in Wisconsin of Mr. Taft's League to Enforce Peace. Just before the armistice, arrangements were made for a big meeting in Madison, Wisconsin. Mr. Taft, President Lowell of Harvard, Mr. Henry Morgenthau, and many others were present. While we were making our preparations, President Van Hise wrote to Woodrow Wilson soliciting his co-operation, at least in the form of a friendly word. He refused. He said that since he did not know what plans might ultimately result, he did not think he should give us any favorable comment.

This lack of co-operation was also felt by the members of Wilson's cabinet, who were more or less dissatisfied because they did not feel they had his full confidence, and still less the sort of co-operative attitude they desired. One day when I was in the office of one of his cabinet members, this member looked out of the window and saw his colleagues on their way to Wilson's office. He said, "Now we are going to have a cabinet meeting." His wistful smile carried the implication that this did not often take place. Another cabinet member expressed in a letter to me this same dissatisfaction with the lack of co-operation and confidence shown by Wilson toward the cabinet.

Ray Stannard Baker described Wilson as a man fired with a passion to abolish the dire evils of racial hatred and international war. As President of the United States, he finally took his place among the immortals. It was then that the ideal of democracy took complete possession of him. It is needless to speak of his consuming zeal to make the world safe for democracy and to attempt to make the World War a war to end all wars.

Wilson was widely regarded as a man of heroic stature, even though he did not have the grace of humility. In my opinion it was not until after he became governor of New Jersey that he began to tower above his fellows, and from that point on he kept growing. I recall one instance in which one of his cabinet officers did a fine thing and it must have been with his approval. When Houston was made secretary of agriculture, Dr. Wood was the administrative head of all the research work in the department of agriculture. From Dr. Wood himself I learned that he had been called into Mr. Houston's office. Houston said to him, "Dr. Wood I have just one job at my disposal, your job. Do you want to keep it?" And Dr. Wood replied, "I like the work and if, Mr. Secretary, it is your desire that I should keep it, I shall be much pleased." Houston then said, "I am well pleased with what you have done. I appoint you. Now, that you have been appointed, you understand that you have the job." "Yes," said Wood. "Now, that you have the job, I want you to tell me what your politics are?" Dr. Wood replied, "I am a Republican." And Houston answered, "That is all right!"

* * *

IV

Sowing the Seeds

* * *

A CRUST HAD FORMED OVER POLITICAL ECONOMY

IN THE YEAR 1885, Adams, Clark, Patten, James, Seligman, and I, fresh from our studies in Germany, were regarded as a group of young rebels. We young men were deeply conscious of the fact that we were human beings as well as economists and that we were engaged in the task of furthering a science which is first and foremost a science of human relationships. We felt the urgent necessity for uniting into a solid group in an effort to break the "crust" which had formed over economics. To accomplish this we founded the American Economic Association.

Until this time little attention was given in this country to systems of political economy. And, indeed, it would have been ridiculous to expect the New World to produce any elaborate treatises on political economy at a time when every effort was concentrated on wresting a living from the soil of recently settled regions. The very substance of the science, the modern complexity of economic relationships, made its appearance later in this country than in the Old World.

Throughout the first half of the nineteenth century our forbears were, generally speaking, too much engaged in the stupendous task of "subduing a continent" to reflect deeply on their activities. In the earlier periods of our national history we were so much absorbed in doing things that we did not have time to think about the philosophic explanation of our activities. This led to something of a contempt for economic theory in general so that the difficulties attendant upon logical and systematic thought were often shirked, or not even realized. Eleven years before the American Economic Association was founded a senator announced one day that he had given his leisure for an entire fortnight to the currency question and had thus been enabled to sound its depths. Today a senator probably would not be particularly proud of the fact that he had spent two weeks in studying the currency question.

The development of any science depends upon painstaking and prolonged reflection. The kind of reflection necessary to advance economic science requires, in turn, an accumulation of wealth in an adequate amount to permit of the leisure necessary for prolonged reflection. The progress of a science depends, too, upon a favorable atmosphere which carries with it social esteem for those engaged in building up scientific structures. It is not enough simply to have wealth, but wealth must find uses which encourage and support science. And these conditions necessary to a flourishing science are the result of the ripening processes of time.

New countries have been less favorable for research in scientific fields than older countries. Germany has, in times past, afforded favorable conditions for the development of science; and our own country down to recent times, less favorable conditions. During the nineteenth century, Germany was a poor country as compared with England or France, but a goodly amount of wealth was devoted to the encouragement of art and science. Nowhere in the wide world did a professor receive higher social esteem up to the time of the World War than in Germany. It always seemed to me that a German professor was a king in his own realm. He had a tenure of office like that of one of our supreme court justices, and was looked up to by all classes of

society, including the military classes. While not occupying
quite the social position held by an officer, a professor's remuneration was relatively high, and conditions were favorable
to the development of thought even in days of comparative
poverty, for one satisfied with plain living and high thinking.
But the living was not always so simple either. I recall that
once while I was at the Johns Hopkins University it was reported that a professor of chemistry at Munich received an invitation from the Johns Hopkins University. He replied that
he would come if he could be given a salary which would equal
his income at the University of Munich. The people of Baltimore were astonished to learn that this would be thirty thousand dollars a year. Of course, this was exceptional, but it
showed that there were material prizes to be gained by those
who distinguished themselves in the scientific world in Germany.

England was at that time a country of greater wealth, but did
not give an equal proportion of pecuniary encouragement to
science in general, and still less to economics in particular, although the universities of Oxford and Cambridge had immense
prestige. Private wealth encouraged individuals in their pursuit
of learning, and in some cases the men of science had considerable fortunes of their own. France, too, honored science, but
the social esteem for men of science was not as conspicuous as
in Germany where the honor in which professors were held
amounted, at times, almost to reverence.

In the United States the case was very different. The best
brains of the country were engaged in devoting their lives to
solving the practical problems of the moment. Able statesmen
—Franklin, Jefferson, Hamilton, to mention only a few, were
in no position to devote much time to economic theories. They
were concerned with them only as guides to the economic needs
of the moment. Few were in a position to devote themselves to

disinterested research, for there were very few chairs of economics in 1885. The first had been established in this country
at Harvard as late as 1871. And the absence of careers for
young men who wanted to devote themselves to economics was
a serious obstacle to the development of the science. My father
said to me, not long before 1885, something like this: "Richard, you are a young man. Some day you will want to get married and have a family. How can you expect that economics
will support you?" It was well along toward the middle of the
nineties when Dr. Henry C. Taylor received the same admonition
from Secretary of Agriculture Wilson. Wilson advised him,
"Take up a practical subject like plant pathology and I will
give you a job."

The development of science also depends very largely on an
atmosphere of freedom of thought and expression, upon what
the Germans call *Lehrfreiheit und Lernfreiheit*—freedom to
think and freedom to express one's thoughts to one's fellows.
When I first went to Germany I seemed to breathe a new and
exhilarating atmosphere of freedom. There was a free and large
spirit on the part of the professors to which I had not been
accustomed. I felt that in the German universities there was
room for growth and the development of individuality. I asked
myself the question, "Was the atmosphere of Columbia College as I knew it favorable to freedom of thought and expression? Did it stimulate and encourage that research which results
in significant thought?" Although I was happy to have had
three years at Columbia as an undergraduate, the only honest
answer I could give myself was "no." The center of attention
was occupied by the classics and mathematics, and the question
of academic freedom did not even arise. Certainly an atmosphere
of freedom like that in the German universities did not exist.
Apparently other American students like Patten, James, Selig-

man, and Clark who had gone to Germany to study and had compared German conditions with those in their native country were reaching the same conclusion. We became keenly aware that the atmosphere of the United States in the seventies and eighties was not favorable to the development of economic science. William Folwell gave the following description of the attitude held by most Americans toward economists: "The opinion prevails far too widely that political economists must be mere doctrinaires and must contend for some set of opinions and some course of policy. Critical study of phenomena is as unpopular as free thinking in religion." [22]

Political economy, as it had been taught in the American colleges and universities, was, generally speaking, rather barren. Sometimes it was called the "dismal science" and sometimes "dry bones." Economics was regarded as a finished product. One could become an economist by reading a single volume. In fact, at Columbia we studied economics from one little book, Mrs. Fawcett's *Political Economy for Beginners.* Mrs. Fawcett defined economics as the "science which investigates the nature of wealth and the laws which govern its production, exchange, and distribution." Man was not mentioned in this definition; it was implied that man is simply an instrument by which wealth is created and not the end for which it exists. In this volume free competition plays the part of the *deus ex machina,* which, if left well alone, will regulate and bring into harmony all the relations that arise among men in their efforts to make a living. Even charitable relief given to the unemployed is condemned as an obstruction to the operation of natural economic laws. During the Civil War in the United States the supply of raw cotton flowing into Lancashire was almost completely cut off. Thousands of men were thrown out of work. Charitable persons organized relief societies in order to save men, women, and children from starving to death. The cry of "permanent pauperization" was raised by some of the "Epigones" of political economy, including Mrs. Fawcett, who wrote:

"Such an instance as this is a most striking example of the harm that may be done by interfering with the operation of competition. Had those who organized the relieving societies during the Lancashire famine remembered that competition tends to make the effect of good or bad trade upon wages only temporary, they would have hesitated before they used such powerful means to check the operation of competition." [23]

In another elementary textbook on political economy, published in 1817, we find "natural liberty" and "natural laws" presented as "liberal and enlarged views," which always lead to the conclusion that "The interests of nations, as well as those of individuals, so far from being opposed to each other, are in the most perfect unison." [24]

It was held that natural laws established certain fundamental principles for all times and places. It was only necessary that we should study these natural laws and follow them to attain the highest state of economic felicity possible to mankind. The ordinary man looked upon political economy as chiefly occupied with a controversy between protection and free trade, and he assumed that every orthodox political economist must be a free trader. At the time of the founding of the American Economic Association and for a good many years afterwards, we used to hear the term "orthodox" applied as an estimate of the value of economic articles and treatises. Either it was said of a man that he was orthodox or that he was not orthodox. In the first case the writer was, *ipso facto,* judged to be an able economist; in the second case, his work was regarded as valueless. The test of orthodoxy was this: Do you or do you not believe in "laissez faire"? Or, in other words, do you or do you not agree that, if the state refrains from all interference with industry, trade, and labor conditions, society will be best organized? The low ebb which academic economics had reached in the seventies was well described by Francis A. Walker, the first president of the American Economic Association, in these words:

". . . While Laissez-faire was asserted, in great breadth, in England, the writers for the reviews exaggerating the utterances of the professors in the universities, that doctrine was carefully qualified by some economists, and was held by none with such strictness as was given to it in the United States. Here it was not made the test of economic orthodoxy, merely. It was used to decide whether a man were an economist at all. I don't think that I exaggerate when I say that, among those who deemed themselves the guardians of the true faith, it was considered far better that a man should know nothing about economic literature, and have no interest whatever in the subject, than that, with any amount of learning and any degree of honest purpose, he should have adopted views varying from the standard that was set up." [25]

Among the most widely quoted and influential exponents of this doctrine were Godkin of the New York *Nation,* Professor William Graham Sumner of Yale, and Professor A. L. Perry of Williams College. According to Perry the economic universe is organized not only by the laws of natural liberty and natural order, but by the express will of the Almighty. A good illustration of Perry's reasoning is given in the following quotations from his *Elements of Political Economy.* Speaking of the Malthusian theory of population Perry says this:

"The abstract antagonism of the law of the increase of population with the law of the increase of food is admitted; but HE who is author of the laws is author also of natural counterworkings of them; so that a practical *tendency* towards their coming into conflict is denied. Each human being is as much constituted by Nature to receive services as to render them, and each is naturally able to become a capitalist; economical laws present no obstacles to all men's becoming rich; most men are unwilling, some are unable, to fulfill the moral conditions of getting rich; while scarcity of food has been caused much more by the maladministration of government than by the law of population." [26]

Perry specifically declared his adhesion to the maxim of "laissez faire." He says this:

"Let alone Legislatures are not wise enough to settle the great questions involved between capitalists and laborers. They are not wise enough, and never will be to say, for example, how much wages capitalists shall pay, or how many hours per day adult laborers shall work. The attempt to regulate any such things as these by legislation is an economic abomination." [27]

An "economic abomination" then in Perry's view consists in any attempt to obstruct the working of the laws of natural liberty.

This whole philosophy was deductively derived from definitions and axioms. Therefore it was not necessary to dig into facts. Jean Baptiste Say once remarked, "Economics is not eager for facts." His position was accepted. Political economy was regarded as a body of truths arrived at chiefly by deduction based on certain traits of human nature and familiar observations, and was to be taught as an almost finished product. Even John Stuart Mill, in whom new life was stirring, said that the theory of value had been so well and so completely established that little remained for subsequent writers to do, except of course to learn this theory.

A caricature of the economics of the day may be found in Dickens' *Hard Times*. Thomas Gradgrind gives expression to the worst of the economics, but it has a truth of caricature which is always in exaggerations.

"Thomas Gradgrind, sir. A man of realities. A man of facts

and calculations. A man who proceeds upon the principle that two and two are four, and nothing over, and who is not to be talked into allowing for anything over. Thomas Gradgrind, sir —peremptorily Thomas—Thomas Gradgrind. With a rule and a pair of scales, and the multiplication table always in his pocket, sir, ready to weigh and measure any parcel of human nature, and tell you exactly what it comes to. It is a mere question of figures, a case of simple arithmetic. You might hope to get some other nonsensical belief into the head of George Gradgrind, or Augustus Gradgrind, or John Gradgrind, or Joseph Gradgrind (all supposititious, non-existent persons), but into the head of Thomas Gradgrind—no, sir!"

Perhaps you recall Sissy Jupe. If her mother had seven children, that was more than the statistical average warranted and nothing could be done about it but to let poor Sissy and her superfluous brothers and sisters suffer the consequences of transgressing the law of the statistical average.

The reason for this deplorably unscientific attitude was that each succeeding generation of American economists throughout the nineteenth century had turned to the writings of the English classical school, without looking into what had been accomplished in the field of economics by their own compatriots. The early American economists had little or no personal connection with one another. In only a few cases were they even acquainted with each other's writings. Each generation examined the English theories afresh, and most of the American writers endorsed these theories, even though they found it difficult to fit the facts of American economic evolution to them. The more original-minded of them began painfully to construct systems of their own, but their efforts were rendered less fruitful than they might have been, because each succeeding generation began the work all over again, with a strange disregard for what had been done by their American predecessors. A few American economists had the courage to reject the general principle of natural liberty. One of these was Daniel Raymond, who emphatically denied Adam Smith's contention that, if every man were left perfectly free to pursue his own interest, the result would be to secure the welfare of the community. On the contrary he claims that "Public and private interests are often entirely at variance." Adam Smith's essential error, he maintains, lies in his idea that national and individual interests are never opposed. Not only is this an unsound doctrine, he says, but it is a doctrine "abominable in its consequences." The government must step in, he thinks, whenever the welfare of the many makes it expedient to do so. His point of view is clearly shown in the following quotation from his *Elements of Political Economy:*

"A government should be like a good shepherd, who supports and nourishes the weak and feeble ones in his flock, until they gain sufficient strength to take their chance with the strong, and does not suffer them to be trampled on, and crushed to the earth, by the powerful. The powerful ones in society, however, are not usually those who are so by nature, but those who have been so by art—by the inheritance or acquisition of enormous wealth; and these are they, who ordinarily engross all the attention and care of the government." [28]

Mathew Carey, too, condemned the policy of "laissez faire." Though Mathew Carey's condemnation of the "laissez faire" doctrine is based mainly on his rejection of free trade both as a theory and as a policy, he shows himself to be not averse to governmental intervention on behalf of the weaker members of the community. A government, he says, is only estimable insofar as it fulfills its sacred duty of protecting the public and of coming to the aid of the oppressed. While the more obscure followers of Adam Smith and of Ricardo were interpreting their doctrines to mean that the community at large had no right to interfere with the free play of economic forces and that unbridled self-interest would secure the welfare of all, Mathew Carey has this to say of the "let alone" doctrine:

"A physician who found his patient in a raging fever and let the disorder take its course, or 'regulate itself' would be deservedly reprobated as unworthy of his profession. But his conduct would not be more irrational than that of a statesman, who says the agriculture, manufactures, trade, and commerce of his country are going to decay, and let them 'regulate themselves.' Government is instituted to guard the interests of the nation confided to its care; and, by whatever name it may be called, is no longer estimable than as it fulfills this sacred duty."

Mathew Carey defends poor laws, as well as all forms of charity, whether public or private, on the grounds that the workers are unable to protect themselves against the constant menace of unemployment. Nothing can be further from the truth, he claims, than to assert that "in the present state of society" every person able and willing to work may procure employment. Even in times of prosperity, he says, "there are always some trades and occupations that are depressed," and in these trades there is bound to be a "deficiency of employment," which results in "pinching distress" for the workers engaged in these trades. He believed that the state should take care of these workers. It is quite clear that Mathew Carey was thoroughly humanitarian in his economic ideas, and refused to accept any philosophy which regarded the distress of the poor as an economic necessity and as part of the "natural order" of things.

The writings of Raymond and Carey attracted much attention abroad; but in this country they had been ignored. Perhaps if some of the ridicule employed to condemn the unorthodoxy of Carey's and Raymond's position had been reserved for some of the "orthodox" economists we would have evolved a system of economics more suited to American conditions.

WE REBELS PROTEST AGAINST LAISSEZ FAIRE
AND ORTHODOXY

We, who had tasted the new and living economics which was taught in the German universities, were depressed with the sterility of the old economics which was being taught in the American colleges. We became weary of the controversies, the wordy conflicts over free trade and protection, and the endless harangues over paper money which seemed to us to savor more of political partisanship than of scientific inquiry. We had little patience with a press which preached conceptions of orthodoxy, and we were prepared to fight these conceptions as not belonging to the realm of science. There was a pugnacious element in our attitude, for we were young and had the pugnacity of youth. We felt that men, who thought as we did, were denied the right to exist scientifically, and this denial we believed to proceed from certain older men able to exercise a very large influence over thought, particularly thought in university circles. Therefore we felt called upon to fight those who we believed stood in the way of intellectual expansion and of social growth. We were determined to inject new life into American economics.

Two aspects of the early history of the American Economic Association should be stressed: First, it represented a protest against the system of laissez faire, as expounded by writers of the older school of "orthodox" American economics. Several of the founders of our association, particularly Simon N. Patten, wished to register their protest against this aspect of orthodox economic theory. The second aspect, and the one on which we were all in complete agreement, was the necessity of uniting in order to secure complete freedom of discussion; a freedom untrammeled by any restrictions whatsoever. It was this second point that came, in final analysis and after much debate, to be accepted as the foundation stone of our association.

But the protest against the "laissez faire" philosophy must not be underemphasized in the history of the foundation of the American Economic Association. In this connection, an attempt was made to organize an association which was to have been known as the Society for the Study of National Economy. The idea of this society, sponsored particularly by Simon N. Patten and Edmund J. James, was that we young economists should organize in order to advocate a definite program and a definite platform, as well as to encourage objective, scientific research. The Society for the Study of National Economy was to have resembled the German *Verein für Sozialpolitik* (Society for Social Policy), which had been organized in Germany during the years 1872–73. The *Verein für Sozialpolitik* included a group of German economists who had broken loose from the "laissez faire" economic philosophy characteristic of the English classical school, which they described rather contemptuously as "Manchesterthum." "Manchesterthum" represented, in their eyes, the advocacy of unrestricted individual freedom from any form of governmental intervention in matters of industry and trade. At the Eisenach Conference (1872), which led to the formation of the *Verein für Sozialpolitik,* Gustav Schmoller made his celebrated speech in which he emphasized the necessity for state intervention in trade and industry. One of the most ardent advocates of this aspect of Schmoller's economic philosophy was Professor Johannes Conrad, under whom both E. J. James and Simon Patten had studied at the University of Halle. Professor Conrad impressed upon his American students the necessity of founding an organization similar to the *Verein für Sozialpolitik* on their return to the United States. In the paper E. J. James wrote for the twenty-fifth anniversary of the American Economic Association he said this about his former teacher and about the *Verein für Sozialpolitik:*

"I remember very distinctly Conrad's speaking to us Americans who were in his seminary one evening, urging us to organize a similar organization in the United States upon our return, emphasizing the fact that times were changing. The old order was passing away, and if economic students were to have any influence whatever upon the course of practical politics, it would be necessary to take a new attitude toward the whole subject of social legislation, and if the United States were to have any particular influence in the great social legislation, and the great readjustment of society on its legal side which seemed to be coming, an association of this sort would have very real value. I decided there that, as soon as I could, I would begin the agitation for such an association."

Thus Edmund J. James and Simon N. Patten were in favor of an organization with a definite program and platform —that is to say, as definite a program as the *Verein für Sozialpolitik* had. The draft of the constitution of their proposed "Society for the Study of National Economy," which I quote in full in Appendix III, lays special stress on the necessity for governmental intervention in order to secure "all the conditions of a sound industrial system."

As an indication of the thoughts stirring in the minds of young Americans, the draft of the constitution of the proposed Society for the Study of National Economy has had great significance in the history of economic thought. We soon found, however, that the proposed constitution rested on too narrow a basis to enlist the sympathy of a sufficiently large group of American economists. The attempts at the formation of this society were, in a sense, preparatory; they indicated a stirring of the soil, and they exerted an influence on me in my efforts to draft a satisfactory statement of principles for the American

Economic Association. However, my effort was not a rival one. I had already intended to form an association of American economists before the efforts of Dr. James and Dr. Patten took any definite shape. That sort of thing was in the air at the Johns Hopkins and was encouraged by the authorities. When the society sent out a draft of its constitution I held back until it became absolutely certain that success could not be achieved along that line.

OUR STATEMENT OF PRINCIPLES WAS NOT A CREED

When it became evident that the "Society for the Study of National Economy" could not be established, I undertook to draw up a project for the formation of a society to be called "The American Economic Association," which should be broad enough to appeal to all the younger economists who, irrespective of their personal views, felt the stirring of the new life in economics and who wished to unite in order to secure complete liberty of thought and discussion, even if their thought led them to "unorthodox" conclusions. In the statement of our "objects" and "declaration of principles" I retained the central idea of the authors of the constitution of the "Society for the Study of National Economy," namely, that the dogma of "laissez faire" should be abandoned by our leaders. My program was a much simpler one and differed from theirs in two important particulars. In the first place, it emphasized historical and statistical study rather than deductive speculation, and, in the second place, it laid less stress on government intervention and, on the whole, was "toned down" in the direction of conservatism. It was designed to attract as many members as possible. The prospectus sent out read as follows:

AMERICAN ECONOMIC ASSOCIATION

Objects of This Association

I. The encouragement of economic research.
II. The publication of economic monographs.
III. The encouragement of perfect freedom in all economic discussion.
IV. The establishment of a bureau of information designed to aid all members with friendly counsels in their economic studies.

Platform

1. We regard the state as an educational and ethical agency whose positive aid is an indispensable condition of human progress. While we recognize the necessity of individual initiative in industrial life, we hold that the doctrine of laissez faire is unsafe in politics and unsound in morals; and that it suggests an inadequate explanation of the relations between the state and the citizens.

2. We do not accept the final statements which characterized the political economy of a past generation; for we believe that political economy is still in the first stages of its scientific development, and we look not so much to speculation as to an impartial study of actual conditions of economic life for the satisfactory accomplishment of that development. We seek the aid of statistics in the present, and of history in the past.

3. We hold that the conflict of labor and capital has brought to the front a vast number of social problems whose solution is impossible without the united efforts of church, state, and science.

4. In the study of the policy of government, especially with respect to restrictions on trade and to protection of domestic manufactures, we take no partisan attitude. We are convinced that one of the chief reasons why greater harmony has not been attained is because economists have been too ready to assert themselves as advocates. We believe in a progressive development of economic conditions which must be met by corresponding changes of policy.

In drawing up this prospectus I was especially assisted by my colleague, Professor H. B. Adams, who the year before had been chiefly instrumental in organizing the American Historical Association. Adams had a genius for organization, and was probably never happier than when bringing an institution into existence. Dr. E. J. James also co-operated most generously and effectively, never expressing the slightest concern for any egoistic ends, but striving to promote the common aim. No one was more energetic and loyal in co-operation than Dr. E. R. A. Seligman. This is all the more to Dr. Seligman's credit because he held the view that economics had not yet "attained that certainty in results which would authorize us to invoke increased governmental action as a check to various abuses of free competition." [29]

The emphasis I laid on inductive studies was not altogether to the liking of S. N. Patten, who represented the deductive school among our group. He also felt that the fourth article of our platform was too much "toned down." At the time he said this:

"It seems to me that the very object of our association should be to deny the right of individuals to do as they please, and that of course is restricting trade. . . . I believe that our platform should state explicitly what we intend to do . . . we should give in some specific form our attitude on all the leading economic questions where state intervention is needed." [30]

Even in its modified and more conservative form, our platform met with a certain amount of friendly criticism. A mimeographed circular was distributed among all the economists who might be supposed to be in sympathy with the general ideas expressed in the new constitution; and it was proposed to gather at Saratoga in September, 1885, in connection with the American Historical Association, to which nearly all the economists belonged. The response to the invitation was general. On September 8, 1885, a call signed by H. C. Adams, J. B. Clark, and R. T. Ely was read at a public meeting of the Historical

Association. All those interested were invited to meet at the Bethesda Parish Building at 4 P.M. on that same day to take into consideration plans for the formation of an American Economic Association. Among those present at this first meeting, besides the original sponsors of the project (E. J. James and H. C. Adams, and I), were John B. Clark, Edwin R. A. Seligman, Davis R. Dewey, Andrew D. White, C. K. Adams, Katherine Coman, and E. Benjamin Andrews, to mention only a few.

I recall clearly that first meeting we held at Saratoga and I can see, as if it were yesterday, Professor Seligman tramping through the rain with me to the office of the Associated Press to see that we had such publicity as we both felt we deserved. Professor Seligman, then, as always, put his shoulder to the wheel when that was necessary, and always exhibited courage when that was required. At our modest beginning in that first meeting at Saratoga there were less than fifty people—a small room held us all, even counting those who were there because of curiosity. For many years any one of our large universities had auditoriums quite ample for all those who attended. Now, when we hold our meetings, we raise the question when some particular city is proposed for our next annual meeting whether or not the city's accommodations are adequate for our general meetings and for our many conferences. Now we debate questions concerning the investment of amounts like five thousand or ten thousand dollars. In the early days the problem was how to get money for the next step in our activities or for the publication of a monograph. Perhaps if I can claim credit for any virtue it is that of persistence. I was almost ready to go out on the street corner and pass the hat. While I never did quite that, once when our finances were in a bad state, I recall writing to a distinguished New Yorker, Abram S. Hewitt, and asking him to help us out with a life membership. This he generously did and mildly reproved me because I had not written to him earlier. Need I say that the gentleman holds a warm place in my heart?

Since I was elected "temporary secretary," it was my duty to state the aims of the newly formed association, as I saw them. One of the main points I made on this occasion was that the doctrine of "laissez faire" implied that the laws of economic life were "natural laws" like those of physics and chemistry, and that this life must be left to the free play of natural forces. The scientific attitude towards this question was, however, I said, one of inquiry, and, necessarily, one of modesty. I spoke as I felt when I said that:

"Our attitude is a modest one, and must, I think, appeal to the best intelligence of the country. We acknowledge our ignorance, and if we claim superiority to others it is largely on the very humble ground that we know better what we do not know. We confess our ignorance; but are determined to do our best to remedy it, and we call upon those who are willing to go to work in this spirit to come forward and help us."

Professor Henry C. Adams said that, admitting that the philosophy of "laissez faire," which regarded the state as nothing more than a necessary evil, was untenable, our problem was still unsolved. The doctrine which presented the state as the "final analysis of human relations" was, he maintained, as untenable as the doctrine of "laissez faire" itself. And he concluded that, "The great problem of the present day is properly to correlate public and private activity so as to preserve harmony and proportion between the various parts of organic society." [31]

Much the same idea was expressed by E. J. James, who said that he wished to make it clear that there was "a legitimate sphere of state activity" and that the question of government intervention ought to be judged, in every case, on its own merits.

John Bates Clark pointed out that, in a society such as the American Economic Association, it was hardly fitting to adopt any one platform, upon which all the members could scarcely be expected to agree. He claimed that: "The point upon which individuals will be unable to unite is, especially, the strong condemnation of the 'laissez-faire' doctrine."

In the end, it was decided to refer our platform to a committee of five, consisting of H. C. Adams, the Reverend Washington Gladden, Professor Alexander Johnston, and Professor J. B. Clark and me. The committee decided that it was desirable to make it plain that the founders of the American Economic Association did not intend to formulate any creed which should restrict freedom of inquiry or independence of thought. With this end in view, the following note was appended to the "statement of principles" which was finally adopted:

"This statement was proposed and accepted as the general indication of the views and the purposes of those who founded the American Economic Association, but it is not to be regarded as binding upon individual members."

The statement of principles read as follows:

1. We regard the state as an agency whose positive assistance is one of the indispensable conditions of human progress.

2. We believe that political economy as a science is still in an early stage of its development. While we appreciate the work of former economists, we look, not so much to speculation as to the historical and statistical study of actual conditions of economic life for the satisfactory accomplishment of that development.

3. We hold that the conflict of labor and capital has brought into prominence a vast number of social problems, whose solution requires the united efforts, each in its own sphere, of the church, of the state, and of science.

4. In the study of the industrial and commercial policy of governments we take no partisan attitude. We believe in a progressive development of economic conditions, which must be met by a corresponding development of legislative policy.

It should be noticed that our statement of principles was never regarded as a creed. In the report of the secretary on the organization of the American Economic Association, I find the following words: "This platform, it must be distinctly asserted, was never meant as a hard and fast creed, which should be imposed on all members, and least of all was it intended to restrict the freest investigation." If anyone ever signed the statement of principles, it must have come to my notice, as I held the position of secretary for the first seven years, and I feel safe in saying that absolutely no one ever signed it, and that no officer of the association ever asked anyone to sign it. It was not intended to be signed, and this reply was made by the secretary when once or twice a willingness to sign was expressed. The "note" printed with the constitution precisely expresses the situation.

This statement of principles, it will be observed, was a compromise on behalf of catholicity. First we have the detailed declarations of E. J. James and of S. N. Patten, then the broader and more general "platform" drawn up by myself, and finally the "statement" adopted; each modification representing what has been called a "toning down" process. The changes made were in deference to the fact that various views were represented in the membership of our newly formed association and still more in the membership we hoped to get. We were anxious to win the great body of economists. While not all the original members may have held precisely the views expressed in the "statement of principles," all certainly felt at home and comfortable in the association; and it was hoped and expected that the statement would oppose no barrier among students who held less pronounced views. We all considered ourselves scientific investigators and not propagandists.

What was its purpose then? Let us be perfectly frank. It had an inclusive as well as an exclusive aim. Like the earlier statement in the proposed Society for the Study of National Economy, it aimed to gather together like-minded men, congenial men who it was supposed could profitably work together. Not every economist was at first asked to join, although no economist who expressed a desire to join was refused enrollment. Our statement had doubtless puzzled and perplexed many because, looking upon it as a creed, they asked themselves, "How could this creed proceed from those animated by scientific ideals of freedom?" It was, however, simply a statement showing conclusions which up to that time those of us who were most instrumental in founding the association held. Along with our scientific aspirations, as already stated, we had as a general aim the accomplishment of practical results.

"When I was five and twenty," said Nassau Senior, "I determined to reform the condition of the poor in England." Thornton, who quotes this in the preface of his book on labor, adds:

"When I was myself about the same age, I conceived, not indeed the same ambitious design, but much the same desire as that which it implies. More than five and twenty years have passed since then, and it is somewhat sadly now, with sexagenarianism at no great distance, that I contrast the insignificance of performance with the magnificence of youthful projects. But the passion of a life is not to be extinguished by any failures that do not extinguish life itself, and so long as any strength is vouchsafed to me, so long shall it be cheerfully devoted to continued search after a cure for human destitution."

Doubtless some such thought as this may have animated at least a few of those who were present at the foundation of our association. Perhaps if any of us were quite as ambitious we should not like to have acknowledged it when we reached middle age—or, as one of our presidents has said less flatteringly, "Now that we are old duffers."

Certainly a practical purpose was dominant among those who

were in control at the time. There was a striving for righteousness and perhaps here and there might have been one who felt
a certain kinship with the old Hebrew prophets. Another element perhaps laid more emphasis upon correct thought, holding that so long as men think correctly we need not concern
ourselves with their action. Certainly everyone was animated by
the love of truth for its own sake. Undoubtedly a dominant
note was to do things practically and scientifically and bring to
pass results.

Rightly or wrongly to many, the statement of principles
seemed like a proclamation of emancipation. At this time the
enthusiasm with which we were greeted may appear a little
difficult to comprehend. But a few quotations will help older
men recall their earlier impressions and the younger to understand the situation at the time. The following five quotations
are from letters received by the first secretary before the Saratoga meeting and were replies to a request to join the movement
to organize the American Economic Association on the basis of
the prospectus sent out giving "objects" and "platform."

Dr. Albert Shaw, then editor of the Minneapolis *Tribune,*
wrote: "The time is ripe for the movement. . . . It seems to me
the society will be a decided success from the start."

Professor Henry C. Adams of Michigan expressed himself
as follows: "The more I think of the project that you have set
on foot, the more I am convinced that it is timely, and that the
association may be made the centre of a marked influence upon
economic thought."

Dr. Washington Gladden said: "I hope to cooperate in the
organization of your society, in which I am deeply interested."

Professor J. B. Clark, then of Smith College, wrote: "The
plan proposed is quite in line with my views and wishes. I
shall be glad to be counted in, in such an organization."

President White of Cornell: "I agree with you entirely that

the laissez-faire theory is entirely inadequate to the needs of modern states. I agree, too, entirely with the idea that we must look not so much to speculation, as to an impartial study of actual conditions of economic life, etc. In fact I like your whole statement, and I hope to connect myself with your association after my return from Europe, probably next summer."

After our organization Dr. Elisha Mulford, author of *The Nation,* a book which in its day exerted a marked influence, wrote as follows: "No recent invitation has given me more pleasure than yours to join the American Economic Association. I subscribe to its articles. It places us in the same plane with all the greater universities, and with the age. In the transitions of thought, none has been more significant than the humanization of political economy. Now, as Mr. Toynbee says: 'The long controversy between the economists and human beings has ended in the conversion of the economists.' "

Why this jubilation? Why this feeling of emancipation? It was felt by many that political economy was opposed to the recognition of any ethical element in our economic life, that it opposed all social reforms for social uplift as futile, that it exalted into a principle of economic righteousness the individual and unrestrained pursuit of self-interest, that it almost deified a monstrosity known as the economic man, that it looked upon laissez faire as a law of beneficent providence, and held that free trade must be received as an ethical dogma, being a practical application of the command, "Thou shalt not steal," for here inconsistently an ethical principle was admitted as all-controlling. Now let it be said that no support, or at any rate very little support, for such views could be found in the writings of the great economists of England or any other country; but a false and undue emphasis of certain teachings of the masters had led to this misapprehension; and for this one-sided development, popularization and the exigencies of practical politics were largely responsible. Hence when the recognition of evils was proclaimed as in harmony with science, when it was proposed to examine the actual situation of the wage-earner and to reason on the basis of observation, when it made known that a body of economists was prepared to examine free trade and protection scientifically and not dogmatically, and that economics embraced the whole of the economic life; the simple message, which now no one would think it necessary to proclaim, produced an impression and aroused an enthusiasm which can be understood only by those who by the aid of the scientific imagination work their way back to the situation of 1885.

It has been said by some that the founders of the American Economic Association had absorbed German ideas and attempted to transplant them into American soil, and that this was an alien soil. This is undoubtedly erroneous, for our association was essentially American in its origin and ideas. German influences were felt and we are all thankful for German science, but, as Professor Farnam pointed out, these ideas of the founders, and in particular the opposition to laissez faire and the expressions in favor of an active policy of government, ascribed to a German influence are not un-American. Professor Farnam was quite right in this view that laissez faire is not a peculiar American product. It is worthy of special note that we must look to the prairies of Illinois, swept by the free air of the Mississippi Valley, for the authorship of the constitution of the proposed Society for the Study of National Economy, in which still more emphatically than in our own statement of principle we find proclaimed opposition to non-interference in economic affairs and the advocacy of very large and broad functions of government. What Germany did for us was, in the sense in which Socrates used the term, to serve as midwife, helping to birth the ideas which had been conceived under

American conditions. We were impressed in the German universities by a certain largeness and freedom of thought, which was novel but very refreshing and delightful. Speaking for myself—and I believe for most of us—I may say that the idea of relativity as opposed to absolutism and the insistence upon exact and positive knowledge produced a profound influence upon my thought. I must not fail to mention the impression produced upon my thought (and again I believe I may speak for most of my associates) by the ethical view of economics taught by Conrad, by Wagner, and above all by Knies, under whom I took my degree. These economists had a sufficiently clear perception of the difference between ethics and economics. They had a feeling, however, that ethical influences should be brought to bear on our economic life, and they believed also that those ethical influences which were actually at work shaping economic life to a greater or less extent should be examined carefully as existing forces. And, finally, it is doubtless safe to say that the warm humanitarianism of the German theorists moved the Americans of my day deeply. But we remained Americans whose intellectual life had been quickened by our own life in the atmosphere of the German universities.

The American Economic Association took a stand at its organization for entire freedom of discussion. We were thoroughly devoted to the ideal of the German university—*Lehrfreiheit und Lernfreiheit;* and we have not hesitated to enter the lists vigorously in favor of freedom when we have considered it endangered. Here there has been no apparent difference. Whatever opinions otherwise may have separated our members, we have stood shoulder to shoulder as one man for free discussion. But was this ever necessary? Rightly or wrongly, we did feel at first that it required a struggle to find a place in our academic life for free expression of our views.

For the first seven years my office as secretary was a part of my general office at the Johns Hopkins University and served as the secretarial office, editorial office, publishing office, and I don't know what else besides. There was no appropriation for secretarial assistance and at first not even a typewriter. I took care of the printing, rushing down to the printing office and sometimes exploding with youthful wrath on account of the delay in getting out a monograph. I made all the contacts and contracts with book dealers; if there is no one else who can be designated by the name of advertising manager, I claim that title.

Women have always been welcomed into our ranks, but in our early days there were few of them. When we held our first annual meeting in Philadelphia there were perhaps fifteen or twenty women present, including such distinguished women as Florence Kelley and President M. Carey Thomas, of Bryn Mawr College. Dr. Stuart Wood planned a reception in his beautiful home but he had evidently overlooked the fact that women were members of our association, and according to the inflexible social code of Philadelphia, he did not see how he could receive women and men both in his home. So it fell to me unhappily to tell our women members that they were not expected at Stuart Wood's reception. In an eleventh hour attempt to smooth over an embarrassing situation, Dr. Wood's sister offered them a reception in her home and extended to them all a most cordial invitation to attend. The good ladies boycotted this reception and while the men enjoyed Dr. Wood's hospitality, his sister's parlors, all brilliantly lighted in anticipation of the ladies' arrival, were empty. How times have changed since then, perhaps even in Philadelphia!

The secretary's office also acted as a bureau of information for the members. For a number of years the bureau performed a very useful function in aiding members scattered throughout the country in the selection of works on topics in which they were interested, in giving information about leading thinkers on various sides of controverted questions, and in answering all sorts of questions in relation to economics. It supplied a real need at a time when there were comparatively few economists in the country, and compared with recent years, a very meager American literature.

It was the opinion of some of our founders that detailed reports and recommendations should be made by committees, and that these would be debated and have a direct influence on public opinion and legislation. The original idea was that each member of the association should belong to a committee, and that the work of the association would be essentially a work of standing committees. This idea was soon abandoned because our members were generally too busy with other duties to develop the work of the standing committees. We were building up departments in our universities, schools and institutions (such as the National Consumers League, the Child Labor Committee, and the American Association for Labor Legislation) to make scientific work easier for those who would follow us. Soon the theory of standing committees was modified. A plan for special committees was drawn up by Professor Charles H. Hull in his report to the council at the thirteenth annual meeting, December, 1900. "The theory of these special committees, as the secretary understands it, is that the association makes no attempt to impose the work of a committeeman upon any member, but, wherever a sufficient and well-balanced group of members desires to take up some subject of investigation which promises results, the council is inclined to give them its blessing, and the publication committee is likely to look with favor upon the proposal to print their report." It will be seen that this was a considerable departure from the original theory of the standing committees.

Another line of activity was the effort to encourage popular interest in economic questions by offers of prizes for essays on various economic questions of the day. These prizes performed an extremely useful purpose in their day, in awakening an intelligent appreciation of economics, in helping start at least a few young people in useful careers, and in attracting support to our association at a time when the struggle for existence was keenly felt by those who assumed the burden of our affairs.

DUNBAR DID NOT UNDERSTAND: WE WERE CONCERNED ABOUT LIFE

Although its formation was greeted with enthusiasm by a few, there was a strange failure, on the part of others, to comprehend that it really inaugurated a new era in the history of American economics. Even now, it is sometimes forgotten how much the foundation of the association meant to American economists. At the close of the nineteenth century, it was especially the older group of economists, with comparatively few exceptions, who really did not know what it was all about.

In 1886, one year after the birth of the American Economic Association, Professor C. F. Dunbar wrote an essay on, "The Reaction in Political Economy." Dunbar was one of those of the older school who was especially catholic and enlightened. We all liked Dunbar and some of us had studied under him. In fact, he was unanimously and without opposition chosen as the second president of the American Economic Association. But the following passage, which I wish to quote at length, shows that he was far from understanding the "new economics" of 1885:

"The 'new departure' in political economy then, as illustrated by this typical case, consists at most in the addition of historical inquiry to methods of investigation already in use. The extent of this addition, and its relation to economic theory, ranges all the way from the copious use of history to illustrate theory—as

in Roscher's principal treatise—to the specific investigation of
economic history, with the light afforded by long familiarity
with economic reasoning, of which in English a brilliant example is given us by Thorold Rogers. But, after all, the difference between the old school and the new is essentially a difference of emphasis or of relative weight given to the historical
side of the subject and not a radical change of method in arriving at economic truths. The movement by which historical inquiry is thus brought more or less into the foreground, according to the intellectual tendencies or the opportunities of the
individual, is, no doubt, an important reaction against the
opposite tendency, which has stopped the progress of political
economy. But such a movement can become a revolution only
when the old method and its results are frankly abandoned, as is
demanded by Schmoller and the most advanced section, in the
expectation of reconstructing the whole fabric of the science by
a new process. That this reaction has a close affinity with the intellectual movement which has given new life and meaning to
the study of history and jurisprudence is undeniable. No doubt,
the development of the industrial life of nations and of their
economic institutions, and the causes which, in all that relates
to material life, make one nation a different historical product
from another, could have no complete exposition without the
application of modern methods of research and comparative
study. No doubt, too, the exposition of these subjects in the
light of ascertained economic laws must be one of the conditions of the advance of social science and of wise legislation.
All this, however, is far from carrying with it either the necessary unsettling of established doctrines, or the abandonment of
the processes by which they have been established.

"There is another important subject, however, on which the
new school of political economy is better agreed, and as to
which it is understood to be in strong opposition to the old

economists. This is the vast increase of the functions and activity of the state, now called for in so many quarters. The old political economy, it is declared, was 'atomistic,' and dealt only with individuals; that of the future must be social, and must take the given society, not the individuals composing that society, as its unit; society, as a conscious whole, has duties limited only by the possibility of actively advancing the general well-being of its members; its powers are to be adapted to this end, and, if adapted, are the justifiable, the most effective, and the necessary means of social advancement. A great and not easily definable extension of the activity of government is thus contemplated. That there is a 'law of increasing functions of government' may be an extreme opinion; but, at any rate, the old presumption in favor of individual freedom is at least obscured, and for laissez faire is to be substituted a system of direct and pervasive, although carefully studied, interference. There is no doubt as to the loftiness of the ideal which such a system sets before the government of any modern state, or as to the qualities with which such a government must by some means be endowed, in order to approach this ideal. Such conceptions of centralized and all-sufficient power, we may add, are a natural effect both of imperialism and of democracy and, hence, at this juncture in the world's history, we have a set of the tide from opposite quarters, in favor of extending the functions of government, quite as marked as the *doctrinaire* tendency of the last generation toward non-interference." [32]

It is apparent in this passage that Dunbar did not really understand what it was all about. First of all, he speaks about method as if it were the principal thing with which we were concerned. He seems to think that possibly we wanted to make of economics economic history. He especially singles out Thorold Rogers as giving us a brilliant example of the use of history and as perhaps an outstanding illustration of the new economics.

Thorold Rogers did give us some economic history, but he did not play any considerable part in the development of economics.

Professor Dunbar then speaks about the controversy in regard to laissez faire, and gives the idea that we advocated extending the functions of government as something always to be desired. He says that there is no doubt about "the loftiness of the ideal" which we had before us in advocating the extension of government functions. The situation was quite different. We saw a multiplication of social and economic relations among men which was changing the character of economic society. More and more we were becoming increasingly dependent upon others, and more and more this dependence was becoming interdependence. The forces of life were getting beyond the control of individuals. It was not a question of what we wished, but a question of shaping and directing the forces of life so as to prevent a disaster. Everything that was happening was making it inevitable that we should get away from laissez faire as a condition of prosperous survival.

Dunbar says about the new attitude towards the functions of government:

"Whether the present flow is permanent, or is destined to be followed by an ebb, it is at present an active influence in large sections of existing society, and gives a marked character to the political economy of the new school." [33]

As a matter of fact, there has been no ebb, and there could be no ebb because economic relations were constantly increasing in numbers and in significance. What great invention or development of industry has taken place since then which does not compel us to collective activity? We have collective activity because our life is collective. This recognition of collectivity and what went with it was not socialism. On the contrary, it was something to keep us from socialism, for we emphasized the rights of the individual as well as the legitimate activity of the state.

Some have thought, and perhaps still think, that we were chiefly concerned about differences in method, or what the Germans call *Methodenstreit*. Certainly, most of us emphasized the inductive method of inquiry and, following the German economists who had trained us, we frequently spoke about the historical method. Sometimes we may have used the expressions statistical method and comparative method. All the talk about method, however, concerned things that were merely on the surface, and did not at all get down to those things which were really fundamental, and about which we were seriously concerned.

It has been said, and said wisely, that when a discussion takes place, apparently about words and forms of words, there are always things lying back of words which do have a real and vital meaning. In the Christian church there was at one time a very active discussion moving men profoundly which turned merely upon the spelling of a word. Those versed in theology know that what was called an iota subscript, which was simply a mark under a letter, played a large role in the history of theology. It seems perfectly ridiculous to the ordinary man that people should have got excited about a little mark. Those who know the history of theology understand that there was something real and vital at the bottom of this controversy concerning a little mark called the iota subscript.

What we young fellows were concerned about was life itself, and the controversy in regard to methodology was simply a surface indication of forces operating more deeply. We believed that economics had, in itself, the potency of life. In the vast field of research which lay before us, and through research, the opening up of fields which had been cultivated only to a limited extent, we felt that we had opportunities for service of many kinds. We had found among our teachers in Germany a warm humanitarianism, and that inspired us. Looking about us with open eyes we saw a real labor question, whereas some of the older school talked about a "so-called labor question." We saw a good deal of poverty on the one hand and a concentration of wealth on the other hand; and we did not feel that all was well with our country. We felt that something should be done to bring about better conditions. We had had a glimpse into the fundamental institutions of our economic life, and discovered that these were in a state of flux. We had learned the idea of evolution and never ceasing change as a condition of life. We thought that by getting down into this life and studying it carefully, we would be able to do something toward directing the great forces shaping our life, and directing them in such a way as to bring improvement.

The most fundamental things in our minds were, on the one hand, the idea of evolution, and on the other hand, the idea of relativity. These two ideas meant far more than the debate about methodology. A new world was coming into existence, and if this world was to be a better world, we knew that we must have a new economics to go along with it.

But why did we talk about inductive method? It was because this was the way of breaking down the old barriers in the path of progress and preparing the ground for something new and constructive. Surely no one of us and no one of our teachers in Germany objected to the use of deduction in its proper place; certainly it had its place, but deduction as it was then used, was inadequate. It did not explain the world as it was. We thought that we could get new premises and new generalizations by opening our eyes and looking at the world as it was. When we began to use the "look and see" method, we found a failure in the conclusions reached by the older economists to harmonize with the life that was unfolding about us. We found also that, as a matter of fact, the conclusions of the other economists, as they existed in the popular mind, and as they existed in the minds of leaders of thought and action, especially, stood in the way of real progress. The way to get out of such closed circles was to study life itself. We believed in gathering together facts, in order that they might tell the story of life. Of course if we had common sense and any intellectual acumen at all, we did not think that the mere accumulation of facts could give us scientific light or practical guidance. We did not need to be told that one could gather facts for a century and not be any wiser. The facts had to be gathered in accordance with some hypothesis and arranged in such a way that they might give us new knowledge. Hypotheses, observation—such procedure was fundamental to us.

We did have a new economics. The apathy and indifference with respect to the old economics were replaced by an enthusiasm which has continued from 1885 down to the present time. We had a message and this kindled enthusiasm. Our message was hailed by the best minds in the rising generation with a joy begotten of hope. All of this explains what our "statement of principles" really signified. The crust that had been formed on economics was broken, and real economic inquiry expanded and grew and has kept on growing until this very day.

An English writer who exercised some considerable influence on the "new economics" of 1885 was John Stuart Mill. Mill stands, in a way, between the new and the old in economic theory. He is Janus-faced; and I say this without intending any reproach whatever. The Germans say of John Stuart Mill that he lacked system, using the term *systemlos*. In his early youth he had been rigorously trained in the Ricardian system of economics by his father, James Mill, who was a close friend of Ricardo himself. In his autobiography he tells us how difficult it was for him, during the time of his father, to break away from the old economics. When he did so, he was hard put to it to replace a system that he had come to feel was inadequate and obsolete. John Stuart Mill says that his "eyes were opened to the very limited and temporary value of the old political economy" partly through the early writings of Auguste Comte (at a time when that author still called himself a pupil of the French socialist, Saint Simon) and, to an even greater extent, through the Saint Simonians themselves. From Auguste Comte he learned how great an error it is to mistake the "moral and intellectual characteristics" of one era for "the normal attributes of humanity." From the Saint Simonians he learned to distrust some of the assumptions on which the old political economy was based, and especially the assumption of believing in freedom of production and exchange as the *dernier mot* of social improvement.

Under these influences, John Stuart Mill says that he came gradually to change his earlier and taught opinions:

"I found the fabric of my old and taught opinion giving way in many fresh places, and I never allowed it to fall to pieces, but was incessantly occupied in weaving it anew."

A captious critic might say that he patched the holes rather than wove a new fabric, and Mill himself might have admitted that there was some truth in this statement. For I have a letter from Thorold Rogers in which he mentions a conversation he had had with Mill from which it appears that Mill himself said that he felt the need of rewriting his economics, but that he was too old to do so. What he did was to state the old propositions and then to modify them so radically as almost to destroy them. His influence upon us economists of the younger generation was undoubtedly very great. Many of us were particularly impressed by a passage in which he said that, when discussing how much or how little should be done by the government, or how far the government should go in restricting what the older economists called "natural liberty," it was impossible to draw any rigid line or to say "thus far and no further." Let me quote this passage:

"Enough has been said to show that the admitted functions of government embrace a much wider field than can easily be included within the ring-fence of any restrictive definition, and that it is hardly possible to find any ground of justification common to them all, except the comprehensive one of general expediency; nor to limit the interference of government by any universal rule, save the simple and vague one that it should never be admitted but when the case of expediency is strong." [34] This passage expressed the way most of us felt.

For several years after I began to work in the Johns Hopkins University I used John Stuart Mill's *Political Economy* as a text; and other contemporaries of mine did so for a number of years. We found that, in spite of Mill's half-hearted defense of the "let alone" system, he really justified pretty much of everything that those of the younger group stood for. We, also, all liked his warm humanitarianism and especially his sympathy with the wage-earning classes, and the frank way in which he renounced his earlier wage-fund theory, having the courage to say, "I was mistaken." In the course of a review of Thornton's *Labour* published by Mill in the *Fortnightly Review* for May, 1869, the English economist admits:

"The doctrine hitherto taught by all or most economists (including myself), which denied it to be possible that trade combinations can raise wages, or which limited their operations in that respect to the somewhat earlier attainment of a rise which the competition of the market would have produced without them—this doctrine is deprived of its scientific foundation, and must be thrown aside. The right and wrong of the proceedings of trade unions becomes a common question of prudence and social duty, not one which is peremptorily decided by unbending necessities of political economy."

THE INFLUENCE OF THE AMERICAN ECONOMIC ASSOCIATION

The men who founded the American Economic Association look upon its foundation as the great event in American economics; but they were only the medium through which deep currents of life found expression. We may regard the history of economic thought before this event as leading up to it, and the events of importance since its foundation may be regarded in the main as flowing from it. Eighteen hundred and eighty-five may be designated as our hegira. The American Economic Association is not to be looked upon as the sole creator of the thought forces within our field, but it is one of the thought causes. It is beyond question that had the Economic Association not come into existence we should have had a development of economic thought in this country; but it is certainly true that our association has gathered together the thought forces and has given expression to them. It has served as a stimulus to young and old. It has rewarded youth by recognition.

Our association has stimulated improvement in economic and statistical work. All who have followed our history will recall our critical treatment of the census office and the active part that we took in favoring the establishment of a permanent census bureau. We may fairly claim an appreciable influence in the improvement which is going on in the census work of the country. In 1905, a special committee was appointed to consider the scope and method of the twelfth census. This committee consisted of Richmond Mayo-Smith, Walter Wilcox, Carroll D. Wright, Roland Falkner, and Davis R. Dewey. The resultant volume on *The Scope and Method of the Twelfth*

Census—Critical discussion by over Twenty Statistical Experts exercised a great and beneficent influence on succeeding censuses. The world of railway reform is associated with our history. Railway problems have been discussed faithfully by men representing different points of view, and members of our association are now engaged in bringing about improvements of value both to the railways and the general public. Our association has been one of the forces in favor of sound money, helping the country to weather storms and avert threatened evils. The trust problem has received fruitful discussion in our meetings, and our members have been among those who have thrown light on the scientific and practical aspects of industrial combinations. The good roads movement received an impetus in an able monograph contributed by one of our presidents. Social reform has been guided and stimulated by our efforts.

Our direct influence has been very largely exercised through our meetings and through our publications. In looking through the titles of the monographs appearing in our first three or four volumes, we see revealed the tendencies of economic thought which the American Economic Association expressed.

The functions of the state, in relation to public utilities, were discussed in Dr. Edmund J. James' monographs on "The Relation of the Modern Municipality to the Gas Supply," and on the "Railway Question." The principle of competition, as a regulating factor in the sphere of industry, was ably examined in an essay published by Professor Henry C. Adams, entitled "Relation of the State to Industrial Action." In this monograph, Professor Adams reached the conclusion that, generally speaking, competition may be relied upon to regulate, in the interests of society as a whole, those industries where conditions of "constant returns" or "diminishing returns" prevail. Professor Adams defined conditions of "constant returns" as those in which, when say two units of capital and labor result in two units of product, if a third unit is added, the regulating product will be increased proportionately. Under conditions of diminishing returns, when two units of capital and labor result in two units of product, if a third unit of capital and labor is added, the resulting product will fail to increase proportionately. So far as businesses conducted under conditions of either constant or diminishing returns were concerned, Professor Adams maintained that the entrepreneur's struggle for superior success was usually "a struggle to depress the cost of rendering services rather than to raise the prices of services rendered." But a third class of industries existed, he said: those conducted under conditions of increasing returns. In such industries, when two products of capital and labor result in two units of product, if a third unit is added, the resulting product will increase disproportionately. Businesses conducted under conditions of increasing return could, he maintained, never be regulated by free competition, "because it is easier for an established business to extend its facilities for satisfactorily meeting a new demand than for a new industry to spring into competitive existence." Thus, in the third instance, we have, he said, a case of natural monopoly, where state regulation and control is an imperative necessity if the general welfare of society is to be considered.

It is noteworthy that both Professor E. J. James and Professor Adams arrived at similar conclusions, though by different routes; namely that public utilities, such as railways, etc., must be subjected to public control.

In the early volumes of our publications, we find monographs on co-operation; one by Albert Shaw, entitled "Cooperation in a Western City," one by Edward W. Bemis, entitled "Cooperation in New England," another monograph on the same subject, Amos G. Warner's "Three Phases of Cooperation in the West," and also an "Historical Sketch of the Finances of Pennsylvania," by T. K. Worthington. The monographs on co-opera-

tion and the one on the finances of Pennsylvania were written
by students of mine in the Johns Hopkins University, and, in
their insistence on observation, they show the influence of the
German historical school. I believe that all the founders of the
American Economic Association, whether their writings tend
to be deductive or inductive, have taught their students to use
the "look and see" method. In our third volume, J. B. Clark
published his essay on "Capital and Its Earnings," which contains the essentials of his entire economic system. In the same
volume our first president, General Walker, presented a paper
on the "Efforts of the Manual Laboring Class to Better Their
Conditions." In this paper, General Walker showed that, although the workers had "as real, as large, as vital a part to perform in securing a just and beneficial distribution of the product
of industry," as the employers, it was, nevertheless, unquestionably true that every permanent increase of wages depends upon
the accumulation of capital for industrial uses.

As secretary of the association for the first seven years of its
existence, I was in a position to follow better probably than anyone else the actual influence exerted by our association; and it
is no exaggeration to say that it was a very great one, and very
appreciable in the development of social control in our country.
Our publications went to those persons in a position to exercise
influence, and they went at the right juncture and produced an
impression that was out of all proportion to the number of our
members.

In our early days branches of the American Economic Association were formed in various parts of the country and served
a most useful purpose in their time as leaders of intelligent discussion of questions of theory and in the treatment of local economic problems. Each one was a center of light and leadership.
The following places among others had branches: Springfield,
Massachusetts; Orange, New Jersey; Washington, D. C.; Buf-

falo, New York; Canton, Ohio; Galesburg and Geneseo, Illinois; Kansas City, Kansas. One of the most thriving of these branches was the Connecticut Valley Economic Association, with headquarters at Springfield, organized in January, 1886, probably the first one to organize; and three well-known American economists contributed to its success; namely, Professor J. B. Clark, F. H. Giddings, and Dr. E. W. Bemis.

Our association has exercised an influence on foreign countries. In Glasgow it served as a stimulus for a local University Economic Association. From Oxford, England, came the suggestion made by a well-known English economist of the formation of a local association in alliance with the American Economic Association, but finally the British association was formed and our correspondence shows that our own association served both as a stimulus and a model. The correspondence of the secretary's office shows our influence as a stimulus in the life of similar associations in Australia and Japan.

One feature of our internal history was the council, which kept in its hands the control of the association, electing officers and conducting its affairs; only changes in the constitution being referred to the general body. Occasionally this was criticized as undemocratic and on its account one member resigned, but it seemed to be necessary at the first to prevent our organization from being captured by some economic sect or group of reformers. Our aim was always to elect to the council all economists who attended our meetings and showed a serious interest in our work, also business and professional men in considerable numbers. The need of such precautions having passed, this arrangement was dropped.

Another interesting event in our internal history was the position taken towards endowments. The council at our Detroit meeting in 1900 virtually rejected the offer of an endowment, it being feared by some that an endowment might come from sources that would prove embarrassing and would hamper our free development. The feeling was even expressed that we should from year to year be dependent upon our friends. It is possibly of some significance that the movement for an endowment came first of all from one connected with a state university and that the opposition sprang almost altogether from men associated with privately endowed universities. Now we have reached a period in our life when we make use of the funds which endowments furnish and do so without danger, conscious or unconscious, to our scientific integrity.

Our first president was Francis A. Walker. The men who established the association felt at once and so surely that he was the natural president that no other name was even considered. He had occupied prominent positions in the country, and we looked upon him as our leader, and far more than any other man, prepared to pave the way for the development of future thought in economics in the United States. He was not selected because we necessarily agreed with his views, but because we looked upon him as a champion and emancipator.

In 1892 the personnel of the association was changed so far as the president and secretary were concerned, and the statement of principles was dropped. It has always been felt that the presidency should be changed frequently in order to enable us to give recognition to those who deserved recognition. Very reluctantly, President Walker had retained the presidency for seven years because it was felt that in the early days he could be of service in this office. In 1892, it was felt that the time for change had come. Moreover, it was felt that we should give recognition to Professor Dunbar of Harvard, whom we all admired and liked personally. He was then not in robust health and the feeling was expressed that we ought not to delay in giving him the recognition which we felt was his due. There was not the slightest opposition, so far as I can recall, to his election, certainly no opposition whatever from those who were regarded as the more progressive members of the association. I had been secretary for seven years, and had done a great deal of hard work. I felt that someone else should take over the burden and ventured to nominate Professor Edward A. Ross of Cornell University, one of my former students, who seemed advantageously situated to care for the work of the secretaryship.

The history of the American Economic Association has been an expression of the history of economic thought in the United States; and may this ever continue to be the case. For us old duffers, as Professor Seligman calls us, 1885 was *Morgendämmerung*—the dawn of day. For us it is now *Abenddämmerung*—twilight—the shadows lengthen. But generation follows generation. Young men have come forward to instruct us. Let the young be tolerant—let them try to respect the fathers—"the old duffers," remembering that even the youngest make mistakes and still have something to learn. Let the older men try to keep their eyes ever turned to the rising sun. The sun of science is ever dawning. I see the promise of an advance in economic thinking beyond what we, the founders, have known. It is not *Abenddämmerung* for the American Economic Association. It is *Morgendämmerung*.

I CONFESS MY LOVE

As I review the events of my life from the vantage point of my eighty-fourth year, it seems to me as if some "higher power" has uprooted me at each of the turning points of my career, lifting me up from where I was and putting me down somewhere else. During 1880 when I was tramping the streets of New York City looking for work, I found a friend in Carl Schurz, who wrote an editorial for the New York *Evening Post* about a report I made for the department of state on the purchase of the Prussian railways by the Prussian government. At about the same time as this first public recognition of my work, I learned that there was an opening on the teaching staff of the Johns Hopkins University. This turned the scale for me. I had returned from Germany imbued with the philosophy represented by Roscher's words, "the beginning and end of all is man." Then I had the fortunate opportunity of beginning my career at a university where the motto was: "Men—not bricks and mortar."

I was the first man to be regularly employed the year round as lecturer in economics at a modest salary of twelve hundred dollars. The following eleven years at Johns Hopkins were years of earnest work, free from outside interference, in an ideal atmosphere of friendly co-operation with students and teachers alike. During these years, I reaped the benefits of the intellectual stimulation which attended the teaching of an exceptionally fine group of graduate students. With the co-operation of H. B. Adams and others, I was able to play my part in the founding of the American Economic Association. In this period I wrote seven of my major books and more articles than I can now see how I had time to write.

I look back to those years as the golden years; they were among the fullest and happiest of my life. While I was on vacation in Lexington, Virginia, in 1883, I met Miss Anna Morris Anderson at a Virginia Military Institute ball. I promptly fell in love with her, and on December 30, 1883, I confided in my mother:

"It is needless to say that I am having a delightful time with my most charming sweetheart. She is certainly a lovely girl and has a noble character. I really and truly believe she is the only woman I ever met to draw out all that is best in me as well as all the resources of my heart. I wish I could give you some idea of what she is, but it is impossible, because I am certain no one

ever like her ever lived and besides you would set it all down
to the vivid imagination of blind love. But I am happy in the
thought that you will soon see for yourself what a treasure I
have won. I am glad our natures are as diverse as they are, since
they supplement each other so admirably. If we were quite
alike, we would have nothing to gain from each other, and it
would be insufferably stupid.

"I did not intend to write so much about Anna, but you see
out of the abundance of the heart, the mouth speaketh."

We were married in 1884. My wife, who had been brought
up in the old tradition of the F.F.V.'s, had never cooked a meal
in her life or done any work in the kitchen. I remember the
first coffee she prepared for me. She and her Southern girl
friend set it before me with great pride and glee—which was
soon followed by consternation. It was a flat failure, but it was
the only failure I can recall, for no Yankee girl could have
taken hold more whole-heartedly of her new job. She had no
old customs or traditions to break and she set to work methodi-
cally studying cookbooks, and asking advice. Soon she became
an excellent cook, a far better one than many of the Yankee
girls.

I INVESTIGATE THE EXPERIMENT AT PULLMAN

On our wedding trip we went to Pullman, Illinois, for I had
been asked by *Harper's Monthly* to write an evaluation of the
social experiment at Pullman. This article was later judged by
H. M. Alden, editor of *Harper's,* to be the best magazine article
of the year. It received an immense amount of attention and I
believe it threw some much needed light on the Pullman strikes
which occurred later.

The words "communism" and "socialism" were becoming
international words, understood by people of both hemispheres,

*Anna Mason Ely, John Thomas Anderson Ely, Mrs. Anna
Morris Ely, and Richard Sterling Ely*

printed daily in ten thousand journals. They were evidence of a momentous social movement; they bore witness to a widespread discontent with things as they were. The pretty dream of a perfect, natural order of things brought about by the free play of unrestrained social forces had vanished. It gave way on the one hand to pessimism; on the other, and more generally, to a determination not to let things go on of themselves, but to make them go in such a manner as was desired. The conviction had become general that the divine order never contemplated a social and economic world left to itself. Co-operation was looked upon as a new social form. Many attempts were made by "captains of industry" to step in between those they led and the unrestrained action of existing economic forces. Insurance, gratuitous instruction, amusements, reading rooms, participation in profits were provided by many employers for the benefit of their employees. Several employers attempted more far-reaching schemes, which embraced the home lives of laborers and thus included wives and children in their beneficence. One extensive experiment of this type was in progress at Pullman. In my article, I expressed the belief that "For this reason it challenges attention and discussion at a time when dynamite bombs and revolutionary murmurings terrify monarchs, when an enlarged human sympathy encircles the earth with beneficent institutions, and when an eager interest in social and economic facts more than atones for the general indifference to the dogmatic assumptions of classical political economy."

In the belief that the only way I could fairly judge what was being done at Pullman was by first-hand experience, after the manner of the "look and see" method, I went there to see for myself. My wife and I went to the Hotel Florence, named after Pullman's daughter Florence, settled down and determined to stay long enough to find out what was going on in all its aspects.

In the way of material comforts and beautiful surroundings, Pullman probably offered to the majority of its residents quite as much as they were in a position to enjoy, and in many cases, even more. Its purpose was to provide both a center of industry and homes for employees of the company. My first superficial impression was that Pullman had attained a high ideal. But after a few days of careful observation, I noticed certain unpleasant features of the social life, which moderated my initial enthusiasm. I soon discovered it was not easy to get all the information I desired. The city was full of spies and the people were unable to discuss things freely. I was not discouraged but I saw that it was necessary to begin casting about for ways to get beneath the surface. One thing immediately attracted my attention. There was a beautiful church, the doors of which were closed on Sunday. I inquired the reason and was told that no regular church organization in Pullman was able to pay the rent. Mr. Pullman believed in philanthropy but he also believed in a six percent return on his investment. There were two or three organizations, but none could afford to pay six percent.

I had not been in Pullman long before I learned that a picnic was to take place. My wife and I accepted an invitation to take part in the festivities. As I talked with the people in the party I began to get light on certain problems that perplexed me. Then I began to resort to various other devices to get the necessary information.

My wife wore buttoned shoes and one day when a button came off we gave it to a shoemaker in Pullman to repair. Shoemakers are often philosophically inclined; the nature of their work seems to develop a disposition to think things over. This particular shoemaker, we found, was quite willing to discuss his ideas and we found that his comments were well worth careful attention. Strangely enough, the buttons on my wife's shoes tore off quite regularly.

While I was in Pullman, Professor Simon Patten, who was teaching in a country school in Illinois, and whom I met in Halle, called upon us and spent some time with us. During Patten's visit it occurred to us to drink buttermilk. The man who served us was one given to observation and reflection, and was in the habit of talking freely while we drank. We drank many glasses of buttermilk.

Still I did not feel I had got at the bottom of things. At the time there was a Presbyterian preacher from Philadelphia who had charge of a church in Pullman. He was bright and friendly and entirely sympathetic with my purpose. One day when I told him I was not getting all the facts I desired, he suggested that I go with him to call on his parishioners. I gladly accepted his invitation and I set out with a note book as small as the palm of my hand. As soon as he saw it the preacher said, "Put that in your pocket. It will arouse suspicion." As we went from house to house we asked the natural questions, "Did Mary get over her whooping cough? What about Johnny's accident? Did his bones set?" Finally we got around to asking questions about the father, who was employed in the Pullman works. In this way we got the reaction of workers.

This was the time of the campaign between Blaine and Cleveland. One day I was standing on the porch of the Hotel Florence with the superintendent of the Pullman works. We were watching a torchlight procession of the supporters of Blaine and Cleveland. I remarked to the superintendent, "I see that the employees are free to express their political views." He answered, "They are in national elections." His emphasis on national did not escape my attention. I began to make inquiries about local elections and I found that employees were anything but free. A local election had taken place and this was a time when it was considered right to pay a man five dollars to distribute ballots in behalf of a candidate. A gentleman in favor

of a local ticket opposed to Pullman said that after repeated
efforts he found a man who agreed to distribute ballots of this
local candidate. However, the night before the election he returned the five dollars and said he could not carry out his agreement. This led to further inquiries. Then I looked into the
assessed valuation of land for tax purposes and was amazed to
see how low it was.

At the time of my visit there was a Baptist organization. The
pastor of the Baptist church had taken up the cause of an
evicted Pullman worker. His congregation dwindled away until
there was nothing left of it.

The social life was so restricted that I think every resident
must have had the feeling that it was impossible within the
realm of Pullman to escape from the overshadowing influence
of the company. There was a repression of individuality and
initiative. Laborers were not allowed to acquire property; there
were no publications or means of getting information which
did not emanate from the company; strikes were regarded as
the chief of social sins; there was unfair administration in respect to employment, retention, and promotion of employees;
there was a prevalence of petty jealousies, a discouragement of
superior excellence, a frequent change in residents, and an all-
pervading feeling of insecurity. For these reasons, I wrote:
"The idea of Pullman is un-American. It is a benevolent, well-
wishing feudalism, which desires the happiness of the people,
but in such a way as shall please the authorities. No! the body
is more than rainment and the soul is more than the body. If
free American institutions are to be preserved, we want no race
of men reared as underlings with the spirit of menials."

It must not be supposed from what I say that I did not find
any good things at Pullman and that I was without admiration.
Mr. Pullman was one of the great industrial leaders of our
generation. Today the leaders in our business schools and uni-

versities tell us that business should attain the standards of a profession. This is an ideal most desirable and perhaps essential to our permanent welfare. A professional man is not unmindful of gain but he puts quality of service first and will sacrifice gain rather than do something which is held by professional standards unethical. It cannot be said of Mr. Pullman that there was any conscientious striving for this degree of excellence. But I believe it can be said that the management of the Pullman Company was really a good deal above the standards that prevailed in business during the past two generations. One could not put anything Pullman ever did in the class of Gould or Fisk. They were below the actual business standard, just as Mr. Pullman was clearly above the general level.

Mr. Pullman naturally desired to have railway presidents among his stockholders, because they would introduce Pullman cars. A gentleman, who afterwards became a member of my staff at the University of Wisconsin and was for some time Mr. Pullman's secretary, told me that one day Pullman had a conference with Gould and sold him some Pullman stock. It was understood that Gould would keep the stock. However, he went ahead and sold it on the market at a profit. This is something that Pullman would not have done. He was not a model employer, but he did give his employees good living conditions, and his ethics were much higher than the average.

On our return from our wedding trip we went to my home in Fredonia, New York. We were both young and very gay and took mishaps with a sense of humor; and it is fortunate that we had such an ample capacity for laughing. At that time we were accustomed to buying through tickets to some place beyond our destination and then have them redeemed. We bought two tickets to Boston when we wanted to go only as far as Buffalo. On our way we stopped at Detroit, at a very "swanky" hotel. After I paid for our breakfast I found we did not have any money left; evidently I had been very careless in my calculations. We had to wait until the evening for our train. We tramped the streets, went to church, sat under trees, and went without supper. The next morning we reached Buffalo and immediately had the balance of the tickets redeemed. I rushed into the station where my wife was waiting and exultantly waved a ten dollar bill in the air and cried, "Now we can eat." How good that first cup of coffee tasted! Then we went on to Dunkirk and Fredonia. Thus ended our wedding journey.

The younger generation of economists may find it hard to understand the hardships under which the first-hand observation of experiments such as the Pullman was accomplished. The research foundations which now make liberal grants of their funds had not yet been established and researches involving any expense were difficult to make. For example, while writing *The Labor Movement in America,* I had to give lectures to defray the expenses of field researches. In these early years I had no secretary and I wrote my articles and books in my own handwriting. How well I remember the night when I wrote the last word of my *Introduction to Political Economy* which was the first edition of my *Outlines;* I sighed with relief, looked at my watch and saw that it was midnight, just six weeks after the day I began writing.

While at the Johns Hopkins I was a member first of the Baltimore Tax Commission, and then for two years of the Maryland Tax Commission. In each case I made a report. My recollection of the report to the Baltimore Tax Commission is dim, but my report to the Maryland Tax Commission was far more important. I worked on it for two years, without the facilities which young men in universities today take as a matter of course. I was granted an appropriation of one hundred dollars to travel to various states and to Canada, to look up data, and to gather by conversation with tax authorities the necessary information. The two other men on the commission were Sommerfield Baldwin, a wealthy manufacturer, and John P. Poe, a gifted attorney and an astute politician. We made a joint report and I made a separate report which was later published under the title *Taxation in American States and Cities*. When we presented our report to the legislative committee which had been appointed to receive it, we were received with scant courtesy. Members of the committee went in and out of the committee room and showed very plainly that they were not interested. However, many years later, I learned that it did have a significant influence in shaping tax legislation and administration in this and many other countries. In Canada, and as far away as South Africa, I am told that certain of my suggestions were adopted. Only six years ago, I received a letter from a Maryland legislator which said, "now we have adopted certain recommendations that you made over a generation ago." This illustrates how great is the need for patience and for adhering to the belief that a good seed planted in good ground may sprout up later.

My experience with the Maryland Tax Commission thoroughly convinced me that any doubts I had concerning my political gifts were well-founded. In Maryland it was the custom to grant a non-paid commission, such as we were, an honorarium on the completion of its work. Therefore, a bill was introduced to the legislature providing that each member of the tax commission receive an honorarium of five hundred dollars. To Mr. Baldwin, the money was a small matter. To my wife and to me, it meant a very much needed spring vacation. To Mr. Poe, it had some significance, even though he was a successful lawyer. But there was another matter which held more interest for Mr. Poe. He had worked on a code of laws and had presented a bill to the legislature for ten thousand dollars to pay for his services. To cultivate the good-will of the legislators and thus insure the passage of his bill, he took it upon himself to speak for the members of the Maryland Tax Commission. He said that we had been appointed as an unpaid commission, that it had been our pleasure to work for the state of Maryland, and we desired no remuneration. We received none. My wife and I had to forego our little trip to Florida. And Mr. Poe's bill for ten thousand dollars was passed.

A more pleasant memory in connection with this report is that of my association with Dr. Finley, who was then one of my graduate students. He was a great help in the preparation of my individual report for publication as *Taxation in American States and Cities*. He did the laborious work of gathering statistics, making tabulations, and more important, the influence of his keen mind was felt throughout the book. I felt that he had done enough to warrant my putting his name on the title page. I said nothing to him about this, and the first time he knew of it was when he saw the first copy of the book. He was highly gratified and he has always held that his part in this book is something which should not be omitted in any biographical sketch of him.

I LEAVE THE JOHNS HOPKINS

When I married my salary was only seventeen hundred and fifty dollars a year, but living conditions in Baltimore were more favorable for members of the faculty and people of culture, who had low incomes, than anywhere else in the United States at that time. We had two colored maids: Mary, the cook, at ten dollars a month, and Cassy, who did all the cleaning, for eight dollars a month. Some of our neighbors protested at the high wages we were paying. The price of food was so low that it seems incredible now. I remember paying twelve cents a pound for bacon, and five cents a dozen for bananas.

I bought my first home in Maryland. It was a three-story brick house at 2400 Calvert Street, next to Goucher College. I think I used good judgment in driving the bargain with the builders. The house was built on a corner lot, about fifteen feet by eighty-five. The builders said they wanted five thousand dollars. They evidently thought that as a Johns Hopkins man I was a good prospect. I offered them forty-five hundred dollars, with a very small down payment, and was surprised when they accepted. The only way I was able to pay the balance was by adding to my salary what I earned by writing articles for the Baltimore *Sun* and other papers and periodicals. I managed somehow to keep ahead of the schedule. And when I left Baltimore, I put a "For Sale" sign in the window and sold my house for five thousand dollars.

During the last year at the Johns Hopkins, I began to feel dissatisfied with things as they were. I wanted to do so much and there was so little money with which to do it. I was not able to secure the books I needed, nor could I get an assistant, although I was doing the work of two men. Both Adams and I wanted to be promoted to full professorships and we were annoyed that Gilman was so slow about advancing any associate. At this time President Harper of the University of Chicago was anxious to have Adams and me come to Chicago where he was to be head of the department of history and political science, and I, head of the department of economics. We had both worked with Harper at Chautauqua and admired his powers of endurance and concentration immensely. But it seemed to both of us that he was too stern a master; we thought that he cracked the whip over his associates in a way we would not like. However, we were not fully decided and we spent one evening together in Philadelphia, discussing the pros and cons. Finally, Adams asked me, "Will you go to Chicago if I will?" I replied, "Yes."

The following day, Adams went to Gilman and told him that if he went to Chicago, I would go along. Adams received his promotion to full professorship; I did not. And I became very angry, not only at Adams, but at the Johns Hopkins University. This was one of the "errata" of my life. Adams was more entitled to the professorship than I. He was four years older, and had been at the university from the very beginning. He probably thought that my promotion would follow in due course. I realize now that my attitude was unnecessarily belligerent. During these years at the Johns Hopkins, I had been attacked many times by the press, and by what the senior La Follette would call, "the interests." I stood firmly for certain principles, and I wanted my fellow-economists to accept my leadership. This insistence made me many enemies, but the university authorities always stood by me. Perhaps, if I had been more conciliatory and appreciative of the work that was being done by other economists, I might have had more whole-hearted support. Alas! I cannot wholly absolve myself from the sin of having adopted the attitude of "holier than thou."

After eleven years at the Johns Hopkins University, the "higher power" uprooted me and put me down in Wisconsin where I became director of the school of economics, political science and history.

* * *

V

Reaping the Harvest

* * *

SIMON NEWCOMB ATTACKS ME AND PRESIDENT CHAMBERLIN DISAGREES

FOR THIRTY YEARS I was to live near the campus of the University of Wisconsin, surrounded by the beauty of Madison's four lakes, in the state of the first brain trust, the home of the La Follettes. The charm of Madison fascinated me from the very start, and when I think of the beauty of Madison's lakes, forests and hills, I remember what Dr. Durlin Rector of Grace Church, used to say—"How beautiful Madison must have been before the white man came!" And his criticism of the white man was justified. Men, whose interest in money had made them callous to beauty, had built the Chicago Northwestern Railway along the shores of Lake Monona. Along the borders of the lake, they built unsightly boat houses. They constructed buildings with no regard for the natural surroundings. It seemed as if the architects were only interested in showing off all they knew about the architectures of ancient Greece and Rome; the buildings on the university campus were examples of eclecticism at its worst. One day I was standing on the campus with a distinguished architect; he glanced at the array of buildings and said, "If they tried hard enough, they could have found two or three more styles of architecture."

But the beauties of Madison outshone the pitiful atrocities by which man had unwittingly defaced them. Soon after I came to

Madison, some aesthetically sensitive citizens took the matter in hand. They did wonders in removing some of the old eyesores. They organized the Park and Pleasure Drive Association and laid out beautiful drives among the hills and forests of Madison. For a long time, these were supported by private contributions from public-spirited citizens. Now, if you drive for forty or fifty miles in and around Madison, you will never forget the delightful trip.

It was President Chamberlin who offered me the post at Wisconsin. His fine appreciation of the importance of research was coupled with a rare courage. Indeed, it required courage and daring to invite me to act as director of the department of the social sciences. During the previous five years, I had been attacked continually by Simon Newcomb and other writers for the *Nation,* who branded me as a socialist and an anarchist. My study of the *Labor Movement in America,* in particular, aroused vehement attacks. This book opens with the following sentences: "The importance of those phases of American life with which the present work deals is no longer likely to be called into question. The labor movement treats of the struggle of the masses for existence, and this phrase is acquiring new meaning in our times. A marvelous war is now being waged in the heart of modern civilization. Millions are engaged in it. The welfare of humanity depends on its issue." Simon Newcomb was bitterly critical of this point of view. He believed, "that labor discontent is perennial in human nature, and is bound to continue, no matter what measure we take to cure it. We may, perhaps, draw the equally encouraging conclusion that it will do no more harm in the future than in the past." He found that my discussion of social movements, as a whole, showed a "lack of logical acumen and a narrowness of view which in a university teacher are most remarkable." He thought my worst defect was "an intensity of bias and a bitterness toward all

classes of society, except one, to which it would be hard to find
a parallel elsewhere than in the ravings of an anarchist or the
dreams of a socialist." He concluded that my *Labor Movement
in America* was "marked by a genuine puerility of tone and
treatment, a scrappiness of narrative and an absence of everything like strength of touch, mental grasp or logical unity—
faults which deprive it of real interest." He concluded, "Dr.
Ely seems to be seriously out of place in a university chair." [35]

Fortunately, President Chamberlin did not agree with Simon
Newcomb. And there were many others who received my books
and articles with great favor. If it were possible to gather the
favorable comments on my work, which appeared in the labor
press and in religious periodicals of the Methodist Episcopal
Church and the Christian Union, they would fill many a volume
such as this. Although I met with criticism from some of the
economists, I found among them many true friends in men like
Taussig, Seligman, and J. B. Clark. Generally speaking, however, the historians have supported me more warmly than the
economists. The men who helped me found the American
Economic Association, C. K. Adams, H. B. Adams, A. D.
White, were largely historians, and because they were not
bound and limited by the traditions of the old classical economics, they were more open-minded than the economists. It was an
historian, Frederick J. Turner, who was responsible for influencing Chamberlin to call me to Wisconsin. Turner had been in
my graduate classes at the Johns Hopkins, and though he was,
primarily, an historian, he was also a good economist. He was
an attractive young man of slight build, medium height, and
with a great deal of personal magnetism, which he doubtless
inherited from his father, who was a prominent politician in
Wisconsin. In 1892, he was the head of the history department
at Wisconsin. He hit upon the idea of combining economics,
political science and history into one department, and he sug-

gested to Chamberlin that he invite me to act as director. The
reason for grouping the social sciences was to justify the un-
usually large appropriation which was granted to organize
graduate and research work in this field. Chamberlin had em-
barked on an ambitious program for developing the new hu-
manities and introducing university methods into the liberal
college. His policy was to spend more money to engage a score
of new instructors and department heads; and in five years, the
annual expenditures for instructors was doubled. When he came
to see me at my home in Baltimore, and talked about the ideals
at which he was aiming, I made up my mind that in Wisconsin
I would have an opportunity to fulfill some of my ambitions. I
wrote to Dr. Shaw on January 25, 1892:

"What I have in mind is university work of the highest
character in economics, political and historical science. Unless
I am convinced that I shall be able to establish a school equal
to any in the country, I shall not accept the position. There are
many things to be considered in favor of the University of Wisconsin. The situation strikes me as in many respects excellent.
It is in the state capital, where we can, for purposes of training,
make use of the bureau of labor and of other offices which exist
there; the courts, state and national, hold frequent sessions in
Madison; and the legislature, which will give us lessons in
practical politics, and upon which we may in time be able to
exercise a favorable influence, meets in Madison once in two
years. Work of a high order is already being done in certain
lines, and the authorities are ambitious to develop the institution. The work in geology I understand to be equal to that
which is going forward at any university in the country. The
observatory, as nearly as I can judge, has an excellent reputation, and the monographs issued by the director of the agricultural experiment station are highly valued. A publication fund
already exists for historical literature. Private philanthropists

Richard T. Ely, 1892

have made some contributions to supplement the appropriations voted by the legislature. I want in this way to secure a fund for books and a lecture fund as well as an additional publication fund. I should very much like to raise money for one or two professorships. In developing my plans in my own mind I have thought of a civil academy to do somewhat for the civil service that which West Point and Annapolis do for the military and naval services respectively, although this is, of course, not all that I should hope to do. You see I have very ambitious plans."

MY EASTERN FRIENDS THINK I AM CRAZY BUT I HAVE HIGH AMBITIONS

When my Eastern friends learned of my decision to leave the Johns Hopkins, they thought I must be losing my mind to go to the "wild and woolly" country of Wisconsin. To them it seemed as it would now if one should leave Harvard to go to the University of Oklahoma. The people of Wisconsin, under the leadership of Professor Turner, gave a great deal of publicity to my departure from the Johns Hopkins University. They made it appear sensational; they said I had left a great university of the highest scholastic standing and had gone into a far country. However, I felt there was a great and unparalleled opportunity at Wisconsin. There had always been a fine flavor about the University of Wisconsin during the period when it was struggling for, and gaining, the right to exist on the same ground as the older and fully recognized universities. Though it was a comparatively small affair, its reputation had always attracted men of high quality. Professor W. F. Allen, a fertile and original writer, had made substantial contributions to historical literature, chiefly on the subject of village communities and land holdings. His essay on the *Place of the*

Northwest in American History contained the germ of the
thesis afterward developed by Turner in his *Significance of the
Frontier in American History*. Under Allen's influence was
founded the history club, the work of which was an expression
of the spirit of investigation which he fostered in his students.
He made a great name for himself and was offered professorships elsewhere, but he always decided to remain at Wisconsin
because of the spirit of fine and honest workmanship he found
there. Professor F. J. Turner's book on the "Frontier" was an
important contribution to the interpretation of American economic history; he also succeeded in introducing seminary methods into the utilization of the collections of the State Historical
Society. C. H. Haskins, also a former student of mine at the
Johns Hopkins, was professor of European history and was regarded as one of the most brilliant men in his field. In the field
of geology, Chamberlin successfully carried on the work, which
had been begun by Bascom, and in 1892, Wisconsin had one
of the strongest groups of geologists in the country.

Although an excellent start had been made in other fields,
before I came no one had ever held a professorship in economics. Economics had been taught along with constitutional law
and other subjects by Vice-President Parkinson. The budget of
my department, granted by the state, was fifty-four hundred
dollars, and I received a salary of thirty-five hundred dollars.
To carry out my plans for developing graduate work and research required a great deal more than the university was able
to give us. With great difficulty, I induced the regents to engage Dr. William A. Scott, who had just taken his Ph.D. under
me at the Johns Hopkins, as assistant professor at a salary of
fifteen hundred dollars. In addition, I felt I must take with me
to Wisconsin a young and promising leader, to be selected from
the men who had been studying with me at the Johns Hopkins.
Among these, I was most impressed by David Kinley, who was

then within one year of completing his Ph.D. degree at Johns Hopkins. I knew his capacity for thought would make him an excellent pace-setter for the graduate students. I felt, also, that it was important that we should begin to give the doctorate degree to men about whose future success we should have no doubt. I therefore invited Kinley to go with me to Wisconsin, and I received an appropriation for him of four hundred dollars a year, with the title, Fellow and Assistant in Economics. Since he could not come without, at least, a salary of seven hundred and fifty dollars, I raised the additional money from private gifts. I also raised money for other scholarships from friends in the East, and by giving lectures in Milwaukee, Cincinnati, Minneapolis, and elsewhere. The fees I received I turned over to the university to cover the expenses of my department for which the state appropriation was inadequate. I carried on my work at the university and gave lectures at the same time, traveling very largely by night to keep engagements. Fortunately, I had strength and endurance, for it required both to start the economics department of Wisconsin on its way.

President Chamberlin had the initiative and daring to give me the freedom and power to develop my department and to help put the University of Wisconsin "on the map."

It is the tendency of able young men on the faculties of smaller and younger institutions to look to the older and well-recognized universities, like Harvard and Yale, for possible openings. I saw that some of the best talent at the University of Michigan was being attracted to the larger universities and I was determined not to let our strong young men at Wisconsin drift away. In order to keep them, we had to make their positions so attractive that they would not want to leave. In each case we had to pay the necessary supply price, which meant the entire abandonment of standardization. When Professor Turner, for example, got a call from Stanford University, with the privilege of spending half his time in research, we realized that the offer might tempt him to leave. I took the matter up with the president and we offered him the same privilege and substantially the same salary as Stanford had. Naturally, such privileges and high salaries could not become standard, except at a university like Harvard which had sufficient resources to apply the same standards to all those of the same rank and keep its strong men. We, at Wisconsin, had to grant additional privileges and salary increases in those cases where they were needed to keep men we wanted. In building up a faculty of superior men, under the handicap of limited resources, I resorted to taking men whose capacities were high, but who were not in demand because they had encountered difficulties in one way or another. I gave these men, who had been discharged from other universities, a chance to make good at Wisconsin; and they justified my belief in them.

My friends in the East had warned me that I would never find at Wisconsin such able students as I had at the Johns Hopkins. But the number of graduate students of high caliber, even in the first years, surpassed what I had anticipated. And my kind of economics seemed to appeal to the young people at Wisconsin. Just as John R. Commons decided to study with me at the Johns Hopkins, after he read Simon Newcomb's attack on me in the *Nation,* so, the vicious attacks made on me in so many quarters, made a strong impression on those who were in revolt against the old economics and against the corrupt politics of the day. Charles Bullock came to Wisconsin after winning the Jacob Sleeper Fellowship at Boston University. The fellowship entitled him to study where he pleased, but it was expected that he would go to Harvard or to Europe. When he announced that he was going to Wisconsin, to study under Dr. Ely, the faculty was astonished, and a little inclined to protest his choice. Bullock, however, was a man who knew what he wanted and was not easily diverted from his course. Like Kinley he became a pace-setter at Wisconsin; in accuracy and scholarship, he was probably the best student I have ever had.

THE LOOK AND SEE METHOD

The graduate work grew rapidly and we soon had as many graduate students as there were at the Johns Hopkins. As I watched the number grow, from year to year, I was satisfied that we were holding our own with the great universities, like Harvard, Yale, and Columbia. However, we never laid emphasis on mere numbers and we did not dilute our work with evening courses and various extension devices, which, nowadays, swell enrollments to such vast proportions.

I was guided by the wish that the training which the ever-growing numbers of young people received at Wisconsin would enable them to contribute directly to human progress. I was, and am, an optimist and a believer in progress. It is true that progress has been called in question by many recent writers; it must be confessed that the hopes of many philosophers, especially those of the latter part of the eighteenth century, have not been fully realized. Those who have had utopian aspirations have been disappointed and disillusioned; those who believed they could retire into a closet, and through their inner consciousness develop an ideal world, have not been practical. Those have been the practical reformers who have carefully and painstakingly studied the forces and currents of our life and have attempted to direct them and act in harmony with them. The world may be conceived of as a life stream. If we are going to accomplish what we desire, we must get into this stream and make ourselves effective in directing it. I wanted the education which we provided at Wisconsin to train our men to earn a livelihood and at the same time, to give them the broader, practical approach to the world, which the classical political economy did not provide.

The importance of the role which Richard Jones played in political economy has not been fully recognized. He was one of the earliest to attack the deductive method of Ricardo and the other classical economists. He pointed out that Ricardo's system was "very ingeniously combined of purely hypothetical truths" and "utterly inconsistent with the past and present condition of mankind." He believed that "the too hasty erection of whole systems, a frail thirst for the premature exhibition of commanding generalities, will probably continue to be the source of error most to be guarded against." Jones' role in political economy was like that of Bacon's in physical science—to preach the importance of experience and the danger of hasty generalization. He wrote: "If we wish to make ourselves acquainted with the economy and arrangements by which the different nations of the earth produce or distribute their revenues, I really know of but one way to attain our object and that is to look and see." This is what I encouraged my students to do for themselves—"to look and see." The animating purpose of the "look and see" method has never been better stated than by John R. Commons when he said: "Academic teaching . . . is merely brains without experience . . . the 'practical' extreme . . . is experience without brains. One is half-baked philosophy—the other is rule of thumb." [36] We encouraged the kind of knowledge which would lead to action, for knowledge without action is dangerous. This danger is illustrated frequently in the lives of men of learning. There are those who become so accustomed to weighing problems scientifically and to looking upon all sides of questions of practical importance, that they become abnormally timid about any action. Thus, knowledge may beget irresolution, and irresolution end in inactivity. A man of knowledge, who habitually fears to take an active part in the work of life, is himself a wretched being and a useless member of society. The importance of knowledge, as a preliminary, should be emphasized, but attention should be called to the importance of letting action follow knowledge. This is a world full of work to be done and knowledge has its practical purpose. Better economic knowledge should bear its fruit in better citizenship. This was the principle which determined the development of the economics department at Wisconsin.

In Germany, I had seen that they developed their economics out of German life, and the German professors were part of this life. Many of them occupied public and administrative positions and contributed in this way to the German Empire. My experience in Germany had first brought to my attention the importance of linking book knowledge and practical experience. In Germany the close connection between the state and the universities made it necessary that men should "look and see," for there the universities were largely institutions designed to train men for the civil service in its various branches, being to this service a good deal what West Point and Annapolis are to our army and navy. A certain realism was forced upon them. Book learning was regarded as of some importance, but not by any means enough. Just as in medicine, a man has to have an internship, after completing his medical work, so, I thought, in the social sciences a man should have practical experience to test his theories, to enlarge them and to understand their application. No man has been more successful than Professor Commons in carrying out this idea. He kept in touch, on the one hand, with labor, and on the other, with the management of industry. He mingled with all classes of people. He introduced to his classes people such as W. F. Foster and Emma Goldman, who were regarded as very dangerous radicals. To him, these people were simply human representatives, whom his students should know face to face. On the other hand, he was just as eager to have his classes know capitalists and leaders of industry. He could admire a labor leader; he could understand the slugger; and he had a great admiration for the big industrial leaders. In order to understand their point of view, he became a member of the Wisconsin Industrial Commission, while on a leave of absence from his university duties. In this way, he came to know the practical side of economic problems.

My daughter, Anna, too, saw the need of gaining practical experience as a background for her academic studies. While she was working for her Ph.D., she got a job in a great tool manufacturing establishment in Milwaukee. Her co-workers in the factory never knew that she was studying for her Ph.D. Once a girl who occupied a bench near her said, "Miss Ely, I want to talk to you about the advantages of getting an education and going through high school." Thus, she acted like one of them and got to know them well. Then she and Alice Van Hise, daughter of President Van Hise, worked in a canning factory in Le Roy, New York. They knew what it meant to work all night when the peas were coming in to be canned. They learned by first-hand observations about the harsh realities which lay behind the theories they studied. And this is what we wanted our students to have—an understanding of economics, based not alone on book knowledge, but on first-hand experience. We wanted them to "look and see" for themselves.

I was very much in favor of including in the curriculum at Wisconsin a training course, particularly designed to prepare students for the public service. Apparently, the time was not ripe for the acceptance of such a proposal, but, I think, indirectly it has had a great deal of influence. I also believed that it was logical to connect the work of the law and economics departments, because these two subjects constitute different approaches to the same territory. They both deal with value and exchange, with property and contract. Perhaps it can be said that economics is the spirit of the law and that law applies economics to practical life. When you read the great original decisions of the supreme court, you find in them sound economics. Only when it comes to procedural and technical presentations in the courts does law enter a field different from economics. President Chamberlin backed me up in this idea, but he left for Chicago just as I began my duties. Since the law faculty did not at all sympathize with my plan, and since President Adams did not have the force to put it across, all that remains of my first efforts to bring law and economics together may be found in the catalogue of the law school where my name appeared. Only after many years did the law and economics departments come into closer practical relationship. And when I went to Northwestern University, I found that Dean Greene of the law school was in full sympathy with the idea. This was one of the times when I thought the seeds dead, but they sprouted and brought a harvest. How often this has happened!

DIFFERENTIATION HAS GONE TOO FAR

The economics department of Wisconsin seemed to develop according to Herbert Spencer's law of evolution, which says that differentiation follows integration. When I first went to Wisconsin, Kinley, Scott, and I were the only men who devoted themselves exclusively to economics. In addition, I myself gave a course in charities and corrections, and at least one course in sociology, and covered the ground of labor economics, money, banking, etc. This had its advantage, for I was compelled to take an over-all view of economics. A few years ago, Bullock said to me, "You and Taussig, who taught everything in economics in the early days, are the only men who have mastered the whole field of economics." This was the time when economics was an integrated whole. However, very soon, the process of differentiation set in. I found it necessary to call men, distinguished in their fields of specialty, to give courses of lectures. I called Dr. Frederick H. Wines to give a course on punishment and reformation, a field in which he had made a mark for himself. His lectures were later published in book form, under the same title as his course. Then, I invited Dr. Amos G. Warner to give a course on American charities. Warner had been one of my students at the Johns Hopkins, and had done such notable work that he had recently been added to the faculty at Stanford. His extremely interesting course on charities was afterwards, also, published in book form, and to this day, is one of the best books in the field. I was particularly interested in having, as special lecturers, those men who had had wide, practical experience. The lecture given by Alexander Graham Bell, who was very rich in practical experience, was one of the most successful.

The process of differentiation and specialization took another step ahead when I appointed as a permanent member of the faculty, John R. Commons, to specialize in the field of labor. Later, I called Edward A. Ross, who rapidly developed courses in the field of sociology. Then, differentiation took place within the field of sociology. John Lewis Gillin devoted himself to the development of criminology, and his work has had an important influence in this country. Another course which had great practical influence on our national policies was that given in 1896 by Dr. B. S. Fernow on forestry.

As late as 1893, we in the United States had heard nothing about conservation, as such. In that year, a German commissioner, representing his government at the World's Fair in Chicago, was asked what most impressed him in America. After some polite hesitation, and after being repeatedly urged to state his opinion frankly, he said: "What impresses me most is that you are a nation of butchers." And, then, he went on to explain that we were butchering, slaughtering the gifts of Nature, wasting our forest resources, our mineral treasures, our soil. Familiar with conservation in his own land, he was more impressed with its absence in the United States than with anything else. Those of us who had attended the German lectures on "Practical Political Economy" by Knies, had learned the importance of conservation. Fernow's lectures were the first ones of the kind to be delivered, not only on this continent, but also in England. Dr. Fernow's vice presidential address, "The Providential Functions of Government with Special Reference to Natural Resources," before the American Association for the Advancement of Science in 1895, was probably the first time that this matter of conservation was discussed in public. At this time, his was a voice crying in the wilderness; but the note was clear and distinct, and who can tell what effect he may have had upon subsequent developments? The teaching of conservation at the University of Wisconsin influenced and paved the way for Roosevelt's great conservation movement and the widespread land programs of the present day.

The University of Wisconsin has been a pioneer in the development of land economics. When things grow up gradually it is so often difficult to fix precise dates. One is thinking of a job and not of making a record. However, I am confident that very soon after I came to Wisconsin in 1892 we began a systematic treatment of what is now called Land Economics. I treated the whole subject under the awkward title, "Landed Property and the Rent of Land."

Among the students I had in the nineties were three men who have played a large role in the development of Land Economics. Dr. Henry C. Taylor, a pioneer in agricultural economics, was chief of the Bureau of Agricultural Economics and is now director of the Farm Foundation. He has always given encouragement and whole-hearted support to work in this field. Dr. O. E. Baker, who has done valuable work in economic geography, with special reference to land utilization and the influence of population on land use, is now Senior Agricultural Economist in the Bureau of Agricultural Economics. Dr. L. C. Gray, who now occupies a commanding position as assistant chief of the Bureau of Agricultural Economics, was another of my students at the University of Wisconsin. One of my students of a later day was Dr. M. L. Wilson, the present Undersecretary of Agriculture. Others, too numerous to mention, occupy important policy-making positions in many of the States.

Since the early days at Wisconsin, the process of differentiation has gone a long way. In my opinion it has gone too far. Economics has been cut up into so many particular fields that an ever-increasing number of economists know more and more of less and less. In our universities today we find many ignorant men, and the cultural value of economics and other subjects is not what it should be. I have noticed that when a group of economists or scientists gets together, conversation lags because each one is afraid to express himself outside his own narrow field. Economics is split up into so many divisions that a dozen men may be carrying on researches along a dozen different lines without the slightest knowledge of each other's work, or without having a complete view of the entire field. The professors in graduate research departments in American universities too generally work alone, each in his own corner, instead of getting together and pulling in teams. Each one is afraid that he will not get sufficient credit for what he is doing and fears that co-operation may lessen his claim to originality. It is because of this that the contribution which economics might make to the enlightenment and prosperity of our country suffers deterioration. Those who have given exclusive attention to money say that the basic trouble in this depression is monetary. Others who have specialized in credit say that this is the source of our troubles. Some who have given special attention to the problems of foreign trade, say that tariffs are the source of all evils. Now all these views are partially true, but they are misleading and injurious because they are only partial truths. What we need today is to get together the results of researches —we need synthesis. We need more of the spirit which was embodied in the round table started by H. B. Adams at the Johns Hopkins. The round table offered an excellent opportunity for the exchange of ideas and for the development of the co-operation and collective action which is so sorely needed. This pedagogical device goes back to the Halle days when Professor Rudolph Haym held a round table at his home. The soundness of this device appealed to me and for forty years I made my round table the very heart of graduate and research work. Members of the faculty and graduate students would meet at my home once a week, at about half-past seven in the evening and discuss various topics and reports. This continued until about ten o'clock and was followed by a social period with refreshments and informal talk which often continued late into the night. In this way the members of the faculty and the graduate students came to know each other very well.

It is a pity that today there are not more seminars or round tables which offer an opportunity for the formation of friendships between those who have mutual interests. Man, isolated and alone, develops no individuality. Such individuality is developed only when he lives with and through his fellows. This is the kind of individuality at which we should aim in our study of economic problems. One of the most serious menaces today is standardization. Classify, arrange, put everyone into an appropriate group and then automatically salaries and tenure, and conditions of service are determined. Treating men individually as Gilman did, and as I did at Wisconsin, made possible achievements that standardization cannot reach. The task of administration is easier with standardization, but not equally creative. Gilman did not like legislation determining standards and rules for the future. I recall hearing him say, "too much legislation, gentlemen," when some past act made it difficult to do what was best at the time. Under Gilman no legislation required retirement of professors at any fixed age. Thus great Gildersleeve kept his active professorship until he was in the eighties. Recently Robert William Wood, a wizard in physics, having reached the age of seventy, in the fullness of his powers, was granted as a great favor, attracting national attention, one year to serve as research professor. The idea of business efficiency is creeping into the universities, and perhaps it was this that led President Conant to induce the Harvard authorities to reduce the age of retirement to sixty-six.

THE CLOISTERS: A HOPE FOR THE FUTURE

We must get away from the curse of standardization and efficiency as it prevails in the great industrial corporations. We must get away from the idea of mass production in education; it is anathema. I recall Pupin's views on this matter. Pupin took great pride in his horsemanship. A New York physician, Dr. Frederick Dennis, made him a present of two splendid cobs, which he trained and entered in a horseshow. At the show Reginald Rives, who awarded the prizes to his cobs, said, "If you can handle your students as well as you can handle your cobs, you are the greatest professor in America." "I could," said Pupin, "if I had to handle only two students at a time, but not two hundred." Rives repeated the remark to his brother, a trustee of Columbia University, and the trustee saw in it quite a chunk of educational philosophy. In his autobiography Pupin asked, "Will American colleges ever adopt it?" I too ask that question and fervently hope that the answer will be "Yes."

Did standardization and efficiency ever produce a great scholar? Is the atmosphere thus created compatible with the highest excellence? Many men approaching the age of retirement at sixty-six still have works of importance to give the world. And yet they must listen to the clock of eternity ticking off the seconds, each one bringing the end nearer. The world would be richer if these men were given the opportunity to complete their work without hurry and anxiety. What we need today is something like the academic grove of Plato to grant scholars of ripe achievement the opportunity to give the world the results of long years of study and experience. I would like to see departments established in the large universities for this purpose. I would call these departments the Cloisters, and admission to them would be the highest honor an American scholar could achieve. The men in the Cloisters would not have regular class work, but small groups of students, because in these days science is too big for the unaided individual. The Greeks were not isolated workers.

Is this a wild dream? I would like to see it—but if I cannot others will. President Butler had something suggestive of the Cloisters when he established the professorship emeritus in residence, but inadequate funds prevented his following up this idea. Senator William F. Vilas in his will, leaving his property to the University of Wisconsin, had something very much like this in view. I believe that the Vilas will is a great educational document, and hope that its provisions will find fulfillment. (Sections of the will are reprinted in the Appendix.)

THE PRESSURE OF POLITICS

The character of the University of Wisconsin has been determined by the attitude of the people of the state. The demand for a university was one of the first expressions of community spirit, and the university has become what it is by and with the approval of the state. While men and leadership are important factors in the upbuilding of every educational institution, yet the history of the University of Wisconsin has shown that leadership outside the university is a powerful factor in determining what men shall be entrusted with leadership within the institution. Public opinion has prescribed the life and activities of the state university, and the people of Wisconsin have never allowed their university to lose itself in academic unrealities. They knew they wanted something different and new, something responsive to their need, something which they called practical. Thus, research in the university has centered about problems of human progress, and many practical contributions have been made to the knowledge of problems in government action, in mastering the forces of nature, and in increasing the amount and variety of production. The presidents and the members of the faculty have always worked in the glare of the public gaze; many have often become tired and have wished they could escape from the intensity of this scrutiny. But while they remained at Wisconsin, they could not.

I got my first glimpse of what effect the pressure of politics had on the university presidents when I spoke to President Chamberlin just before he left Wisconsin. He said, "I came to Wisconsin a young man of forty-five, and now I leave Wisconsin at fifty-two, an old man." And shortly after I came to Wisconsin, Turner said to me, "It is really astonishing that the people of Wisconsin let us have such free scope as we do have. We cannot expect this always. At present the budget of the university is relatively small; when it becomes larger, it will attract more attention from the legislature and the citizens, and criticism is sure to follow." One day, some twenty years later, Turner and I were standing in the corridor of the University Club at Madison. Those twenty years had left their harsh marks on Turner's sensitive face. He said to me, "I have been so annoyed and irritated that I would now accept any one of six calls I have already refused, and do so by wire." His prediction had come true. The university had grown, and with its growth the criticism had become fierce, often merciless, often mendacious. This was the price which the members of the faculty paid for permanence of tenure. Plenty was done to irritate and disturb the faculty, but as far as I know, no one has ever been discharged from Wisconsin because of his views. But the presidents enjoyed no such permanence of tenure. Wisconsin is a virile state and its people like to see blood flow, now and then. When they become discontented with the university, nothing satisfies them but to see the president beheaded, so to speak. Thus, Wisconsin University presidents have served relatively short terms; as long as the people of Wisconsin have allowed them to serve. And each one has gone on his way after making his contribution; in fact, he has been forced to go on his way.

The first president of the University of Wisconsin whom I knew personally was John Bascom, although he left before I came. It has been said that when Bascom went to Wisconsin, the university was on the level of a large high school, and when he left it had become a true university. The university, as Bascom found it, had in many ways the social tone of a big country academy; he left it a college of men and women, earnest, with an interest in important matters and with reasoned opinions about them. In a large measure, this temper of the college came about through the direct influence of the president himself, through personal contact with individual students, through his addresses to the entire college or to representative groups, and through his teaching in the classroom. There he met every student of the senior class. He believed the best form of college discipline to be that which was most personal. Cases of trivial and annoying misdemeanors, as well as cases of dishonesty or serious neglect in connection with studies, were dealt with directly by the president. He gradually acquired influence as a leader of student thought and ethics. The broad improvement came by substitution rather than by repression; by the stimulation of more serious interests; by a judicious allowance of freedom with the encouragement of self-reliance and a sense of responsibility. This attitude is what made the change in the university.

During the period of his presidency, Bascom's teaching was the central fact in the intellectual progress of the university.[37] He held to the principle that we are bound in duty to use the school as a means of helpfulness in the world and that every true educational principle takes issue with any system of instruction that omits to call upon the school to take its place in the state as a constructive agency in the highest social economy. His philosophy prospered so because the community was prepared to receive it and because he had the co-operation of an unusual faculty. He was responsible for calling Turner and Haskins in history; he started the nucleus of what became one of the strongest groups of geologists in the country. He was a man of broad interests. He wrote books on economics, ethics, religion, and philosophy. One of his books on economics I had the privilege of editing. But his services to Wisconsin were not in the field of authorship, he was pre-eminently a great teacher. Men like La Follette and Turner always felt that they owed a great deal to him in the way of ethical uplift and a steadfast determination to fight for righteousness. He expressed his philosophy in the following words:

". . . he who has the power to teach must find this liberty his first condition of success. He who requires dictation is unfit for instruction. We do not see how the public or any portion of it shall say to a college professor what or how he shall teach, what opinions he shall hold, and when and where he shall express them unless they wish to degrade a branch of knowledge, or make its impartation contemptible. When one is called to a professorship these subsidiary questions are settled, and he is then accepted in the freedom and integrity and totality of his manhood. The president is a leader among equals, the weight of whose words is more that of wisdom than of authority." He encouraged in his teaching corps a fullness of deliberation and a democratic participation in the government of the university which has become traditional in the Wisconsin faculty, and makes it impatient of anything which looks toward autocracy in academic matters. He did not interfere with anybody's teaching; he "worked in his place and expected others to work in theirs." President Birge has said, "I question whether the history of any great commonwealth can show so intimate a relation between the forces which have governed its social development and the principles expounded from a teacher's desk as that which exists between Wisconsin and the classroom of John Bascom." [38]

But the relations between John Bascom and the various representatives of the commonwealth of Wisconsin were not always friendly. It has been said that Bascom was a man lacking in tact. He had many New England traits, some of them desirable, and others not quite so excellent. He displayed the typical New England reserve, and perhaps frostiness, in his contacts with others. He was the sort of man who was more concerned with an adequate statement of the truth than with the amenities of an occasion. He regarded the board of regents in the light of an annoyance, and he was not afraid to let them know it. He complained that it was made up of "almost exclusively those interested in politics." He remarked that "rarely, indeed, was any man granted the position of Regent who had any special knowledge of the methods of education or interest in them."

While Bascom was president, the Republican boss (and he was a boss of the old type) was Elisha W. Keyes. Keyes was an honest man according to the standards of the time; but those standards were not high. It had been reported that he made some money on the sale of trees and shrubbery and possibly some other things to the university. These gains were in the form of commissions or profits from sale and resale. In political circles in New York City and elsewhere, politicians doubtless would be unable to see anything unethical in these transactions —but not so Bascom. When he was told about it, he practically called Keyes a thief at a meeting of the board of regents. Naturally the politicians did not like Bascom. Naturally Boss Keyes wanted to get rid of him. Bascom, on the other hand, grew increasingly restive in this hostile political atmosphere. Finally, he told Boss Keyes that if he would give him a year of peace as president of the university, he would quit and return to Williams College. Keyes went into this agreement and kept it. Though Judge Keyes and his party in the board of regents would gladly have scored on the president by making his resignation immediately effective, President Chamberlin, who had been elected to succeed Bascom, refused to lend himself to this project, and the opposition was obliged to content itself with an ambiguous victory.

Thomas Chrowder Chamberlin had passed most of his life within the boundaries of Wisconsin. After a professorship at Beloit College, he was appointed chief geologist of the state at the age of thirty-three. At the time of his election to the presidency of Wisconsin University, he was with the United States Geological Survey as chief of the glacial division. He brought to the job the thoroughly ingrained habit of approaching every problem from a purely scientific point of view, and an amazing ability to forecast the new functions of the university. He saw and grasped the opportunity to extend the functions of the university in area and in depth. His dominant interest was to encourage individual research and leadership in

original study. The penetrating logic with which he planned
the growth of the institution and the boldness with which he
put his plans into execution made him seem distant and imper-
sonal to the public and the undergraduates. But his reputation
for unapproachableness served to mark a change from the old
intimate life of the college to the new and larger life of the
university. Those of us who were at Wisconsin at this time
witnessed the beginnings of the modern university. Life and
innovation were in the air. Within these five years, we saw the
students and faculty double in number. When Chamberlin
came, the university had just been provided with buildings in
excess of its immediate requirements and with a considerable
appropriation for apparatus. With admirable coolness, he seized
the moment of advantage to revolutionize the scope of the institution. In five years, though all other operation expenses
increased only fifty percent, the annual expenditure for instruction was doubled. The efforts by which this growth was accomplished tired Chamberlin. Administration of the University of
Wisconsin carried with it responsibility to political elements in
Wisconsin and this did not content him. Therefore, when he
was invited to become the head of the department of geology
of the new university at Chicago, he eagerly seized the opportunity to continue his scientific career.[39]

The university tradition started by Chamberlin was continued
by Adams, but in a very different way because Adams was a
very different man. Charles Kendall Adams began life as a
farm boy in Vermont, and his early education was bought with
hard manual labor and self-denial. He worked his way through
the University of Michigan, studied in the German universities,
and then joined the faculty of his alma mater. He became dean
of the school of political science and in 1885 he succeeded
Andrew D. White as president of Cornell University. He had
an intimate knowledge of university matters and a thorough

historical and theoretical knowledge derived from the study of educational institutions in this country and in Europe. The first five years of his administration reflected, in some degree, the general business depression that followed the panic of 1893, but the growth of the university was not halted. The temporary stagnation in the outside world of business and industry probably favored the development of advanced study, for it reconciled some men to spending a longer time in preparation for life. Adams's interests were primarily humane, social, and political; and he brought to the position of presidency a homely geniality which Bascom and Chamberlin had lacked. He was favorable to fraternities, and to the development of intercollegiate athletics. Intercollegiate sports flourished after 1890. Within three or four years, football, rowing, and field and track contests became the distinctive college games. Adams held the belief that the prowess of its athletic teams is an important factor in the drawing power of an institution of learning. As soon as the era of business depression was over, the university shared in the revival of prosperity. The years 1898–1900 witnessed a tremendous increase in attendance.[40]

Adams and his gifted Irish wife rendered a great service to Wisconsin in the way of developing the social amenities. Chamberlin had lived in a rather humble, rural house with framed mottoes on the walls like "God bless our home." As soon as the Adamses came with their fine furniture and works of art, a struggle began between the old families of Madison, who before had been on the top of what constituted society, and the university people. The struggle was plainly in evidence, and before long Mrs. Adams had put the university on the top. Adams, himself, would not have done this, but his good wife took the initiative and under her, he was equal to the situation.

Adams was a man of striking appearance. As I think of him

sitting before the open fireplace in the living room of his university residence, somehow the picture of an English lord of
the manor occurs to me. Adams owed a great deal to his wife,
who was the widow of the publisher Barnes. She had some property, works of art, fine furniture, fine laces, etc. I knew Adams
when he was the professor of history at the University of
Michigan before he married the Mrs. Adams I knew. He was
with me one summer at a summer school at Martha's Vineyard.
Then he looked like the typical professor, a little slouchy in his
appearance, and certainly not very distinguished. The Mrs.
Adams I knew was responsible for the change in his appearance and for his delightful manner of distinction. Together,
President and Mrs. Adams rendered a great service to Wisconsin in the way of developing its social life.

After I moved to Madison, my wife and I had a dinner in
honor of President Adams. There was a rather distinguished
gathering assembled on this occasion. One of the guests was
General Fairchild, who had been a general in the Civil War
and who had been governor of the state. He was charming
and was the life of any social gathering. As the dinner proceeded, stories were told, some of which I thought a little
risqué. General Fairchild, after every story of this kind, would
say, "I have a good story too. You must work up to it." As
a matter of fact, however, he never got around to telling any
of them. My wife and I were a little anxious about how Mrs.
Adams, a meek looking woman, would react to these stories.
She soon relieved us, however, by telling the following story:
"Aunt Martha, a pious Catholic, was lying on her death bed.
A priest was called in to administer the last rites of the Church
and to console her. 'Mother,' he began. 'I know, I know,
Father,' Aunt Martha interrupted, 'I will soon be in the bosom
of Beelzebub.' 'Mother, Mother, you mean the bosom of Abra-

ham,' the priest protested. 'Father, when you have been a lone, lorn widow for forty years, it doesn't much matter whose bosom.' Then Martha passed away."

Hospitality is a great force and those who are entrusted with the task of choosing a president for an American university do well to inquire about the social gifts of the president's wife. A president, no matter how great he is in many respects, without the right kind of wife is lame and halt. Mrs. Adams certainly did her part in winning friends and support for the university. I, too, was very fortunate in having a wife who could not be surpassed in charm and social gifts.

I cannot recall all the distinguished persons whom I entertained at my home. Among them were the men who gave lectures in their fields of specialty. After the lectures, I often invited them to dinner, and after dinner we entertained each other with a wealth of good stories. I remember, particularly, the interesting story told by Alexander Graham Bell about his experiences with the telephone. His invention had received little attention when he sent a model to the World's Fair at Philadelphia in 1876. When his wife insisted that he go to Philadelphia, he flatly refused. By a series of clever maneuvers, she persuaded him that they should go to the railway station together. In telling the story, he assured us that he did not know what compelled him to go to the station, or what it was that compelled him to board the train as it was pulling out— his wife shouting to him that she would send his bags after him. Mrs. Bell, probably, could have explained this. At Philadelphia, no one paid any attention to him until one Sunday, Dom Pedro, an emperor of Brazil, was going through the building in company with the distinguished citizens and directors of the fair. Dom Pedro had met Bell in Brazil where he had gone to give lectures on instruction to the deaf. He immediately recognized Bell and asked him what he was doing there.

When Bell told him about his invention he at once showed a great deal of interest and, of course, all those with him became interested too. Royalty means a great deal to Americans! He insisted that Bell give a demonstration. So some of the party went into one room, while Bell and Pedro remained in another. When the demonstration was over, Pedro very excitedly said, "The damn thing talks!" This was a crucial incident in Bell's life and also, in the development of the telephone in the United States.

It happened that nearly every one of the men in the course on charities and correction was heavily built. And after dinner, they often leaned back in their chairs and laughed heartily. The chairs came from an old Virginia plantation and were not very strong; hence several collapsed from time to time—until, at last, my wife said, "No more lecturers in the course of American Charities and Corrections!"

Among the many distinguished persons who came to Madison and whom I entertained at my home was Prince Kropotkin who had come to Wisconsin to lecture to the students and to the general public. At this time, Miss Jane Addams and Robert Hunter were both in Madison. Robert Hunter was the head worker in the University Settlement in New York and author of a noted work on poverty, published in 1904. I invited Miss Addams, Robert Hunter, and others to dinner to meet Prince Kropotkin. What a picturesque figure he was! He had a long flowing beard and bald head and he looked very distinguished. At the table were my two children, John, then six years old, and Anna, four years old. John had been reading his favorite fairy tales in which princes always had crowns. At the table he looked long at Prince Kropotkin and then asked, "Prince Kropotkin, where is the crown on your head?" Then Anna, who echoed everything John said, asked, "Prince Kropotkin, where is the hair on your head?" He apparently did not notice Anna's question, but he replied to John's by telling him that his crown was in Russia. This amused Miss Addams very much and she often spoke of the episode later.

As head of the new School of Social Science, History and Economics, I saw that it devolved upon me to use hospitality in the interests of my own department. I lived in a large house on the top of a beautiful hill in University Heights and my home was a social center for my students. It was there that I held my weekly round table which is something, I am sure, that lingers in the memory of many of my former students, when they return to Wisconsin. As Professor Bullock has well said, they came to the house, less perhaps to see me, than to see my wife. "What a lovable personality she was," writes Professor Bullock; or, to use the words of Dr. Finley, "What a radiant personality!"

After considering for many months the question of a successor to President Adams, the regents of the university on April 21, 1903, settled on a professor of geology, Charles R. Van Hise, who had the backing of La Follette. He had risen to eminence in science, in teaching and in administration, and he had never been connected with a university other than Wisconsin. His administration coincided with that period in our history which began with Roosevelt's first term and ended with the close of the World War. The earlier years of his administration were coincident with the so-called "progressive movement" in Wisconsin. From the very start, he laid emphasis on the relation of the university to the material interests of the state. In the university he saw the agency, beyond all others, through which advancement was to be procured; he believed in the university and he trusted popular government. He was in favor of research and of extending the benefits of the university to the entire population through university extension courses and other services. He believed that the university should be one with the state; that the campus of the university should become the State of Wisconsin. He tried to convince the people of the state that the university was "a good business investment," because it returned directly to the state, in economic benefits, more than was expended on it. Contacts with public affairs increased and the sense of public duty was stimulated. Some said we did not have simply a university—but a university state. The La Follette wing of the Republican party had come into power and under its progressive program a large use of public money for the public good was contemplated and the university as a recognized instrument of the public service was to share in this liberality. By 1910, there were thirty-five professors of the university who were giving part time to some branches of the state service. The cry arose that the university was in politics and many complained that it was becoming too expensive. Van Hise was attacked on all grounds; he was called everything but a downright thief, and perhaps even that. But he stood firm in his purpose; few could have stood up under the abuse he had to take. His wife once told me, "Charles takes it as part of the day's work. After the most violent abuse he lies down and sleeps like a child."

After Van Hise's death, Birge took over the presidency for a short time. Birge was not a bold and daring man like Chamberlin or Van Hise. He was rather cautious, and under him we had slower and less spectacular progress and less opposition from the people and the legislature. The short but calm period of Birge's presidency was followed by the presidency of Glenn Frank, who had a stormy time with the political elements. He was finally ousted by the regents, and was followed by Dr. Dykstra, who is now president of the university.

LA FOLLETTE RALLIES THE FORCES OF GOOD GOVERNMENT IN WISCONSIN

There was no state in the union, not even Massachusetts, which was in as favorable a condition as Wisconsin in the matter of good government. It is well said that a stream cannot rise higher than its source and the source of good government in the final analysis must be its citizens. The success of the University of Wisconsin has been, in large part, due to the character of Wisconsin's population, which consists largely of those of German and Norwegian ancestry, with a large element of New Englanders and a sprinkling of Southerners. I think most credit is due the German strain in the population, for they were men of high ideals and they brought with them some of the best things from Germany. They had the idea of service to the state and they were firm believers in education. As I write one instance comes to my mind. Soon after I came to Wisconsin, a bill was introduced to make an appropriation for a splendid historical library building. Opposition to this scheme developed, and we on the faculty were ill at ease on the day when the voting took place. The speaker of the house was ill, and had to be brought in on a cot to cast his vote for the appropriation. This added drama to the tense situation. But what I recall more vividly and what impressed me most strongly was an old man at the back of the assembly who rose to say a few words. He was a rather rough looking German and as he began speaking in his broken English, my heart sank. "Here we have a negative vote," I said to myself. In his halting speech, he explained that he had never had a sufficient education to enable him to profit by the splendid collection of books which we proposed to house in the new library building. His children, however, and many other young men and women, who were getting a better education than he had had, could profit by this collection. In

REAPING THE HARVEST   209

conclusion, he exclaimed, "I vote, 'Aye.' " The bill was passed,
and many speeches were made, but no other speech moved me
as deeply as this one.

Most of these Germans, who had come to the United States
after the Revolution of 1848 in Germany, were people of
strong convictions, who had suffered in Germany and who on
account of the strong conservative reaction which followed the
Revolution were unwelcome there. They believe in law and
order, and in learning; and they have a high appreciation of
the nobility of service to the state. This was illustrated by Judge
Romer, chairman of the Wisconsin Railway Commission. He
and his wife thought it a great thing to be of service to the
state and he refused higher salaries elsewhere so long as he felt
he was really accomplishing something.

Some mention should be made of the prominent residents
in Madison who were in close relation with the university and
without whose efforts the university could not have kept on its
fine course. One of the most distinguished of these was W. F.
Vilas, who became secretary of the interior in Cleveland's
cabinet and who was thoroughly devoted to the university.
When the Democrats came into power in 1894, Peck was
elected governor of Wisconsin. We felt some anxiety about
Peck, for we knew him as a humorist and the author of the very
successful *Peck's Bad Boy*. But he proved himself to be more
than a humorist; he was an excellent governor and was very
liberal about appropriations. Once he said to the legislature, "I
dare sign anything you legislators dare to pass." The appropriations he agreed to were very generous and the Democrats were
hungry for the spoils; to some politicians the university jobs
were particularly attractive. Vilas realized the danger of the
situation, and he came back from Washington at this crucial
time and said, "Boys—hands off!" Thus, the raid was stopped.
Later, when a contest was raging between the groups favoring

Van Hise and those favoring Birge for the presidency of the
university, Vilas showed the same admirable quality. There was
a strong faction in the faculty which felt that Dr. Van Hise
should be president, but Vilas strongly favored Birge. Frederick
J. Turner, often called the King-Maker, led the movement to
bring Van Hise in. He had the support of Governor La Follette
and regents were appointed one after another, who were favorable to Van Hise. When a meeting was called and Van Hise was
made president, Vilas, at first, raged like an angry lion in a
cage, pacing up and down angrily. However, after the initial
outburst, and when he realized that the selection of Van Hise
was an accomplished fact, he gave Van Hise all his support just
as if he had been his own choice. Upon the death of Colonel
Vilas in 1908, President Van Hise was immensely gratified by
the fact that Vilas left his magnificent private fortune to the
university for the endowment, at some future time, of ten
research professorships. This trust agreement has been called
a great educational document. The hours of instruction were
to be limited and the professors were to be given every opportunity for research. This fund still continues in the hands of the
trustees, but the depression has caused losses and the accumulation has not been large enough to warrant the trustees fully
to carry out Vilas's great purpose. (See Appendix IV.)

Another Wisconsin citizen of high character and rare charm
was General Lucius Fairchild, who had been governor of the
state from 1866 to 1872, and who gave generously of his time
and strength to the development of the university. The Honorable Breese Stevens, regent of the university, was a handsome
man of commanding presence and a charm equal to that of
Fairchild. I remember how warmly he welcomed my family
and me when we first came to Wisconsin, and how he stood
beside me and helped me during the distressing period of my trial
for heresy. And there was no one who was more helpful to the

university and to me personally than Reuben Gold Thwaite, librarian of the historical society. He was a fine scholar, a good writer, and a delightful companion with a fondness for anecdotes and good stories. He helped in every way he could to acquire books and various manuscripts for those engaged in research.

The forces of good government in Wisconsin are to be found in its citizens of high intelligence and noble ideals. But leadership was needed to rally these forces and this was furnished by the senior La Follette. Born in Wisconsin, reared in an atmosphere of agrarian discontent, he became the outstanding spokesman of the oppressed elements. Rural pioneer life, a long struggle against near poverty, and the oratorical education he received at Wisconsin cast him in the role of agitator and critic. His policies as governor (1900–1906) were a pronounced heresy from the viewpoint of the national organization of the Republican party. His major political ideas were democratization of electoral devices and the control of industry by government. The aggressive assertion of these policies finally led to a rift between him and Republican liberals and eventually led to his unsuccessful independent candidacy for President in 1924.

His chief work was to transform Wisconsin into a political laboratory for advanced measures. He backed every progressive movement in Wisconsin, and although it is not necessary to endorse everything that La Follette said and did, we must admit that he fought a good fight and that he often won out. La Follette had the zeal of a reformer. He wanted an office to fulfill his mission in life and he wished to make a name for himself. He recognized what so many reformers overlook—that to secure office he must make himself a master of political methods. He knew he must outmaneuver the old politicians—beat them at their own game. This he did—and it is an amazing story. He went to work to study politics with all its devious ways and did so with a skill rarely exhibited even by a Tammany politician. He appealed directly to the people. "Restore government to the people" was his watchword. With his astounding gifts for oratory and his magnetic appeal, he carried the people with him. He could hold audiences spellbound for hours at a time. He was as good a popular speaker as William Jennings Bryan and a far brainier man. He presented an attractive personality and a striking appearance with his pompadour hair and pleasing countenance. It was easy to understand why he intended to become an actor in his youth. His personal magnetism brought him a powerful following. I remember taking my sister-in-law from Virginia and my wife to a reception at Governor La Follette's home. When we asked her afterwards what she thought of Governor La Follette, she replied, "He has powerful taking ways." My German neighbor, Louis Backhaus, was a typically devoted follower of La Follette. He once said to me, "When the governor goes by on horseback, he says, 'Hello, Louis,' and that is enough."

After the senior La Follete got into politics, he conducted his campaigns with rare skill and used tactics which always kept his opponents guessing. His personal appeal always played a large part in his political life. Sometimes he would depend very largely on correspondence. A friend of mine who had an office near La Follette's told me that his last senatorial campaign was conducted in large measure over the telephone. He would call somebody up in Green Bay, we will call him "Sam," to inquire how the campaign was going and to give him his instructions. The conversation would go something like this: La Follette would say, "Hello, Sam." Sam would ask, "Who is this?" "Bob," would come the reply. "Bob who?" "Bob La Follette." Then Sam would say in delight, "Why, Bob! Is this you?" "Yes, Sam," La Follette would answer, "this is Bob." Then he might call up another man, say a "John" in Superior, and carry on the same sort of conversation with him. This contact enabled him to exert his personal magnetism even over the phone. Thus, by exerting an extraordinary political skill, he gained control over the state, which he and his family, with a slight interruption, have kept ever since.

It was La Follette's objective to develop the state government into a power suitable to cope with the great business organizations so that it might protect unorganized interests against oppression. At the time when La Follette began his career at Wisconsin, the state was owned by the railway interests, perhaps as much as any other state in the Union. They had various ways of keeping control. One was by the distribution of free passes while the legislature was in session. The first year that I was at Wisconsin one of the state senators distributed a thousand passes and before that session closed he had probably distributed another thousand. Any voter could get a pass. I recall that one day our German cook, Mary, asked my wife if she could not have a couple of days off to go down to Milwaukee. My wife asked her why she wanted to go there, and she said she had a free pass. Once while the legislature was in session, a conductor from one of the coaches walked by and waved his hand, without going in. This evil was soon corrected by La Follette and the employees of the state were forbidden to accept passes.

In order to make it more difficult for special interests to influence the personnel of government, the direct primary system of party nominations was adopted in 1903. In 1903, also, the ad valorem taxation of railroads was put into effect, involving the creation of a railway rate commission with powers that would prevent the railway companies from passing the tax on to the public. Its jurisdiction was soon extended to all so-called "public utilities."

A NOTEWORTHY CIVIL SERVICE IN WISCONSIN

Especially noteworthy was the kind of civil service he established. He recognized and acted on the truth that without a good civil service there cannot be good government. He requested Professor Commons, whom I had called to Wisconsin, to revise the civil service bill, in order to remove the majority of civil servants from political influence. Naturally, Commons supposed that those who had already been appointed to civil service positions would be exempt from the new civil service test requirements. To his surprise, Governor La Follette said that all must have some kind of civil service test. In this way good government was established in Wisconsin. It is no exaggeration for me to say that from that day to this not a state in the Union has had a better administration than Wisconsin. Without this administration, many of the reforms introduced would have been failures. On the whole, they have worked out well. What has taken place has not been revolution, but reform within the framework of the Constitution. The limited experience I have had in administering civil service strengthens my conviction that it is very easy to inspire those engaged in the civil service not only with a sense of duty, but with a desire to do their best possible work. Once I was elected to an office that is called side-supervisor of Wisconsin. My duties were to take care of the roads and to make assessments of the properties in my district. My neighbor, Louis Backhaus, had a team and wagon, so I employed him for the road work. He was a good-natured and easy-going old German. He would not cheat, but naturally his "stroke" in working for the community would be a slow one. I inspired him with the idea that we must make our money go as far as possible and we must not let any other district beat us. It was admirable how he responded to this idea of service as I put it to him. It gave me satisfaction to do something, in my very small way, to promote the delightful atmosphere fostered by the governor in the civil service of Wisconsin. Men in the civil service in Wisconsin put their best into their work and paid little attention to the clock. I used to take pleasure in bringing my friends down to the capitol to see the lights burning in the evening. They worked just as professors in a university work. There was something like this in the atmosphere in Washington when Theodore Roosevelt was President. Something of the spirit, something of the original zest may have disappeared in recent years. I still think, however, that it remains true that no state, not even Massachusetts, has a better administration or government than the state of Wisconsin.

Madison's real estate board as well as the landowners deserve a great deal of credit. The real estate board of Madison is of a higher order than is generally found elsewhere. Perhaps we in the university had something to do with it. When I was a member of the faculty, a rule was passed that no one could become a member of the real estate board without passing an examination. Members of my department often made up this examination. It was not an extremely difficult examination, but it was a good examination, not a farce. This one thing did a great deal to raise the standards in real estate which was in my day becoming a real profession in Madison. Control was exercised by a state commission and they could establish as high standards as they desired for the real estate business. Anyone who had any complaint could bring it to this commission, and this was a very serious matter for the realtor. At one time Governor Kohler removed the whole state board because he thought they tolerated sharp practices in the sale of land in and about Milwaukee as well as elsewhere. So far as I know this had never happened in the United States. We were trying to establish standards in Wisconsin like those in England.

In order to obtain a more scientific and disinterested solution of the tax problem, a tax commission was created in 1911 and resulted in the adoption of the income tax system of 1911. La Follette also secured the passage of an Employers' Liability Act, which provided for the adjudication of claims. Permanent state commissions were created to supervise the practices of banks, of insurance companies, etc. In formulating this new mass of legislation, which was amazing in its extent, the Wisconsin legislators had the assistance of the legislative reference library, under the direction of Charles McCarthy, who came from Brown University, where he had been a classmate of John D. Rockefeller, Jr. He had all the political gifts of the Irish, and he did a great piece of work as a backer and co-worker with La Follette.

When I came to Wisconsin, La Follette greeted me with the remark, "You have been my teacher!" He had never been my student, but what he meant was that he had got a great deal out of my writings. I was never his close personal adviser, but I saw him frequently; often he was a guest at my house as I was at his. I stood shoulder to shoulder with him and I think he continued to feel, as he had at the start, that I was his teacher. When I was attacked bitterly, in an attempt to oust me from Wisconsin, he said he would take the stump in my behalf before he would allow my enemies to prevail. Once on a matter of great importance, he drove out to my house, seeking advice. B. H. Meyer, who had been chairman of the Wisconsin Railway Commission, was nominated for membership in the Interstate Commerce Commission. This disturbed La Follette because he felt that Meyer was too conservative. He consulted me about the nomination and I persuaded him to withdraw his opposition to Meyer's nomination. As a result, Meyer's nomination was confirmed by the Senate. La Follette was satisfied with his decision, for Meyer has been one of the most upright and competent men in the I.C.C. He has held the post for twenty-seven years, a longer time than any other commissioner has served.

My break with La Follette came at the time of the World War. We in the University of Wisconsin felt he was pro-German and was siding against his own country. Some of us, like John R. Commons and myself, had boys at the Front and we felt he was shooting at them from the rear. My son John experienced some of the heaviest fighting of the war, and naturally I joined the ninety-two percent of the faculty which signed a protest to the United States Senate. The feeling ran so high that his picture which hung on the university walls was taken down and kept in hiding for a good many years. I was not one of the ring-leaders, as La Follette thought, in circulating this petition among the faculty, but I certainly was in sympathy with them. La Follette was very bitter and warned us that he was going to have the entire ninety-two percent of the faculty fired. This threat was made in the heat of anger; he realized it was too large an order and he said he would be satisfied with naming the next president. He wanted Dean Roscoe Pound of Harvard, but Pound rejected the offer. Another prominent scholar declined the nomination; and then Zona Gale, a member of the board of regents, suggested Glenn Frank. She knew Frank when he was editor of *Century Magazine* and had been a guest at his home. He was elected, and then fired by a board packed by Governor Philip La Follette. Whether the senior La Follette was ever satisfied with Frank, I do not know. I am inclined to doubt it, although he never made any protest.

In looking back from 1938 to the time of the World War, I do not feel so sure as I did then that La Follette was wrong and Woodrow Wilson right. If La Follette had been nominated and elected in 1912, it is quite possible that the country might be far better off than it is now. How clear it seemed to all of us then that we were doing the right thing! The experience that we have had in trying to make the world safe for democracy has convinced a great many people that La Follette was right, that Woodrow Wilson was wrong. We have all been bitterly disillusioned. I frankly confess that I have been. What would have happened if La Follette had prevailed, no human being knows. Certainly, I do not presume to know. I am inclined to wish that La Follette had been elected in 1924. So far I can go and no further. The World War ended my personal relations with Robert M. La Follette. I am ready to throw a wreath upon his grave.

I AM CALLED A COLLEGE ANARCHIST

In 1894 the nation was in the throes of a depression; unemployment and misery reached new heights; radical sentiment was rising. The tide of the workingman's discontent swept about 750,000 employees in the various industries into a series of strikes. The Pullman strike of June and July was a dramatic climax to the passion and bitterness which had been aroused. For the first time, the unions were able to weather a major financial shock.

In this year of distress and excitement, I was teaching economics at the University of Wisconsin. All my energies and all my thoughts were devoted to the task of building up a great graduate and research department. I worked unsparingly, but happily, in an atmosphere of approval and encouragement on the part of the authorities and my associates. I was aware, however, that in some quarters outside of the university, I had aroused antagonism. Had I not written on Marxian socialism, a topic as full of dynamite as Darwinian ideas had been twenty years earlier? Had I not conducted and written about labor investigations? Had I not attacked corporate abuses? For these activities such periodicals as Godkin's *Nation,* which was a citadel of conservatism in all matters affecting property and labor, branded me as a radical and a dangerous man. For years, the *Nation* never lost an opportunity to attack and malign me. Its efforts reached a climax on July 12, 1894, when it published the following letter:

THE COLLEGE ANARCHIST

To the Editor of the Nation

SIR: Your statement in the last *Nation,* to the effect that there is a sort of moral justification for attacks upon life and property based upon a theory which comes from the colleges, libraries, and lecture rooms, and latterly from the churches, is supported by the teaching and the practice of the University of Wisconsin.

Professor Ely, director of the School of Economics, believes in strikes and boycotts, justifying and encouraging the one while practicing the other. Somewhat more than a year ago a strike occurred in the office of the Democrat Printing Company, the state printers. An agitator or walking delegate came from Kansas City to counsel and assist the strikers. He was entertained at Professor Ely's house and was in constant consultation with him. A little later a strike occurred in another printing office in this city, in which Professor Ely was also an abettor and counsellor. He also demanded of the proprietors that their office should be made into a union office, threatening to take his printing away if they did not comply. (They were publishing a paper for him as secretary of some organization or association.) Upon the refusal of his repeated demands, Professor Ely withdrew his printing, informing them that he had always been in the habit of dealing with union offices. In conversation with one of the proprietors he asserted that where a skilled workman was needed a dirty, dissipated, unmarried, unreliable, and unskilled man should be employed in preference to an industrious, skillful, trustworthy, non-union man who is the head of a family. He also stated that the latter would have no ground of complaint, as he could easily remove the objections to him by joining the union, and that conscientious scruples against joining the union would prove the individual to be a crank.

Such is Ely the citizen and business man—an individual who can say to citizens and taxpayers, "Stand and deliver, or down goes your business," and to the laboring men, "Join the union or starve with your families." Professor Ely, director of the School of Economics, differs from Ely, the socialist, only in the adroit and covert method of his advocacy. A careful reading of his books will discover essentially the same principles, but masked by glittering generalities and mystical and metaphysical statements, susceptible of various interpretations according as a too liberal interpretation might seem for the time likely to work discomfort or loss to the writer. His books are having a considerable sale, being recommended and advertised by the University and pushed by publisher and dealers. Except where studiously indefinite and ambiguous, they have the merit of such simplicity of statements as makes them easily read by the uneducated. They abound in sanctimonious and pious cant, pander to the prohibitionist, and ostentatiously sympathize with all who are in distress. So manifest an appeal to the religious, the moral, and the unfortunate, with promise of help to all insures at the outset a large public. Only the careful student will discover their utopian, impracticable and pernicious doctrines, but their general acceptance would furnish a seeming moral justification of attack on life and property such as the country has already become too familiar with.

Very truly yours,

Oliver E. Wells

At first my reaction was one of bewilderment. At the close of the academic year, in the summer of 1894, I had gone to Chautauqua, New York, to lecture in the summer school there. Certainly I had done nothing outside my customary routine within the past few months which would even remotely warrant such an attack. Furthermore, I had never even heard of the person who wrote the letter. He had never given me an opportunity to discuss his charges. He never was a member of my seminar, nor in any of my classes. I am not sure that he even attended any of my lectures. Although the charges were entirely false, I was completely at a loss as to how to get the truth before the public. I was particularly confused and indignant because of the underhand manner by which my accuser had chosen to attack me. One might think that the proper course, the courteous course, the direct and honorable course for my accuser to follow, would have been to lay his charges before the president of the university and the board of regents, who were the responsible officers in the case. But, no! One may be excused for thinking that he chose the course he did, publishing his charges in a journal a thousand miles away, in sensational language, in order to direct attention to himself as a defender of the faith. Then, as now, people who appealed to prejudice in making charges against those with whom they disagreed, found ready and gullible audiences. Such people write a definition to suit the case and then, of course, the case fits the definition. What socialism was to the writer of this letter was not at all what other people conceived it to be. However, the writer did not like my views and so I must be socialistic. Then, as now, many critics and their followers failed to note that there is a difference between teaching and inculcating a doctrine.

My bewilderment deepened into alarm at the wide publicity this letter received. A few days after the original letter appeared, it was reprinted in the New York *Post*. Anyone who will read the press of that time will readily see how large the event loomed in the eyes of the public. Now it may seem like a trivial episode, but then it was a rather sensational event. Not only were the charges serious, but my accuser was the state superintendent of education in Wisconsin. Such strong accusations made by a person in so responsible a position could not fail to make an impression on the public mind. Dr. Shaw, in an effort to cheer me up, wrote at this time: "You must remember that everybody now understands so well the fact that the Evening *Post* has a blacklist and has not the slightest desire or intention to be fair and just, that its assaults against a man of high character and standing usually help such a man more than they hurt him. For the immediate present, it seems to me, you can well afford to ignore the whole business."

By this time, however, my only feeling was one of intense indignation at the injustice which had been done me. I felt that my career which had just fairly begun at Wisconsin was being threatened. I realized that all my hopes and ambitions to play a significant role in the educational history of the country were in danger of frustration. And as the seriousness of the situation became daily more and more apparent, I knew I could no longer ignore the attack. The first investigation of Mr. Wells' background revealed that he held office only as a result of an upset in the Wisconsin election of 1892. It appears that the Republicans had offended the Catholics and Lutherans with the Bennett law, which placed the parochial schools, many of which were to be found in Wisconsin, under state supervision. The Democrats had never won in Wisconsin and they went to the convention thinking that their nominees would never get beyond the stage of nomination. As the convention was about to adjourn, someone called attention to the fact that they had not nominated anyone for the post of superintendent of public instruction. Someone shouted out the name of Oliver E. Wells, formerly an unknown teacher in a public school, and the nomination was carried. The people's reaction to the Bennett law was so unfavorable that the Democrats elected their slate, including Mr. Wells.

After his unexpected election and newly won authority, his suspicious nature came to the fore. He began accusing people of dishonorable and dishonest actions. He attacked one of the men on the regents board of the university who had taken an option on some land, which he thought the university might want in the future, in order to prevent a possible increase in the price of the land when the university did desire it. It was a perfectly unselfish move on his part, and one on which he did not make a dollar. Wells, however, accused him of speculation in land at the expense of the university. In the same way, and with as little factual support, he accused me. It has been said that Mr. Wells, while in the office of the New York *Nation* one day, voiced what he thought about me. Of course, the *Nation* must have been delighted with his comments, and the story goes that he was asked to sit down and write them out; thus, the *Nation* was the vehicle used to bring about my trial.

In a letter to Amos P. Wilder, editor of the Wisconsin *State Journal,* dated July 22, 1894, I gave vent to my anger at these trumped-up charges and wrote in my defense:

"Mr. Wells' letter contains nothing but lies. He may have heard them from others and believes them, but nevertheless, they are lies, and nothing but lies—not facts twisted and distorted, but lies, without even the semblance of truth. Everything can be refuted by demanding specifications. I am accused of believing in strikes and boycotts, 'justifying and encouraging the former and practicing the latter.' When and where? Quote from my books, accurately, showing justification and encouragement. Of course, no one can do it, for the exact opposite is the truth. 'I entertained a walking delegate from Kansas City.' Demand his name. It is a lie. Never to my knowledge did I see a walking delegate from Kansas City—'in constant consultation with him.' I never exchanged a word with such a man, so far as I know. This can be easily proved. I was an 'abettor and counsellor' in another strike—Tracy and Gibbs, he means. Let him name a striker with whom I counseled. I never to my knowledge have exchanged a word with a striking printer in the city of Madison, I never, so far as I know, knew one by name or sight. I never attended a workingman's meeting in Madison. I was never asked by a striker for any advice."

This letter, however, was personal and confidential; so far as the general public was concerned, the whole situation remained embarrassing and depressing. At the university it was vacation time, the president was away, the regents had scattered, and I, myself, was kept from Madison by my contract at Chautauqua. The independent action of my friends at this time, however, eased the tension considerably and gave me the courage I so sorely needed. The attacks were becoming more serious, but my friends stood by me without flinching. Bishop John H. Vincent, who looked upon me to some extent as his teacher in economics, read my statement of defense before a large audience in the vast amphitheater at Chautauqua. In his forceful and dramatic presentation, I noted especially the tones of approval with which he read the following passages of my statement:

"Taking up, first, the series of charges brought against my conduct and character, I deny each and every one in each and every particular. I defy the author of these base and cruel calumnies to prove one statement that he has made, and until he does so, I shall hold him up to the public as an unmanly and shameless slanderer.

"As to my views, I have nothing to retract. I may have modified my opinions, for only fools never change, and as the years have passed, I have shared a common fate and become, on the whole, more conservative. But in the main, the views I now hold I have held for years, and they are so clearly expressed in my writings that no honest and intelligent man, who reads my books, with care, need misunderstand them."

In this statement, I laid special emphasis upon my views on anarchy. "I was the first writer to examine exhaustively, to expose and to attack unsparingly anarchy in the United States. This I did in my *Labor Movement in America*. The propaganda of anarchy is a dire national calamity against which all right-minded people should work with all the resources at their command. Especially should the wage-earning people shun all connection with it. . . . Anything more foreign to my thought and feeling than anarchy, I do not know; anything more diametrically opposed to my social philosophy, I cannot conceive. In obedience to the laws and constitutional authorities of the land lies our only hope of progress."

MY FRIENDS SUPPORT ME AND THE ATTACK TURNS OUT A FIASCO

While Bishop Vincent was thus lending me his valuable support in Chautauqua, my friends in Wisconsin were not idle either. One of them, David Kinley, a former student, who afterwards became president of the University of Illinois, was spending his vacation in Madison. As soon as he learned of the situation, he wrote a note to the Wisconsin *State Journal,* making light of the whole matter. As he had been under my instruction for three years, he certainly knew whether or not I was a socialist. Then, he went to Superintendent Wells of his own initiative, and suggested to him that in view of the fact that it would be difficult, if not impossible, to prove his charges, even if he believed them to be true, the best course to pursue would be to withdraw them. The state superintendent declined to do this. Kinley accordingly began to organize my defense. At the same time, the regents had been obliged to take notice of the serious charges made against me in so public a way by appointing a committee of investigation, consisting of H. W. Chynoweth, John Johnston, and H. B. Dale.

A few weeks before the trial came on, I was physically ill as well as terribly depressed. Not only was I under a severe mental strain because of the pending trial, but I was deeply affected by the death of my little daughter Josephine. She was a beautiful baby of nine months, who twined herself about my heart strings as no one of my babies did. She was with her mother in Richmond, Virginia, where my wife was visiting her father, when she died. I hastened to Richmond from Madison, but on the train I received word saying she was gone. I was badly shaken by this tragedy and utterly incapable, physically or mentally, of making a defense, which required a considerable amount of investigation and careful, painstaking detective work. But my good friend, David Kinley, carried on for me. Gratitude wells up in my heart as I think of him and the service he rendered me.

In the interval between his efforts to induce Mr. Wells to withdraw his charges and the meeting of the committee of the regents, Kinley undertook some investigation on his own account. He thought that the most serious charge against me was that of aiding and abetting a strike in Madison. He remembered that in the preceding winter, when he was still a student in my seminar, there had been a strike of the employees of one of the newspapers. If I had conferred with any agitator, it must have been, he reasoned, in connection with that strike. Therefore, he set about finding the strike leader or agitator. He did not know either the name or the whereabouts of this man. However, he wrote a letter asking when he had been in Madison, whether he had conferred with Ely about the strike, whether Ely had given him any advice, and if so, what it was. He also asked the man to describe Ely as he remembered him. My friend then took this letter to the officers of the printers' union and asked them to find this man and send the letter to him. They kindly agreed to do so, as they remembered the strike very well. In due time, a reply came, full of surprise, from this agitator, stating that he had been in Ely's seminar, which was on the third floor of the Madison opera house, one afternoon during his stay in Madison, and had had a long conversation with a person whom he supposed was Richard T. Ely. He then proceeded to describe the gentleman with whom he had conversed. The description did not fit me at all, but it did fit a student-member of the seminar. People who knew both myself and this student recognized him at once from the description. He had evidently been found in the seminar room and permitted the stranger to assume that he was "Ely."

In the meantime, some of my friends, such as Professor Frederick Turner and David Kinley, after some correspondence with me, and by my authority, employed the Honorable Burr W. Jones, one of the ablest attorneys in Madison, to conduct my case. When Kinley received the agitator's letter, he passed it on to my attorney but let the fact that he had such a letter leak out, thus arousing considerable speculation as to its contents and causing some uneasiness to my accuser.

The regents committee finally appointed the date for its first meeting. I was ordered to produce all my articles and books. When the prosecution made this order, it did not appreciate fully what it signified and what a task they would have to read my writings. At the time set for the trial, several of my students, their arms loaded down with books, marched down State Street with me to the auditorium where the trial was to be held. Herbert Chynoweth presided. He had all the dignity and impartiality of a judge of the supreme court. There was a gathering of my students and associates and a sprinkling of the city's distinguished citizens. I recall the stately form of the Honorable Breese J. Stevens, who was one of the regents of the university, and a distinguished citizen of Wisconsin. Also, there were several strikers present from the Democrat printing office union to testify against me. The auditorium where the trial was held was not large nor was it brilliantly lighted. Looking back, it reminds me of the "Inquisitions" of the Middle Ages. To be sure there were no instruments of physical torture, but there was cruel mental torture. What would be the outcome of this unprovoked attack upon me?

After the meeting was organized, my attorney arose and asked the chairman of the committee whether the inquiry was to be conducted in strict accord with the rules of legal evidence or whether the committee was inclined to seek the truth through any avenues that they could find. The reason for raising this question was, of course, to determine whether the letter from the strike leader would be accepted as evidence. Counsel for my accuser arose and insisted that the inquiry be conducted in strict accord with the rules of legal evidence. My counsel, of course, did not object, and the committee was obliged to grant the wishes of the counsel for the other side. However, my opponents obtained no advantage from their attitude, because it alienated the sympathies of the audience, the meeting being open to the public.

The second question to be raised was the order of consideration of the various charges. Counsel for my accuser, apparently believing that it would strengthen his client's case if he could create a prejudice against me in the minds of the audience and the committee by convincing them that I was a socialist, demanded that the charge of teaching socialism be taken up first. My friends, anticipating this, urged my counsel, Mr. Jones, to oppose such a demand and to insist that the charges be taken up in the order in which they were made. This course would necessitate inquiry into the charge of aiding and abetting the printers' strike and would focus attention upon the fact that my opponent's insistence on legal procedure would rule out the evidence contained in the letter from the strike leader of the preceding winter. The committee, of course, was not influenced by this view, but nevertheless, decided that the charges should be met in the order in which they were made. That decision practically ended the session. One of the striking printers, who was put on the stand, was asked the question, "When did you last see Professor Ely?" He replied, "I never saw him until tonight." Evidently, they wanted to show that I had been associated with the strikers. It was amusing to see the confusion of Mr. Wells and his attorney at this unexpected answer. Mr. Wells and his counsel declined to proceed further at that meeting. Accordingly, the session was adjourned to a later date.

When the committee reassembled a week or two later, Mr. Wells and his counsel failed to appear. In the interim, they had published a statement to the effect that they had not been fairly treated at the first session, but they did not specify in what respect. Their failure to appear opened the way for my counsel to raise again the question whether the procedure which had been previously determined upon should be followed or whether the committee would not now accept evidence from any reliable source, irrespective of the technical correctness of its admission. They decided that they would do so and my attorney at once produced the letter of the strike leader of the preceding winter. When it was read in open session, everybody present recognized at once that the description given by the writer of the man with whom he conversed did not fit me at all. Therefore, that charge broke down.

The committee then took up the charge of my teaching socialism. Some of my friends, again, especially Professor Turner, Kinley, and my brother-in-law, had compiled a series of extracts from the works of Adam Smith and John Stuart Mill which, considered by themselves, conclusively proved that both Smith and Mill must have been radical socialists! Of course, the extracts, in their proper context, had no such significance. The point was that Mr. Wells' evidence that I was a socialist rested largely upon isolated extracts and statements from my lectures and writings. The parallelism at once broke the strength of his charge. Moreover, the gentlemen referred to above had also taken to the meeting copies of all my published works and all my lecture notes. These they put at the disposal of the committee in charge, with the suggestion, made through my attorney, that no fair conclusion as to the character of my teaching could be reached in any other way than by reading these books and lectures. However, the withdrawal of my accuser and his attorney from the case was regarded by the committee and the public at large as a confession of failure to establish their charges, and the committee refused to read them.

As soon as the inquiry reached this point, my attorney produced and read letters from numerous friends and many former students, including such authorities as President Charles Kendall Adams, the Honorable Carron D. Wright, United States Commissioner of Labor, Professors Turner and Haskins. They all expressed amazement at the charges that had been made against me. With respect to my influence on students, my former student, Albert D. Shaw, wrote:

"I have a very clear impression from Dr. Ely's teaching and writing in its totality, that reverence for government and for organic institutions was inculcated by him as a great cardinal doctrine. Far from influencing his pupils in the direction of destructive socialism, Dr. Ely's economic teaching as a whole has been constructive and conservative. Unlike certain teachers of economics who have not favored his methods, Dr. Ely has based his work upon facts rather than upon theories, and has been eminently an inductive investigator in economic fields. It has seemed to me, if I understand something of German economic method and thought, that Dr. Ely has been more closely allied to the German historical school than to the German school of so-called socialists of the chair."

With reference to my approach to economic problems, Albion W. Small, head of the social science department of the University of Chicago, wrote: "In my judgment no man in the United States has done so much as he to bring economic thought down out of the clouds and into contact with actual human concerns. Nothing could be more grotesque than to accuse him of encouraging a spirit of lawlessness and violence." As to the charge that I had an anarchistic leaning, H. B. Swaine, a former student of mine, and later president of a normal school in Montana, wrote: "If there is any one thing, which more than another, characterized all Dr. Ely's references to current problems, it was his very manifest conviction that the evils of society (which he was never disposed to exaggerate) could be remedied by patient, careful and intelligent means which should take the utmost precaution to guard the interests of all concerned."

In regard to the so-called pernicious effect my philosophy and writings had upon workingmen, Carron D. Wright, United States Commissioner of Labor, wrote: "His influence upon the workingmen has been the influence of the pulpit. He has undertaken to teach them broad and catholic views of their relations to industry and to society, and I believe if they would follow his advice and teachings, it would be much better for them. I do not believe that there is a thing in Dr. Ely's life, in his teachings, in his utterances through his books, or in his association with workingmen that can for a moment be considered as inducing discontent among the workingmen, or that can in any degree render him responsible for strikes and violence. I know from my personal knowledge that Dr. Ely's views would lead men away from strikes, away from violence, and to adopt a better mode of settling their difficulties."

These testimonials made a strong impression on the committee. But, beyond that, they were a magnificent personal tribute which warmed my heart. The splendid way in which my friends rallied around me at this critical point has always been a source of deep satisfaction to me. I deem myself fortunate in having had, and in still having, so loyal and fine a group of friends and students.

The committee, after taking the whole matter under consideration, published their decision, completely exonerating me and giving to the world that famous pronunciamento of academic freedom which has been a beacon light in higher education in this country, not only for Wisconsin, but for all similar institutions, from that day to this. Their declaration on behalf of academic freedom which has come to be regarded as part of the Wisconsin Magna Charta follows:

"As regents of the university with over a hundred instructors supported by nearly two millions of people who hold a vast diversity of views regarding the great questions which at present agitate the human mind, we could not for a moment think of recommending the dismissal or even the criticism of a teacher even if some of his opinion should, in some quarters, be regarded as visionary. Such a course would be equivalent to saying that no professor should teach anything which is not accepted by everybody as true. This would cut our curriculum down to very small proportions. We cannot for a moment believe that knowledge has reached its final goal, or that the present condition of society is perfect. We must, therefore, welcome from our teachers such discussions as shall suggest the means and prepare the way by which knowledge may be extended, present evils be removed, and others prevented. We feel that we would be unworthy of the position we hold if we did not believe in progress of all departments of knowledge. In all lines of academic investigation it is of the utmost importance that the investigator should be absolutely free to follow the indications of the truth wherever they may lead. Whatever may be the limitations which trammel inquiry elsewhere we believe the great state University of Wisconsin should ever encourage that continual and fearless sifting and winnowing by which alone the truth can be found."

The last section of the regents' statement of exoneration

is now inscribed on a tablet in Bascom Hall which was dedicated in 1915. From the day those words were written to this, no responsible party or no responsible authority has ever succeeded in restricting freedom of research and teaching within the walls of the university. There are no "sacred cows" at Wisconsin. There is no such thing as "standardized" teaching in any subject. Professors and instructors present faithfully the various sides of each problem. Their duty is to train the students to independent thinking. They are in no sense propagandist for any class or interest. A university to be worthy of its name must be progressive—not progressive in the partisan sense, but in the dictionary sense. The tablet in Bascom Hall typifies the spirit of research and the principles that animate the university as a whole.

The attack on me turned out a fiasco. Madison roared with laughter, when after the ludicrous collapse of the accusations, an article appeared in a Madison newspaper, containing selections from Superintendent Wells' latest report, which considered by themselves would make him out a "dangerous man"!

The people of Madison gave me a grand reception after the trial, and their support left no taint on their reputation as upholders of free and untrammeled academic freedom. To the regents of the University of Wisconsin, I can give nothing but praise for their treatment of me. They supported me magnificently. Before I reluctantly left to go to Chicago and Northwestern University, they had removed, in my particular case, all upper age limits for retirement. They gave the LL.D. degree to me, while still in active service, a thing never done before, and they made me honorary professor of economics, a position which I still proudly hold, so that I am still a legal member of the faculty. May this once for all dispose of the slander that I was dismissed from the magnificent institution, to which I have given over thirty years of my life.

THE MOTTO OF THE INSTITUTE—
UNDER ALL THE LAND

My good friend, Frank Fetter, has said, "My own conviction has long been that the land question far transcends any restricted field of economics and that it is fundamental to national survival and national welfare. It is truly a problem calling for statesmanship of the broadest type."

I, too, was firm in my conviction that planning the uses of land is at once the most fundamental and the most difficult and intricate of all problems with which we have to deal. I believe that in economics, as in medicine, the greatest advances are made by men of scientific training, following scientific methods, working on practical problems. The truth of science should not be divorced from its practical application; it is only when truths are discovered and formulated by the scientist that practice can proceed with assurance. And that is exactly what was *not* happening in the field of land economics. There was an acute dearth of scientific data. Year in and year out, for many years, I had seen the problems of land economics dealt with by costly trial and error methods. The fact that in a prosperous state like Wisconsin farm lands to the value of hundreds of thousands of dollars should be sold for taxes pained me because of the tremendous economic loss involved—and even more because of the tragic stories of poor settlers who lost their all, in many cases as the result of mistaken judgment in the purchase of land.

Throughout all recorded history the relation of people to land has been an important factor in civilization. Land is the original source of wealth; the earth is utilized to supply us with food, clothing, shelter, recreation, and culture. The field of land economics reaches the ends of the earth and to the minutest detail of economic interest. It is so large and touches life at so many points that the practical problems involved in it are

numerous and various. The scope of land economics is as large
as that of property rights in land and natural resources. One of
the first marks of civilization is the definite allotment of specific
rights in the gifts of nature. As soon as the half-civilized nomad
strikes his tent for the last time and settles down to an approach
to civilization, he reaches out for control over natural resources
which he wants to appropriate to his own purposes; and problems connected with the land have begun. The extent of the control which he will be allowed to exert, the conflict of his interests with those of his neighbors, the desires of others for the
things over which he has established control, all these give rise
to land problems. In the complex civilization in which we live
today, nearly every phase of life to which we turn presents
problems of property rights in land or in natural resources.
Moreover, these will continue to emerge, and also to change as
time goes on; for there can never be any final solution of the
problems connected with land as there can never be any final
solution of the problems arising from human relationships. It
is because of the ever present character of these problems that
research in this field should be constant and continuous. For
this reason I feel I was filling an important need in establishing
the Institute for Research in Land Economics and Public Utilities. The more earnestly and successfully we deal with these
problems, the higher the civilization we shall leave to our
posterity.

When we look at the causes of war in the past we find that
they were largely due to failure to establish satisfactory land
policies. If we dare to hope for peace we must realize that we
must have economic foundations of peace and this means that
plans must be arrived at for the equitable distribution of food,
minerals, and other raw materials among the nations of the
earth. The wars of the world have been from the beginning
wars for the control of natural resources. My readers will recall

the story of Abraham and Lot. The land became too small for their growing families and for their increasing flocks, so Abraham said to Lot, "You go this way and I will go that way." They separated in peace and sought elsewhere for a more ample supply of land. This story is a rare exception in the world's history. Generally, war is resorted to for the satisfaction of land hunger. The wars of ancient Greece, the wars of Imperial Rome, and all wars down to the most recent ones have been waged to satisfy the need for more land. If we are to avoid wars, we must plan out the uses of land so that adequate food and raw materials will be available to all nations. And to this end we must reconstruct national boundaries so that the best use may be made of the land. It is true that for the attainment of world peace something more is needed than planning out the uses of land, but this is essential as a foundation for other efforts, and without this, the other efforts are futile. Surely we have here a staggering job worthy of our best efforts for solution. It was my aspiration in founding the Institute for Research in Land Economics and Public Utilities to join with others who are working for world peace and to make some worthy contribution to that great end.

The individual farmer plans out the uses of his land. He divides it into fields and uses which in his judgment will enable him to secure from his farm the largest and most valuable product. But before the farmer begins his operations, various agencies, public and private, have been at work. If they have functioned efficiently, hard work and thrift will make the farmer prosperous. His farm, for example, must be of the right size, but often the size of his farm may have been determined by the Homestead Act with which he had nothing to do. This act established one hundred sixty acres as the proper size of a farm. In some parts of the country this one hundred sixty acres is a proper unit. In other sections it may be altogether inadequate. Some years ago I made an investigation of the Montana dry wheat country. There we found a farm of 3000 acres was the right size. A farm of one hundred sixty acres meant ruin, and a farm of even 1000 acres was too small for the overhead of machinery and the human overhead. The world over, the right size of a farm is an urgent problem. Its solution requires public action supported by social and individual effort.

When we turn to the cities we find many landowners in distress. Roughly speaking, we may say that real estate in some of our great cities has become bankrupt. Foreclosures, rent assignments, and other indexes of distress in New York and Chicago tell the sad story of inadequate and shortsighted land utilization. Individual buildings may be beautifully planned as individual buildings, but if they do not fit properly into some general scheme, they may become bankrupt or operate at a heavy loss. We hear a great deal about city planning; we have a profession of city planners. Just as planners, some of them are excellent. Two or three of them can get together and replan the whole of New York City. Nevertheless, if their plans do not rest upon a solid economic foundation, and generally they do not, the result is loss and keen distress. The poverty that results from bad utilization of the land and that passes on from generation to generation is evident to every careful observer of what is taking place in city and country. Countless needless tragedies exist. They can be seen on every hand in the struggle of men who cultivate poor farm land and in every city in the efforts of men and women to pay for the land that in a generation will not be worth the price paid. A great practical purpose of the Institute for Research in Land Economics and Public Utilities is to join in the labors of those who are striving to abolish poverty and hope in time to achieve their purpose.

Parallel with the land studies, The Institute has undertaken a comprehensive and far-reaching program of research in public utility economics. Why public utilities should be associated with land in the Institute's research work is not difficult to understand. In the case of urban land, all the problems of city development are related more or less closely to transportation. In the case of agricultural land, the marketing of farm products is of great importance. Such a public utility as water power cannot be considered except in connection with the land. These relationships, we may expect, will become increasingly vital to public welfare as our economic society grows more complex and its members more interdependent.

In 1920 the Institute for Research in Land Economics and Public Utilities was founded at the University of Wisconsin, and in 1922 it was incorporated as an independent research and educational institution. Before the Institute was established, work in land economics and public utilities was more or less scattered and unsystematic. It was our purpose to bring together facts that serve as material for scientific analysis and are of value to courts, legislators, administrative officials, public utility executives, real estate dealers and owners, and many others. In gathering together the results of the best work of scholars in the various fields and in proceeding systematically with our research, we have been engaged in pioneering. The work we have done is essentially new work and has been recognized very generously by those who have carefully followed our activities. The following is an excerpt from an editorial which appeared in *The New York Times:*

"It is clear that the findings of this research institution will be of national and international concern. Its studies cannot be limited by state or even national boundaries. It has ultimately to do with the world's natural resources. 'It is no wild guess,' says Dr. Ely, 'that two hundred years or five hundred years from now, when the earth has multiplied its population, the Institute may be rendering more far-reaching service to mankind than it is

possible now to foresee.' They are fortunate who are privileged
to lay its foundation."

The motivating idea has been to gather together existing
knowledge, interpret it cautiously, and then to conduct researches in order that we might go forward to new and better
generalizations. We were criticized because in our early mimeographed volumes of the *Outlines of Land Economics* we stated
certain conclusions. It was said that we should have waited until
we had finished our researches and then given our conclusions.
If this had been done, no conclusions or generalizations would
ever have been reached, because researches must be continuous
and never-ending. Even if we reached perfection in generalization on the basis of facts at a given moment, and this is, in the
nature of things impossible, we should need to continue our researches, because evolution, like life, never ceases and the situation that exists at one particular time is something that the world
has never seen before and never will see again. We have
never advocated panaceas. We stand ready to revise conclusions
as we get new light. But first of all we must gather the essential
facts; then we must look at these facts dispassionately and interpret them objectively. This is the spirit of the Institute's work.
It has been so well expressed by words uttered by Herbert
Hoover and Owen D. Young, that we had painted on the walls
of the Institute's quarters at Northwestern University the following quotations:

"The nation today needs more support to research. It needs
still more laboratories. . . . And scientific research means more
than its practical results in increased living comfort. The future
of our nation is not merely a question of the development of
our industries, of reducing the cost of living, of multiplying
our harvests, or of larger leisure. We must constantly strengthen
the fiber of national life by the inculcation of that veracity of
thought which springs from the search for truth. From its

pursuit we shall discover the unfolding of beauty, we shall
stimulate the aspiration for knowledge, we shall ever widen
human understanding." (Herbert Hoover)

"Facts can be applied in any field. Our curse is ignorance.
Facts are our scarcest raw material. This is shown by the economy with which we use them. One has to dig deep for them,
because they are as difficult to get as they are precious to
have. . . . I shall be happy if we can substitute the calm findings of the investigator for the blatant explosions of the
politicians." (Owen D. Young)

The Institute's research has been organized under four divisions. The first—general land economics—dealt with the
relation of the different kinds of natural resources to the distribution and movement of population, standards of living,
industrial development, distribution of wealth, property rights,
national policies, and international relations. The ultimate objective of this field of study and research is a group of integrated policies by national, state, and local governments and
by business interests for the most effective utilization of all
natural resources.

The second, urban land economics, concerns the problems of
land utilization caused by the aggregation of population in
cities and metropolitan regions. The prime objective is the securing of intelligent planning by governmental units and by
private interests which will make possible satisfactory living
conditions and efficient economic life for the growing numbers
of city dwellers.

Third, in the field of public utility economics, the Institute's
aim is progressively to uncover the facts upon which sound
public policies and wise private practices in administration can
be based.

Our fourth field of interest was taxation. Tax students foresee the necessity of a readjustment of many antiquated features

of state and local taxation to modern social and industrial conditions. Such a readjustment must particularly be one which
will contribute to the wiser and more effective utilization of
land and natural resources. The Institute believes that scientific
work must constitute the essential basis for working out these
adjustments.

OUR AIM—TO BETTER HUMAN LIFE

What has the Institute done for the bettering of human life?
It has made a thoroughgoing study of the factors relating to
housing for the greater part of our population, considering "not
only the dwellings themselves but the social institutions and
activities that affect and determine living conditions." The financing of home-building has commanded the Institute's attention,
and interesting suggestions on this matter have already resulted
from the studies that have been made. The Institute has made
studies of the factors determining the location and growth of
cities and the concentration and shifting of districts given over to
special uses within cities.

We have been concerned with the basic causes of farm
distress. We are not interested in mere palliatives; still less do
we care for any man's panacea. It is well known that the reason
for the shrinkage of the farmer's share in the nation's income
is found in the maladjustments due to changing price levels.
Most of the vociferous political advocates of farm relief get as
far in their analysis as this price discrepancy, but some of them
get no further. We were not content to stop at that point. We
are seeking in the history of American agriculture causes that
have contributed to bring about the present situation. Two such
contributing causes may be found in the over-stimulation of
agriculture and in the farming of land unfitted for the purpose.
More research will be required to determine how far these
causes have operated, and how they may be checked.

Another objective of the Institute was to secure balanced production on agricultural land. Some land now given over to farming might be better used for growing trees, of which there is now an under-production. It was the aim of the Institute to show by careful surveys of land under cultivation how some of these mistakes may be rectified and to lay the basis for a wiser policy of land utilization for the future. In Michigan and Wisconsin fact-finding studies for this purpose have been conducted.

Farm tenancy and farm ownership are subjects that have claimed a great part of the Institute's attention. The aim is to bring together the facts on ownership and tenure of agricultural land, and therefrom to discover the underlying principles of land tenure. Everything that is known to help or hinder the acquisition of farm land—credit, taxation, the farmers' standard of living—is subjected to the most careful scrutiny. A district in Manitowoc County, Wisconsin, known to have a low percentage of tenancy, was selected as one of the areas for intensive, qualitative study. Land transfer and inheritance in that district from its settlement in 1847 were searchingly examined, and genealogical and sociological factors were taken into account. The data on twenty-five hundred mortgages, bonds, and contracts thus obtained showed land credits, encumbrances, and interest rates over a period of eighty years. A similar study was conducted in an Illinois township where the tenancy percentage is high.

OUR WORK IN ADULT EDUCATION

Planned utilization of land requires education and research of the highest type. Land planning is dependent on the classification of the land with respect to its various uses, and to make such a classification of the land is an extremely difficult complex problem. Education must secure pertinent facts and the knowledge of these facts must be widely diffused. The education of all social groups must proceed until desirable social action is secured. Learning what the costs are in the best construction of a well-planned modern city is an educational process and some of the findings are of vast significance.

Training of workers is necessary; textbooks must be prepared. We must embark on a vast adventure in adult education. Ultimately education in land planning will mean many things —such as better homes, less waste and more economical utilization of land, more abundant and widely diffused property, better understanding of past and present history, and a laying of the economic foundation of world peace.

Therefore our work has largely been one of adult education in which I have always been interested. Perhaps I may again mention the fact that for seven years my association with Bishop John H. Vincent of Chautauqua gave me an interest in adult education that I have never lost. In adult education our work, apart from the work in universities, was directed particularly toward those in the real estate business which we wanted to help put on a professional basis. The importance of this cannot be overestimated, because it is through the real estate business that men acquire farms and homes and real estate generally. In 1931 and 1932 the real estate situation throughout the country was becoming critical. Banks, insurance companies, and lending institutions were foreclosing property to the total of billions of dollars annually. For the most part, these institutions did not have good real estate departments, and as their real estate portfolios increased, they assigned men from their credit departments, their lending departments, and others, to handle their real estate.

It has always been my thesis that, to successfully cope with real estate problems, a sound knowledge of what is known as land economics is necessary; therefore, I put before the trustees of the Institute for Economic Research the question as to whether we should establish a school of land economics.

I was delighted when the trustees approved of my plan, and we started in a modest way and held four courses pertaining to real estate—one was a course in land economics, given by myself—another in appraising was given by Mr. John Burton— a third in real estate management was given by Robert H. Armstrong—and a fourth was given by Robert Whitten. While we were only fairly successful, judging by the numbers registered in our school, we acted as pioneers in the field.

Though the men who worked with me in this school may have felt disappointed at the small numbers we attracted in the beginning, nevertheless each one of them should hold the satisfaction that I do, in having initiated a movement that is now spreading throughout the nation.

The International Committee of the Y.M.C.A. has been particularly interested in this work. Mr. T. H. Nelson, who is the leader in their efforts to impart sound education to those in the real estate business, has been cordial in his recognition of our service. I quote from a letter that he wrote some time ago:

"We are almost wholly dependent upon the Institute for Research in Land Economics and Public Utilities [our former name] for the formulation of reliable real estate literature and for that determination of what we might call real estate science."

One of the main contributions of the Institute has been the public and civic services rendered by members of the research staff. It is believed that, within reasonable limits, these services are justifiable, insofar as they contribute towards the development of sound public policy.

Eventually, the time came for the Institute to leave the home of its birth. I felt that my work at Wisconsin was over. I had made my contribution. I decided to leave the pleasant fields where I had spent thirty years of my life and to accept an offer to go to Northwestern University, taking the Institute with me.

We were splendidly welcomed at Northwestern. I was under Dean Ralph E. Heilman, a fine speaker and a gifted man, who treated us magnificently. Through his instrumentality large funds were placed at my disposal and I had a large staff, which at one time must have numbered twenty-five or thirty. The Institute occupied nearly the whole seventh floor of Wieboldt Hall in Chicago and I had fine offices overlooking Lake Michigan. Nearly my whole force in the Institute moved with me from Madison to Chicago. I took with me, also, my splendid private library which was housed in a room especially prepared for it.

From the beginning it has been our conviction that an institution of research should have some real and vital connection with a university. We have felt that with this connection a great deal more would be accomplished in the way of research for a given expenditure than would otherwise be possible, and at the same time give to men of special talent, training that they could not receive in ordinary graduate work. The problem has been well stated by Mr. Bernard De Voto in these words: "The existence of a higher caste of intelligent students is, and always has been, a fact. But it is only by frankly recognizing its existence and enfranchising its members that the present instrumentalities of liberal education can be made fully effective." The best results for the talented few can only be obtained if they work together with the leaders in research on definite projects. Classwork should not be entirely omitted, but it should be reduced to a very few hours a week. The results which can thus be achieved are seen in the careers of those who have been associated with the Institute and, in my opinion, are a demonstration of the soundness of our pedagogical methods. It has been my good fortune since I began my educational career with the Johns Hopkins University to have among my students many who have achieved distinction. Those who have been turned out by the Institute, however, give every promise of taking their rank with the best of these. Among them were Dr. George S. Wehrwein, Dr. Herbert D. Simpson, Dr. Coleman Woodbury, Dr. Helen Monchow, Dr. Morton Bodfish, and Dr. Adrian Theobald. Although still comparatively young, they have already attained distinction in their respective fields and show remarkable promise of further growth.

Dr. George S. Wehrwein has gained an enviable reputation in the field of land economics, both in this country and abroad. In time to come, I have little doubt that he will rank among the highest in his chosen field.

Dr. Herbert D. Simpson has made a name for himself in the field of public finance. He now holds a full professorship at Northwestern University and is considered an expert in that subject.

Dr. Coleman Woodbury has attracted attention by his activities in the housing movement. As a Rhodes scholar, for one year, he traveled on the continent and studied housing developments. On his return, he became a member of the staff of the Institute and taught housing at Northwestern. At the present time, he is executive director of the National Association of Housing Officials.

Another one in the round table was Morton Bodfish who is now executive vice-president of the United States Building and Loan League and the American Savings and Loan Institute, and who has already attained distinction in this capacity. He is, also, an Associate Professor in Land Economics in Northwestern University. Associated with Professor Bodfish is Adrian Theobald who is director of education and research, American Savings and Loan Institute and assistant vice-president of the United States Building and Loan League.

The name of Paul Raver must be mentioned in this connection. He specialized in the field of public utilities and he is now an associate professor of public utilities at Northwestern. He is, also, executive officer of the Illinois Commerce Commission.

Certainly in this list of the products of the Institute for Economic Research at Northwestern, the name of Helen C. Monchow should not be omitted. A graduate of Mt. Holyoke College, at first she was my personal secretary, but she gradually advanced and is now managing editor of the *Journal of Land and Public Utility Economics.* This magazine is, in my opinion, the equal of any economics periodical of our time.

Also, I must mention the name of Herman Walther who trekked with us in the odyssey from Wisconsin to Northwestern University. Herman Walther was a man who combined to an unusual degree the practical and the theoretical. In Chicago, he soon attained recognition and he became associated with Henry G. Zander & Company, one of the best real estate firms in that city. He later became associated with the HOLC as Chicago district manager, and at present holds the position of vice-president and managing director, First Federal Savings and Loan Association of Chicago. He is, also, a lecturer in real estate at Northwestern University, giving courses in real estate finance and real estate valuation.

In Wisconsin, the relations between the Institute for Economic Research and the university had been ideal. The Institute as such was not a part of the University of Wisconsin; it had no representation on our board, nor did it desire any. At that time we were receiving a grant from the Carnegie Corporation and it was a condition of this grant that we should have suitable office space provided us. But the University of Wisconsin went beyond the letter of the law, so to speak; they provided us with splendid quarters. My own offices were spacious and no visitor could fail to be impressed by the beauties of the fine paintings and lithographs which adorned their walls. They were presented to me as a gift by my Irish friends, after my return from Ireland, at a colorful ceremony held under the auspices of the Ancient Order of the Hibernians. President Van Hise was so impressed with my office that he once offered to trade rooms with me. "You move into my office," he said, half in earnest, half in jest, "and I will take over yours."

So far as members of our staff were engaged in teaching, as several were, they had to be regularly appointed, even if their salaries were paid by the Institute, as they were, except in my own case. When I wanted Dr. Wehrwein, for example, to be appointed to conduct classes, I made the recommendation to the dean and then it went to the president of the board of regents and the appointment was made just as it would have been if the salary had been paid by the university. No possible objection could be made to this arrangement. It would have created chaos had men been brought into the faculty otherwise. My nominations could have been rejected, although they never were.

At Northwestern, I had many friends and former students. Dean Alton James of the graduate school had been my student at the Johns Hopkins. Professor Frederick S. Deibler, head of the department of economics, had been one of my students at Wisconsin. Dean Heilman told Professor Deibler that I was bringing a group of men with me who were to have special privileges, teaching only classes in connection with research, and to be paid higher salaries than the other professors were then receiving. Professor Deibler said, "It does not harm the rest of us at Northwestern, instead it gives us hope that later on we, too, may have higher salaries and privileges we do not now enjoy."

Difficulties soon appeared. The trustees at Northwestern obtained final authority over the Institute, which was unfortunate in several ways. The recommendations of the board of trustees of the Institute for Economic Research had to be confirmed by Northwestern University. And this led to a division of authority which weakened the Institute. Actually, these recommendations were always confirmed, but in effect this procedure lessened the responsibility of the Institute's trustees, and Northwestern, in turn, would not assume responsibility for our finances.

It happened, too, that our potential sources of funds were also prospective donors to the Northwestern University and that led to difficulties of a financial character. When I appealed for funds it would often be said, "It is up to Northwestern University to support you." In this connection, one particular incident occurs to me. I had met Cyrus McCormick. The McCormicks had come from the same part of Virginia as my wife, with whom Mrs. Leander McCormick was very friendly, calling her "Cousin Anna." It was a natural thing for me to turn to Cyrus McCormick for support of my work. But President Scott spoke to me about this matter. He said, "We are trying to get a generous endowment from Mr. McCormick. You must wait until we see what we can do." This I did. Northwestern University did not receive any large gift from him. My opportunity had passed and I received no support from that quarter either.

So, as time went on, it again became clear to me that I must once more leave the pleasant land where I had hoped to spend the rest of my life. I decided to move the Institute to New York and to work independently. New York was an ideal place for the Institute, for here was to be found the center of those activities with which we were scientifically concerned.

Looking back, I still think that the movement to Northwestern was a good one, when considered from the point of view I had at heart. Friends say that so far as graduate work in

economics is concerned, we "put Northwestern on the map."
Certainly we had a fine group of graduate students and a good
number still are there in various capacities. I think there is not
a university in the country in which better work is carried on in
land economics and public utilities than at Northwestern, unless
it be Wisconsin.

It was at Northwestern, also, that I found the young woman
who later became my wife. Margaret Hale Hahn was a member
of my round table, a dynamic personality, with many varied interests. She was a Northwestern graduate and had attained distinction in athletics, as well as in scholastic work. She was a member
of the debating group and was one of the first women to represent
the university in a joint debate with Wisconsin; she was also
president of the hockey team and had obtained her letter. We
were married in 1931. Her companionship and her vitality have
greatly enriched my life. We are now the proud parents of two
lovely children, Billy, six, and Mary, four.

My romance seemed to climax the long successful career of
the Institute as a sort of matrimonial bureau. I have been called
a "wonder man" at pairing off young men and women. But,
although I am happy to say that all the marriages between the
young men and women in the Institute's employ have turned
out successfully, with one single exception, I must disclaim any
responsibility for being a matchmaker. Luck and chance were
the determining factors. Young men and women worked together in pleasant surroundings on mutually interesting work,
and nature took its course.

And so, at the age of eighty-four, I am again in the city of
my youth. And as I look about me, I am still fired by an ambition to "set the world right," just as my father before me. It is
a great comfort to me to know that after I am gone, many of
my students and friends, now in the prime of life, will remain
to carry on. I give them my blessing.

Mrs. Margaret Hale Ely and William Brewster Ely,
Radburn, New Jersey, 1932

I HAVE CHANGED MY MIND ABOUT
MUNICIPAL OWNERSHIP

A scientific person dislikes creeds. Science is not religion; it is a progressive upbuilding of truth. I have often been asked, "What is your social creed?" I have answered, "I have no creed." Yet mature thought reveals to the man of science that he may go too far in his opposition to a statement of his opinions. As a result of his studies and his experiences he may have reached conclusions of value to others. There is no impropriety in a statement of these conclusions provided it is understood that he reserves the right to change his opinions if longer investigation and riper experience reveal mistakes. I find I have changed my views on a great many economic subjects, as well as on topics of a different sort. Sometimes I have been vehemently reproached for changing my opinions. Among my severe critics, the more charitable have said that it has been due to the growth of conservatism with advancing years; the less charitable have asserted it is due to corrupt influences. The truth is that the world has changed and I have endeavored to keep an open mind and have tried to change my views with the increasing knowledge that this economic world of ours is in a constant state of flux.

Writing in 1891 I had this to say: "The chief modern industrial problem is often stated to be the distribution of property. What is wanted is widely diffused property and it is desired to bring about this wide diffusion without injustice and without injury to the springs of economic activity. Wise social reform will always seek for the line of least resistance. At the present time I feel inclined to classify the chief things required to bring about an improved condition of society under three heads: (1) Education in its broadest sense, including kindergartens, manual training, technical schools, colleges and universities. (2) Abolition of private monopoly and substitution therefor of public ownership and management of all those enterprises which are by nature monopolies like railways, gas and electric, telegraph, telephone. (3) Reforms of the laws of inheritance." [41]

My views on education have remained the same; my views on inheritance laws I will discuss later. But I have been bitterly criticized for changing my opinion on the question of public vs. private ownership of natural monopolies.

It seemed to me that if we sharply defined the field of our industries into those that were competitive and those that were monopolies, and left to private ownership and initiative the competitive industries and had public ownership and operation of the natural monopolies, we would have an ideal situation. Competitive industries are suitable for private ownership and operation because they are regulated by competition. What I thought was especially needed then was a certain amount of regulation of competition in order that there should be fair competition. I was especially influenced, as were many of my contemporaries, by a monograph written soon after the American Economic Association was formed, by my friend Professor Henry C. Adams, called "The Relation of the State to Industrial Action." His idea was that through the agency of the state and other social forces, competition should be placed constantly upon a higher and higher ethical level, but competition should be maintained.

Now, what were we to do with natural monopolies? I started my reasoning with the assumption that the regulation of natural monopolies is necessary because the nature of the service rendered is, in such a peculiar degree, a civil service, and because the effective control of full and free competition is absent. There were two alternatives to be considered—public control of private corporations and public ownership with public control.

When I began writing, we had very few agencies of control. The Interstate Commerce Commission had not yet been established. The Massachusetts Railway Commission, based on public opinion, was in existence, but it seemed to me rather ineffective, although it may have worked better in Massachusetts than elsewhere. Public regulation of private monopolies did not look very promising to me—and that for the following reasons:

I saw that control meant a necessary antagonism of interests in the civic household. Human nature is such that those who are to be controlled cannot be satisfied with the control exercised. However righteous the control may be, those who are controlled will feel themselves aggrieved and wronged and will try tc escape control. It is probably a necessary outcome of human nature that those who are to be controlled should enter into politics in order to escape control or shape it to their own ends. The efforts of patriotic and high-minded citizens in their self-sacrificing neglect of their private affairs to look after public concerns may grow weary—but not so the activities of the corporations to be controlled. And who are those whom we are asked to control? They are frequently friends and neighbors. When one is asked to resist what is esteemed the extortion of a gas company, one of the magnates may be his neighbor and friend, perhaps his employer. Perhaps I am a college professor and the street-car magnate whose rapacity I am called upon to help hold in check has endowed the chair which I occupy. Is it strange that many of us who are called upon to control others of us should simply refuse to do it? As I saw it, regulation was not feasible; in advocating public ownership I was following the theory advanced by Jevons in England and emphasized by Edmund J. James and others in this country, that the way to improve government was to give government essential tasks and make it real and vital to us all. As I saw it, the problem was to secure men of talent and experience and keep them in office during good behavior—to engage men for all positions on the basis of merit—to enact such legislation and administrative reforms as could prevent employees of the city from using their political power for their own selfish ends or for partisan purposes. This line of reasoning emphasized a thorough-going reform of civil service. I thought that public ownership would bring home to everyone the importance of good government.

I had seen public ownership operate well in Germany. There is no question that, on the whole, it did operate very well. German railways at that time were, in many respects, better operated than our own. Frequently I was aroused by the unwise attempts on the part of those interested in our natural monopolies to belittle the success that Germany was achieving. There was much talk about the slow German trains, yet I think that any critical examination of the facts would show that the average speed was greater than ours, and for a long time the fastest train in the world was a German train operating between Hamburg and Berlin. I recall a controversy that I had on this point, I think it was in a paper called the *Railroad Gazette,* and finally it was conceded that I had proved my point. Then there were a thousand and one little conveniences offered by the German railways, due to the fact that they were publicly owned and operated. If one bought a ticket between Berlin and Frankfort-on-Main, one could travel on any one of several different routes. Also, one could simply drop a card into a postbox and have someone call for freight to be taken to the freight station; and the freight could be insured for a very small sum even including delivery at a specified time. There were classifications of freight, and "Eilgut" or fast freight which corresponded to our express, was I thought not only cheaper, but better.

In Fredonia, where I was brought up, there was a considerable amount of municipal ownership of public utilities, and it seemed to work very well. I noticed a real pride on the part of the people in the fact that they collectively owned so many things, and that they operated them so well. What was true of Fredonia was true, to a greater or less extent, of other places in western New York, with which I was familiar. People owned many things; they were proud of their common ownership, and local government on the whole reached a relatively high stage, both in regard to honesty and efficiency.

I have always recognized that we do not have natural law in the economic world, and that economic laws are different from the laws of external nature. Nevertheless, I felt that, in predicting the success of public ownership, I had discovered an economic law which closely resembled the laws of nature in the regularity with which it would operate.

I thought that human nature, such as it is found in our country and in modern civilization, would respond to public ownership of natural monopolies with all its implications. I thought that we would remove the sources of corruption, and certainly at the time I was writing, these sources of corruption were very largely connected with private ownership of natural monopolies. I thought that if we could have public ownership and operation of natural monopolies, we would have pure government; we would have excellent operation of these natural monopolies through a highly trained and capable civil service in the nation, state, and city. I thought that we would have the beginnings of a much better and more prosperous society.

I am not altogether filled with pleasurable emotions when I think about a statement that I once made in an address on natural monopolies in Boston. This was many years ago, and I said that I would no sooner expect to see a city fail in the ownership and management of natural monopolies than I would expect to see stones flying away from the earth instead of to the earth—disobeying the laws of gravity.

It seems to me that this is perhaps the most absurd statement

I have ever made. I would feel worse about it than I do if other economists had not made statements just as false. They have been made when other economists felt, just as I did, that they were dealing with economic laws which operated with the certainty of the laws of the physical universe. Malthus, in his theory of rent in 1815, uses these words:

"It may be laid down, therefore, as an incontrovertible truth, that as a nation reaches any considerable degree of wealth, and any considerable fullness of population, which of course cannot take place without a great fall both in the profits of stock and the wages of labour, the separation of rents, as a kind of fixture upon lands of a certain quality, is a law as invariable as the action of the principle of gravity. And that rents are neither a mere nominal value, nor a value unnecessarily and injuriously transferred from one set of people to another; but a most real and essential part of the whole value of the national property, and placed by the laws of nature where they are, on the land, by whomsoever possessed, whether the landlord, the crown, or the actual cultivator." [42]

Malthus uses exactly the same comparison that I did. He says that the law according to which rent increases is as invariable as the action of the principle of gravity. This is a real consolation to me when I think about that one of my statements which, perhaps more than almost any other, I would rather not have said. It reminds me of letters that I have seen from time to time in the daily press under the heading "a most embarrassing moment."

General Walker, also speaking of the law of rent, declared himself to be ". . . a Ricardian of the Ricardians, holding that the great thinker, who has given his name to the economic doctrine of rent, left little for those who should follow him to do; and that any wide departure from the lines laid down by him can only result in confusions and error." [43]

I comfort myself with thinking, nevertheless, that Malthus and Walker were great economists.

Malthus and Walker overlooked the way certain forces were going to operate in the future. Malthus had a theory of demanders which he said applied only to agriculture. This theory of demanders was that, however great the supply of food, there would always be a demand for it. This was the result of his theory of population—that population would increase to the limits of subsistence, as established by whatever standard of living might prevail. Walker had evidently the same underlying assumption.

Now we have seen, on the one hand, a great increase in agricultural production, and we see that population does not find its limits set by the productivity of agricultural land. The productive power increases far more rapidly than the population. We have relative over-production, and we have a fall in land values and unearned decrements rather than unearned increments in the rent of land.

If we grant the premises of Malthus and Walker, they were right and the premises wrong. This was also true of my premises, and I want to examine some of the premises I assumed when I felt so confident that, under our American conditions, public ownership of natural monopolies would surely prove a success. I am interested in reviewing in my own mind the mistakes that I made in my forecasts, and the nature of these mistakes.

One thing that I did not understand sufficiently was the psychology of the American people. I believed the great mass of our people would not only be interested in what was their own property and its management, but intelligently interested. I thought their interest would increase if we had public ownership of things of real and vital concern to the great mass of people, like agencies of transport, gas and electric light, and many other things monopolistic in their nature. I thought that the interest would show itself in a real pride in good management, and that to secure this management, the great mass of the people would appreciate excellence of administration and be willing to support measures to secure excellence in administration.

My hope and belief was that, as a result of public ownership of natural monopolies, we would have in the civil service an enlistment of a due proportion of the talent of the country, and that those in the civil service would have satisfactory monetary remuneration and would receive honor and consideration, just as justices of our Supreme Court do. I had it in mind that we would approximate the excellence of the civil service in Germany where those in the service received very moderate remuneration, but where they enjoyed security of tenure and where special excellence was honored by generous recognition of those in control of government.

The rulers of Germany were not, generally speaking, especially gifted—and I am speaking of things as they were before the World War—but they did show an interest and appreciation of faithful and meritorious service, and they rewarded excellence by awards of distinction. We are apt to laugh at medals and the various orders in European countries, but they are a real force. We must remember that the ancient Greeks exerted themselves and put their best powers into efforts to achieve a wreath of bay-leaves of no pecuniary value. We find in our own country, so far as we have established suitable methods for public recognition of merit, that they are a real force. Universities have long been in the habit of conferring honorary certificates for recognition of merit; agricultural colleges select annually a few farmers to whom they award certificates of no pecuniary value, but they are a real force in bringing about better farming.

Once when I was in Munich, Germany, I lived in the same

house as two very able students of the University of Munich. They were students in the faculty of law, and were taking their final examinations, which were very severe. In discussing their futures, they said that if they got sufficiently high grades and won distinction in their final examinations, they hoped for positions in the civil service, but that if they fell below what they hoped to reach in their examinations, then they would take service with banks or insurance companies. How far away are we from a sentiment of this kind! It was a question of high social esteem that they felt would be obtained in the civil service rather than in private employment.

Now when it comes to public ownership of natural monopolies in the United States, things have not turned out as I anticipated they would. The situation in Germany was different from ours in many ways. The permanent head of the civil service in Germany was a ruler, who had no interest in changing employees, but who magnified his office by establishing the best kind of a civil service and cultivating the right spirit among his civil employees. In fact, in earlier days he had a pecuniary interest in the excellence of the administration because his own income, in no small measure, depended upon the fostering of industries as well as the promotion of agriculture. He was more in the position of the head of a great corporation in this country than in the position of the President of the United States.

A generation or more ago we did establish civil service reform, and there has been a real improvement, but after all, the improvement has not been sufficient to attract and keep in the civil service a large part of the best talent of the country, or to give to those in the civil service all possible inducements to cultivate their powers and to put forth their best in the common service. Government becomes more and more significant in its economic aspects but there is not a corresponding general interest in public administration, and a corresponding increase in the comprehension of its significance. The great mass of the people are interested in games—baseball, movies, radio, and football. They devour articles on these subjects as well as on crime, but generally skip anything that relates to the administration of government—national, state or local, regarding it all as extremely dull.

Moreover, the condition of western New York which interested me, as well as my experiences in Germany, were something exceptional. Western New York is largely settled by New Englanders of a relatively high type of intelligence and character. Common ownership and operation of public utilities was something new and exceptional, and the community was small enough so that there could be a general appreciation of what was happening. In western New York today, I think there is a good deal less interest and pride in public ownership than there was thirty or forty years ago. It has become something commonplace, and people are not quite so sure as they were formerly that they are doing things which deserve general commendation.

However, there have been some notable instances of the success of public ownership in the United States.

On the Pacific Coast I had some interesting experiences, in connection with the Bureau of Light and Power of Los Angeles, which is municipally owned and administered. This bureau has been excellent. This has been largely due, however, to two older men to whom credit should be given for efficiency in the operation of the Bureau of Light and Power. To a certain extent, it was their own creation, their own child. I thought in my different contacts with this bureau that there was danger that the younger men and women in the service of the bureau might not have the same feeling of devotion to this great enterprise as the older men have who have devoted their lives to it. However, those in charge of the Bureau of Light and Power of Los Angeles have always tried to keep up the *esprit de corps* by establishing classes in economics, engineering and other subjects, so as to have trained employees, and to help them realize the significance of their own jobs. I took particular pleasure in addressing one of these classes several years ago. I tried to instill in them the spirit of service and a comprehension of the significance of their jobs. I tried to show them that they had jobs, but that they also had something more.

How all this will turn out, remains to be seen. I have pointed out a danger which has to be met if we are to have the right kind of public administration of publicly owned natural monopolies. The great mass of the people, even very intelligent people, have little sympathy with the idea of giving permanent tenure with advancement, and a higher position for those in the civil service. They still have the idea of office as more or less of a special favor—"a plum," to use a common expression.

After I had spent some time in Los-Angeles and vicinity, I went north to San Francisco and then to Portland and Seattle. In San Francisco there was a bad condition of public utilities— competition of private industry with public industry. One of the privately owned lines had not been very prosperous. It was said, and apparently with some grounds, that the owners of this line wanted to sell out to the city.

I found in Seattle that the street-car lines had been bought by the city and were being operated by the city. There was a fair degree of excellence in the administration of the car lines, but there was no prospect that this operation would prove remunerative. It appeared that the privately owned lines got out of a difficult situation.

There were two electric light plants in Seattle, one owned by the city and the other by a private company. According to my theory, there ought to have been a sentiment on the part of the citizens of Seattle in favor of the publicly owned plant. They should have felt that the publicly owned plant was their own and that they should therefore foster and encourage it. Apparently there was little, if any, feeling of this kind, even among the professors of the University of Washington, located in Seattle. I would have supposed that the professors of the university would respond to this sentiment. If they did not respond, what hope was there that others would respond?

In New York City today how many citizens take special pride in the Independent Subway and patronize that rather than the other lines? Among the riders perhaps one in twenty is especially concerned about the fact that he is riding on a muncipally owned line.

During the past thirty or forty years commissions have been established to regulate great natural monopolies which are privately owned. The purpose of these commissions is to regulate service in the general interest, and to see that rates are established which will give not more than a fair return—or we may say, a socially desirable return—for the investment of capital and enterprise. This has been the avowed aim of the Wisconsin Railroad Commission, the work of which I was well acquainted with. Their purpose is to establish rates high enough to attract the necessary capital into various industries to which these rates apply, but no higher. Now these commissions have not been entirely satisfactory. Many of them have been inefficient, and some of them have doubtless been corrupt and controlled by other interests than those of the general public. Nevertheless, these commissions have constantly improved and are improving. We have still a long way to travel to make them what they should be. It is obvious that the American people are determined, first of all, to try out the commission control of private industry, rather than public ownership. There are certain exceptions, to be sure, but in general this is the direction of American development.

The whole question seems to be extremely complex, and there is no easy solution of the problems involved. We have political interference of various sorts, whether under commission control or whether we have outright public ownership. And the occasional corrupt influence exerted by private industry upon the commissions is even more discouraging. Nevertheless, I am convinced that the task of making the commissions what they should be is a far easier task than that involved in direct ownership and operation by various public agencies of natural monopolies. This is evolution more in harmony with the history of conditions in our own country, and thus I have come around to changing my views. I have changed my mind in this changing world.

I am not disposed to fight public ownership, and so far as the Institute is concerned, my only desire is to bring forward impartially the facts, and then let the general public decide what it wants to do. I am always glad to see a case of successful municipal ownership like that of the Bureau of Light and Power of Los Angeles, and I deprecate unfair attacks of private interests upon municipal ownership; likewise I deprecate the still more unfair and distorted misrepresentations of private ownership of monopolies which proceed from partisan advocates of municipal ownership.

At the present time, however, big business has been cowed, and is in many cases an under dog. Big men in the business world are now often afraid to come forward boldly and assert their rights, even though they are undoubtedly at the same time in the social interest. The world has changed, and they are the true progressives who have changed their mind in this changing world. Those who hold tenaciously to views which were sound forty years ago are belated progressives. They think they are progressives, but they have not changed as the world has changed. They are dwelling in past times. I think in this connection of my former student, co-worker and dear friend, Dr. Albert Shaw, who stood shoulder to shoulder with me in my earlier attitude toward these monopolies, and who, with the changing mind in the changing world, still stands shoulder to shoulder with me. He is one of the true progressives, fighting for the right in the public interest, and stating facts, even if they should happen to be facts which seem to be favorable to big business.

Dr. Shaw wrote two or three books on municipal ownership in different foreign countries, and spoke highly of municipal ownership as found in various places in Europe. He gave true pictures and his books were stimulating and instructive. One of the foolish things done by some of those interested in private ownership was to send Hon. Robert P. Porter, former superintendent of the U. S. Census, to England, to write a partisan account to show the inaccuracy and misleading character of Dr. Shaw's books. Those interested in private ownership have done a great many foolish things that reacted against them. Fortunately, however, many big leaders among the railways and electric light and power concerns have shown that they have the changing mind in the changing world. Who can fail to think of men like President Willard of the Baltimore and Ohio Railroad, and Owen D. Young, among those interested in light and power? We have had in our Institute some financial help from these men and others like them, including George B. Cortelyou, and we have also had money from those who take a very different attitude in respect to public ownership. But money which comes to us must be free from any restrictions or limitations of any sort whatever. We have been told simply to state the facts, and the following is the sentiment of one of the leaders of the light and power industry who contributed to the Institute—"If there is something wrong with our methods, we want to know it. We must adjust ourselves sooner or later anyhow." This is simply long-headed business as well as good citizenship.

IS COMPETITION SELF-ANNIHILATING?

The industrial question which has overshadowed in importance all other questions is this: "Is industrial evolution naturally leading to the domination of substantially all the great fields of industry by monopoly?" Every thoughtful person, living through the period during which I have lived, must have had the feeling that discussions of monopoly have been vague and unsatisfactory. There can be no doubt that in economic literature, as well as in the periodical press, this one-word-sign, monopoly, has been made to stand for many different and more or less antagonistic ideas, and as a consequence, the controversies in which we have been engaged concerning monopoly have produced comparatively little action and even less light.

Undoubtedly the economists are quite largely responsible for the confusion of thought which has been introduced into the discussion of monopoly, for extending the term to cover related but quite different economic concepts they have departed from the best usage of the English language. The agitation of the so-called trust problem was active when I went to Wisconsin in 1892. It was the burning question of the day and all varieties of business were lumped together under the one term —monopoly. Every combination doing business on a large scale was almost sure to be called a monopoly, even though it was exposed to competition to such an extent that it was on the verge of bankruptcy. Unfortunately, it cannot be said that the discussions of the economic theorists were far in advance of popular discussion. The popular speeches on monopoly and the so-called scientific articles on combination brought forward one thought—"Competition is our salvation; competition is the life of trade; combinations prevent competition, consequently they are injurious and should be abolished." It was not generally realized that "competition is not always a good thing; competition does not always lower prices; competition is not always a possibility; competition has produced marvelous results in those pursuits which are adapted to competition, and the unwarranted conclusion—drawn from this fact that competition everywhere and at all times is a good thing." In attempting to force the application of the principles of competition to those pursuits which are not adapted to competition we do more harm than good. There are certain businesses which are in their very nature, by reason of their own inherent qualities—monopolies. These we call natural monopolies, and any endeavor to regulate natural and artificial monopolies by the same law is predestined to failure in the future, as it always has failed in the past.

Monopoly signifies unity. This is what the word has meant from time immemorial when employed by careful writers. We have monopoly in any line of business when we have unity of control over the products of that business. We have unity of control when all those who have services or commodities of a particular kind for sale have so bound themselves together that they act as one man. It is not necessary that we should have absolute unity; if we have what may be termed a substantial unity, that is enough. If a combination controlling 80 percent of the supply of a product is able to dictate one uniform policy for those outside the combination, then we have a true monopoly. Monopoly means "unified tactics with respect to price." "Monopoly means that substantial unity of action on the part of one or more persons engaged in some kind of business which gives exclusive control more particularly, although not solely, with respect to price." [44]

At the present time monopoly has a new significance, and

that for two reasons. The first is that it is incomparably more far reaching than in any previous age in the world's history, and the second is that its operations are so complicated, and so interwoven with our entire life that it is difficult for the plain citizen who is not a trained expert in economics to detect its presence and manifold ramifications. Even when the presence of monopoly is clearly perceived the highly complex character of our industrial civilization renders it difficult to apply remedies. The consumers of the country believe that monopoly exists and is expanding rapidly and it is their conviction that monopoly price must mean high price. Other producers tremble when they contemplate a billion dollar trust with which they must have relations. The wage-earner feels that isolated and alone, he is a pygmy, a nothing, when his individual interests are pitted against amalgamated hundreds of millions, and he is zealous in the formation of labor unions to prepare for conflict. When the citizen reflects, he feels that the potentialities of political power residing in a billion dollar trust are vague but certainly vast, perhaps illimitable. At bottom, protection is sought in the appeal to good will—to the benevolence of our industrial conquerors. What are the lessons of history? Does past experience teach us that we may place our hope for economic well-being wholly or in part in the benevolence of any class of men, even the most estimable? Or turning to the deductive argument, does our observation of human nature, even at the best, lead us to think this is a safe procedure? When we question ourselves, do we think we could stand such a test? Noteworthy and impressive in this connection is the following utterance of the late President Benjamin Harrison, "The man whose protection from wrong rests wholly upon the benevolence of another man or of a congress is a slave—a man without rights."

The desire for monopoly is about as old as the human race.

It could not be described better than it is in Isaiah v. 8: "Woe unto them that join house to house, that lay field to field, till there be no place, that they may be placed alone in the midst of the earth." We have admitted that a certain large portion of the industrial field is a monopoly field. The question still confronts us. Is competition self-annihilating? Is it self-annihilating through the entire industrial field? Here is the point at which the socialist separates from the non-socialist. It is the assumption of the socialist that in this respect there is no inherent difference between businesses ordinarily designated as natural monopolies and other businesses. They say simply that some lines develop more rapidly than others, and that some exhibit sooner than others the monopolistic character. To admit this is to admit the claim of socialism. But I do not believe we must admit this; for this reason I am not a socialist. I believe that we have superadded to the competitive field a new noncompetitive field. So far as we now see, we have a large field belonging to monopoly; but outside of this field we have another in which, under right conditions, competition is a permanent social force. I believe that the causes of competition are found in human nature and in the laws of the external physical universe. The essential truth has been philosophically stated by the late Professor Franklin H. Giddings of Columbia University: "That competition in some form is a permanent economic process is an implication of the conservation of energy. Given an aggregate of units of unequal energy, their unequal activity is an inevitable consequence. With the complexity of social environment that every quarter of the earth everywhere presents, and the limitless variations of heredity, a society composed of individuals of equal energy is an impossibility. Therefore when market competition seems to have been suppressed, we should inquire what has become of the forces by which it was generated. We should inquire further to what degree market competition actually is suppressed or converted into other forms, and within what limits combinations can hold together and act effectively. The combination equilibrium may be at best an unstable one." [45]

We can then never allow competition to cease. Combinations of labor and combinations of capital may expand freely, so long as these combinations mean merely association and co-operation. But when combinations mean monopoly, either competition must be restored or, where this is impossible, the ends of competition must be secured by other methods of social control; and if these methods of social control in some cases mean public ownership and management of industries, a place must be opened for the competitive principle in the terms of admission to public employment.

PROPERTY AND CONTRACT—THE FOUNDATION STONES

Competition rests on the basis of the existing legal and social order and therefore undergoes a process of evolution as the bases of the legal and social order evolve and change. But the element of rivalry must not be removed. Competition rests on a basis of property and contract, and certain laws and customs which regulate personal conditions; it changes as property and contract themselves are regulated and change with economic development.

In the course of my life-long search for fundamentals I spent many years studying property and contract. In 1911 it became clear to me that if I was ever to finish my *Property and Contract in their Relation to the Distribution of Wealth* I must get away from Wisconsin where my administrative duties absorbed too much of my time and strength. The University of Wisconsin very generously made it possible for me to go to Germany in that year, and also in 1912 and 1913. I went to Munich, and during the three years (1911–13) I spent perhaps two years away from the University. This enabled me to finish my *Property and Contract* which I regard, in many ways, as my most important work.

The book appeared in 1914, just a few weeks before the outbreak of the World War. At the start the sales were very satisfactory. The fate of the book, however, is a good illustration of luck and chance in human life. One or two favorable reviews appeared and, if I recall correctly, a good review appeared on the front page of *The New York Times*. The book, however, had not attracted public consciousness before the World War began. When the world was aflame, who cared for a book on property and contract? Considering the circumstances, it had, on the whole, a fair sale and I think it was reprinted several times. At the end of the World War in 1918, it was no longer a news item. It was impossible to revive the interest in this work that had been aroused when the book first appeared. Consequently, the book never attracted the general attention it otherwise might have had.

The manuscript of this book was read by Justice Oliver Wendell Holmes, always a good friend of mine. I recall a criticism he made of my style. I had a habit of saying "gotten," an old English form, where I should have used "got." When this expression is used instead of "got" it may lead to confusion. He related the following story to illustrate the confusion and misunderstanding that may thus be caused. An American had made arrangements to go to the theater with an English friend if he could get tickets for the show. He telegraphed to his English friend, "I have gotten tickets." The Englishman interpreted him to say, "I have got ten tickets." So he appeared with a party of friends, much to his friend's surprise.

I recall that the main criticism Justice Holmes made in his

notes on the margin of my manuscript, outside of those in respect to style, was in regard to endowments. The eighteenth century social philosophers had found fault with perpetual endowments because they perpetuated the ideas of their founders. I had something to say in favor of these endowments. Justice Holmes wrote in the margin, "I think you stand here on rather shaky ground." I believe, however, that I was right, although I freely acknowledge that there must be some social control of old endowments to fit them to new conditions.

I brought forth the view that property and contract were established and are maintained for social purposes and find their limitations in social welfare. I elaborated, and I think successfully, the social theory of property and the social theory of contract. I stood for both property and contract, but not as absolute categories. I maintained that there is no such thing as an absolute right of property or of contract, but that they are both flexible and must be modified to meet changes in economic conditions. What I said then was not new, but to some my contentions may have seemed radical. Now, however, my theories have been generally accepted by legal and economic theorists in this country.

But my theory of vested interests or rights has not been so generally accepted in this country and our ideas in regard to this are in a state of confusion. The following is the definition I gave of vested interests: "Strictly speaking, vested interests are economic interests which are legally recognized to be such that they cannot be impaired by public action, directly or indirectly, without indemnification."

Certain rights are acquired under the laws and customs that have prevailed in a particular country. These may be changed in the general social interests, but, when they are changed, those who suffer loss should be indemnified. Let us suppose, for example, that property in land, which has existed from time immemorial, was considered undesirable, and that public ownership, through the single tax or otherwise, was to be substituted for it. If it is accepted that private property in land ought to be abolished because public ownership is better calculated to promote social well-being, then the burden of the change should be socially borne. Those who have acquired private property in land should be indemnified. They should bear simply their share of any loss involved in the change which it was assumed was made in the public interest.

Let me give another illustration. Let us suppose it was decided that Mr. John D. Rockefeller's properties in oil and the facilities for reproducing, refining, etc., were to be taken out of private ownership and put into public ownership, for the good of the community. Now, according to our assumption, Mr. Rockefeller has acted according to the laws and customs of the country in acquiring his vast properties. He should, therefore, be paid a fair price for his properties. If he is a member of the community, as a taxpayer he will carry an appropriate share of the burden of this change. That is all that can be required of him.

This idea of vested rights has been extended by Mr. and Mrs. Sidney Webb, in their writings, to jobs, in which the worker should have a vested interest. On account of technological changes, the worker may lose his job. The changes, in the long run, may be in the general social interest and the community is wealthier on account of the change. But the displaced worker must eat from day to day, and the burden involved in the change should not be placed upon the shoulders of the worker. He must be taken care of somehow. One may take the familiar illustration of the stagecoach drivers and the owners of the stagecoach properties. When a shift took place to railway transport, this was a change in the general interest, but the burden of the change should not be placed on the persons affected thereby. Auguste Comte, something like a hundred years ago, elaborated this idea very satisfactorily.

An illustrative case may be found in the purchase of the Prussian railways by the Prussian state, in the late seventies of the last century. The owners of the private railways which had been purchased by the Prussian state were paid a fair price, and I think, no more than a fair price, for their properties. They were given to understand that if they would not accept a fair price, the state-owned railways would enter into disastrous competition with them. They took the fair price offered to them, which was paid by long term bonds.

On the other hand, the railway presidents who lost their jobs were indemnified. They were regarded as having a vested right. They had served in the capacity of presidents of the privately owned railways and, generally speaking, there was no place for them in the publicly owned railways, although there was a place for most of the workers. They were indemnified and given a fair remuneration for what they had given up.

England is regarded as the classical land of the vested interests. In England relatively rapid progress has taken place with less disturbance. In this country when we want to make some great change, as, for example, public ownership of railways and other public utilities, naturally those who stand to lose their all in the change are opposed to it. If they could be assured that they would have a vested interest and be properly indemnified, the opposition would not be so strong. From time to time a change may be proposed which would deprive a great many who hold office of their jobs. Naturally they will fight it and the opposition will become formidable. A man will fight for his job because he is fighting for his life and the life of his family. If, however, a man once has a permanent position in the civil service, he knows he is going to be taken care of. He can look at the change in a more fair-minded manner and he will be less hostile to it. We cry out against the opposition of government job-holders to changes which would deprive them of their livelihood and we talk scornfully of bureaucrats. Often we have done cruel and wicked things against those who have positions in the civil service. At times vast numbers have simply been thrown on the street without warning. It would be simply asking too much of human nature to expect that they should take a different attitude.

When I was in Munich in 1913 I found that so far as employment was concerned, there was no need to worry about a man who was regularly appointed in the civil service. He had a life-long job if he was faithful and did his work efficiently. There was very little unemployment in Munich in 1913. The private charities were largely Catholic and they worked together with the government and took care of the question of employment.

I think if we are going to have satisfactory progress in this country, we must go as far as the English have come and recognize vested interest. In my book on property and contract I contended for this idea of vested interests. All that has happened since then and especially what is happening now confirms the view that I then took. For example, turn to the T.V.A. at the present time. Private utilities cannot stand up against government competition any more than privately owned railways in Prussia could stand up against government competition a few generations ago. The owners of private property in business must accept the verdict whether it is for public ownership or for private ownership. They should, however, be paid a fair price for what they have—a fair price—neither more nor less.

CALVIN COOLIDGE AND THEODORE ROOSEVELT

My contacts with three presidents of the United States may have some significance in my autobiography. Elsewhere I have spoken at sufficient length about Wilson.

I first saw Coolidge when he was Governor of Massachusetts at the time of the police strike. My former student and friend, Professor Charles J. Bullock, took me to his office and brought me into contact with Mr. Stearns, his supporter who helped to make Calvin Coolidge President of the United States.

The only other time that I have a clear recollection of meeting President Coolidge was at a dinner given to him by Secretary of Agriculture Jardine. Each member of the cabinet traditionally gives the President a dinner once a year and this is the only time he is supposed to dine outside the White House. Secretary Jardine once invited me to his annual dinner to the President and of course I gladly accepted. At that time I was professor at the University of Wisconsin. The dinner was given at the Mayflower Hotel in Washington. Before the dinner the fifteen or twenty guests assembled in a large reception room in the vice-presidential suite. We gathered together in a semicircle at the end of the room, and awaited the coming of the President. We all hoped that Mrs. Coolidge would be present, but on account of some ailment she was not with us. The President finally appeared, wearing white kid gloves. Each one of us was presented to the President who kept on his white kid gloves while he shook hands with us. We were introduced in these words, "Mr. President, let me present to you Senator McNary, Professor Ely, etc." In each case he replied, "I am glad to see you." These were the only words I heard from his lips that evening. After this ceremony, we all filed out, led by the President, through a long hall to the dining room. The President sat down in the place which was obviously the seat of honor. I sat opposite him. The table was beautifully decorated by flowers; the dinner was excellent.

To the President's left was Mrs. Jardine, at his right was Mrs. McNary. Both these ladies were good talkers, and Mrs. Jardine soon tried to engage President Coolidge in conversation. I think finally she gave up in despair and threw down her hands, so to speak. Then Mrs. McNary attempted to engage the President in conversation. At last she gave up in despair, and threw down her hands. All this while the President stared straight ahead and said nothing.

After the dinner, the President led the way back to the room where we had first met him. Secretary Jardine ushered me to a seat on a sofa opposite the President. To make conversation he said jocosely, "Mr. President, here is Professor Ely, dean of American economists. If anything is wrong with the country it must be his fault." The President turned slightly towards me, a half smile playing around the left corner of his mouth, which opened and shut, but said nothing. This placed me in a very awkward position. It is the etiquette of the White House, as at the royal courts that the President must begin and end a conversation. If I had, at this point, begun a conversation, he would have thought me impertinent. He said nothing, I said nothing.

My friend French Strothers, long an editor of the *World's Work,* while he was a guest at the White House, wrote an article entitled, "A Week at the White House." A year later when he was again a guest at the White House, he wrote another article entitled "Coolidge a Year Later." He told me the following story about Coolidge. One evening, he, Mrs. Coolidge, and President Coolidge were in their private rooms. It was along about half-past nine or ten o'clock. President Coolidge was obviously half asleep. Strothers thought surely it was time for him to retire and he started to rise from his chair. Mrs. Coolidge beckoned for him to sit down, which he did. About a half hour later the President appeared so sleepy that my friend thought he would surely fall from his seat. He started to rise again, thinking that he certainly should leave at this point. Mrs. Coolidge again beckoned with her hand for him to sit down. At this moment President Coolidge roused himself and said, "You must not pop up until I do." There is no doubt that President Coolidge insisted on the observance of all the formalities due him.

I was once a guest at the palace of Queen Wilhelmina at The Hague. She was out of the city but her husband Prince Henry received me, along with the other guests. The master of ceremonies on that occasion had such perfect manners that he did not seem to have any at all. He came up to me and said, "Dr. Ely, the Prince wants to meet you." His tone and voice implied that for the past three years or so the one desire of the Prince had been to meet me, of whom he had obviously never heard. He escorted me to the Prince and beckoned me to sit at his right. After the formalities of the introduction were completed, the Prince began the conversation by asking me what I thought of the proceedings of the International Statistical Association which I was attending as a delegate from the United States. In the course of our conversation I remarked that I had been a student at Heidelberg where I had taken my doctoral degree. He then proceeded to carry on a conversation in German. Finally the master of ceremonies brought another guest up to see the Prince. The Prince extended his hand and we shook hands. That was the end of the conversation. He had begun and ended our talk. However, unless he had told me to go I would have had to stay and even if it were three o'clock in the morning and the Prince were fast asleep, I would not have been able to leave. This was the sort of etiquette which ruled at the White House during Coolidge's administration.

I cannot recall when I first met Theodore Roosevelt, but I saw him at the time I was bitterly attacked by the *Nation*. Coming out of the inner room of his office he hailed me with some such words as these, "Hello, Ely. Is the *Nation* still after you? No man can read the *Nation* and remain a gentleman."

He was always very encouraging and stimulating. Once before he was president, he was at my home in Madison, Wisconsin, for dinner. What a delightful guest he was! At that time I was very fond of sapsago cheese, which I spread very liberally on my bread. I recommended it to him. But Mrs. Ely said, "Mr. Roosevelt, be a little sparing in spreading that cheese on your bread, not everybody likes it as much as Professor Ely does." He tried some and then turned to my wife and said, "You have saved me from an awful experience." After dinner we went to Governor La Follette's house where he was having a reception. We had a delightful evening and La Follette and Roosevelt were very cordial to each other. During the course of the dinner he accidentally spilt a cup of coffee down Mrs. La Follette's dress, injuring her gown. He was profuse in his apologies but Mrs. La Follette passed it off with a jocose remark. He afterward said to Mrs. Ely, "Mrs. La Follette is an angel, she is an angel."

I must have had some influence on him through my student and friend, Dr. Albert W. Shaw. He was his adviser and an excellent one, far better than I could have been. I believe also that Roosevelt was familiar with my books and had been influenced by my writings. Long before he took up the conservation movement, I had been teaching conservation at Wisconsin and must have had some influence on his thought whether he fully realized it or not. I was to a certain extent a forerunner in the conservation movement and I must also mention in this connection Dr. E. J. James, later President of the University of Illinois, who was one of the pioneers in this movement.

If I recall correctly, the last time but one that I met President Roosevelt was at a banquet in Madison, Wisconsin. I did not sit at the speaker's table but at the next one. After the dinner, Vice-President Parkenson started to introduce me to Roosevelt. The President said, in the presence of all these people, "I know Dr. Ely. He first introduced me to radicalism in economics and then he made me sane in my radicalism."

MY BELIEF IN EQUALITY OF OPPORTUNITY

My belief in the importance of equality of opportunity has never wavered or changed. The struggle for equality of opportunity is what has made America great from the point of view of social philosophy. This struggle runs through our entire complex history like a red thread, giving it unity and explaining what is American as nothing else does. In the eighteenth century it was based on the philosophy of natural equality; later this philosophy was modified by the recognition of the existence of natural inequalities. Today we know that there are vast natural inequalities of native ability among men. Upon this knowledge is based the attitude which characterizes America at its best, the attitude expressed by the words, "Give him a chance."

Some years ago, Mr. von Bethmann-Hollweg, son of the old Chancellor, who is famous for his remark that the treaty with Belgium was merely a scrap of paper, visited me in my office in Chicago. We talked about many things and at last I said to him: "You have been in this country three months, you have traveled extensively, you are a keen observer, your impressions are vivid; tell me what is it that characterizes America above all other countries?" He replied quickly that what characterized America above all other countries could be summed up in the phrase, "Give him a chance." He did not speak about the speed of our life, our acceleration; he did not refer to America as a land of "unlimited possibilities"; the four little words, "Give him a chance" expressed his outstanding impression.

On its positive side this struggle for equality of opportunity expresses itself in a multitude of ways which aim at giving every individual a chance to develop all his powers, whatever they may be, to the fullest extent. We want every American to have an effective right to be provided with material goods for physical growth, to maintain his health and strength in a favorable environment. Our public-school system cannot be explained otherwise. Even now, in publicly supported colleges and universities, the struggle is going on to give those, who are qualified to benefit by it, the opportunity for research and scientific investigation. Every step forward in the history of public education has met with obstacles and those which have not been overcome are gradually yielding to the irresistible pressure for equality of opportunity. However, there still lingers on in our public-school system the idea that all men are born essentially equal, that they should all have the same kind of training. This is fallacious and socially injurious. Generally speaking an academic high school education is desirable but there are many who cannot profit by it. It has been said that "there is no greater inequality than equal treatment of unequals." George Washington did not believe in equality of powers. He thought that each should have an equal chance to develop what powers he had, so that our government might function as the makers of the constitution intended it should. In his farewell address he said, "Promote, then, as an object of primary importance, institutions for the general diffusion of knowledge. In proportion as the structure of a government gives force to public opinion, it is essential that public opinion should be enlightened." The makers of our constitution expressed their belief in equality of opportunity when they safeguarded, to all alike, the fundamental rights which are stated in the first ten amendments. No agency of the government may abrogate these rights.

On the negative side, this struggle for equal opportunity expresses itself in the determination to render adequate service for material goods that we receive. We are determined that men in our country shall no longer receive something for nothing because if they do so they abstract from the wealth produced that which should go for service. Through stock exchange manipulation, through dishonest manipulation of real estate, through unfair practices in merchandising, millions are given to those who have taken something for nothing. We are trying to reduce this amount to a minimum. Property which is inherited by passing from generation to generation includes a vast amount of surplus value. In 1891 I made the following plea for reform of the laws of inheritance: "Excessive wealth discourages exertion, but a suitable reform of the laws of inheritance will remove from us many idle persons who consume annually immense quantities of wealth, but contribute nothing to the support of the race, and who, leading idle lives, cultivate bad ideals and disseminate social poison. For the sake of the sons of the rich, as well as for the sake of the sons of the poor, we need a reform of the laws of inheritance. A reform of the laws of property will help us to approach that ideal condition in which the man who does not work shall not eat, and it will also tend to the equalization of opportunities so as to give all a fairer start in life, allowing each one to make such use of opportunities as his capacity and diligence permit, and thus rendering inequalities, economic and social, less odious and injurious, more stimulating and helpful." [46]

Many objected to my proposal to reform inheritance tax laws. They said, "You are proposing measures which impair the rights of private property." This is not a valid objection. The right of inheritance is one right and the right of private property is another and distinct right. The right of property means an exclusive right of control over a thing; the right of inheritance means the transfer of this right. The state or local political unit must be recognized as co-heir, entitled to share in all inheritances. A man is made what he is by family, town or local political circle which surrounds him and by the state in which he lives and by the nation. A tax on inheritance is the means whereby the claims of the town, state, and nation may secure recognition. No wise man wants to abolish the inheritance of property, but a great deal is being done, and more is going to be done, to bring under control the passage of property from generation to generation and thus to cut down very greatly the receipt of something for nothing.

In these ways we are trying to carry out the philosophy of equality of opportunity expressed in our Constitution. We must not run all the people through the same mill, educational or otherwise. We must give each one an opportunity for educational, spiritual, and religious training in accordance with the character and makeup of the individual. We provide opportunities and "give each his chance"—that is America.

UNTIL WE MEET AGAIN

Gentle Reader—I am not saying good-by. I have reserved these last few words in which to be more personal, in which to come closer to my reader. I am telling what is now happening and is to happen. Present and future are one. As I write, present becomes past. As I project the present into what I am doing it becomes the future. I have tried to look through the open window of life and tell you how the world seems to me as it goes by so swiftly. It is a long story measured in the years of a single life; it is an instant of time in human history. If what I have written is to some small degree entertaining, I am pleased. If it shall contribute a mite to making the world a bit happier and better, it is an answer to my father's daily prayer—and that is compensation for years of struggle, years mingled with sorrow and suffering.

I am living as my father admonished, "Live as if you were

to die tomorrow and work as if you were going to live indefinitely." So I plan ahead, D.V. The older generation, for the
sake of decency, if not piety, would use the letters D.V. I wonder if every young reader at once recognizes D.V. as "God
Willing."

I feel as if, so far, I have been guided by this Higher Power.
If I say "God" some may feel that I show myself to be hope-
lessly unscientific. Yet what arrogance to assume that God has
no place in human affairs! We are told that many scientists
have found no place for God in their researches. Why should
this disturb anyone? Why should it be expected that physics,
mathematics, logic, pure reason should ever reach anything beyond pure materialism, should even get so far as Matthew
Arnold's "a power outside of ourselves that makes for righteousness"? Belief in the "Higher Power" requires an act of faith.
Search the Scriptures—the Old and the New Testament alike.
Do you find a religious leader who lived and died for the world,
who has said a word that would warrant us in the belief or even
the hope that the processes of a Darwin or an Einstein could ever
find God? We enter into a different realm from that of natural
science when we would discover God. This is the realm of
faith. Take St. Paul, the most learned of the Apostles; did he
ever say "he knew"? He hoped, he saw, through a glass—darkly,
and yet for this faith he lived and died. It was and is foolish-
ness to the Greeks.

Do I believe in prayer? Do I believe in miracles? Again and
again in distress and despair, relief has come in strange ways
and differently from what I could have expected. The blind
man whose sight was restored, in reply to mockers said, "One
thing I know, that whereas I was blind, now I see." I knew
dire need and distress and help came, shall I say miraculously?
Once, when speaking to my cousin, Robert Erskine Ely of the
Town Hall, about a deliverance of this kind, I remarked, "My

Presbyterian father would have called it Providential." He replied, emphatically, "I, too, call it Providential."

It is gratifying to me to read the confession of religious faith of the late Michael Pupin, like myself a Columbia graduate and a Columbia fellow. He repeatedly speaks of events in his life as providential and even ascribes good fortune to the love of God. Speaking of his sorrow at the death of his mother he writes, "I soon found myself enjoying the warm personal friendships of German fellow students and of the professors and it was a very fortunate thing; it was providential. Nothing but the love of God and the friendship of man can give that spiritual power which one needs in moments of great sorrow." In explaining electricity, Pupin said that no electrical generator generates electricity because electricity is made by God. This is the final ultimate. In saying this he speaks as a child. Child and wise man come together. If we are to inherit the Kingdom of God we must come like little children with the kind of faith which made Pupin say "electricity is made by God."

Once, two or three years ago, after a luncheon at the Salmagundi Club, several in a group of which I was one fell to discussing the wonders we had seen in our lifetime—the telephone, the motor-car, the radio. The question was asked, "What marvels remain to thrill our little children?" The motor-car is no more to them than the horse and buggy to us when we were youngsters. The telephone is a mere matter of course—so is the radio. These are past. Someone suggested that suppose there are intelligent beings like us on the other planets, and we should be able to communicate with them; that would be a greater thrill than we have known. Then someone, equally daring, observed that if we learned to communicate with our loved ones who have taken that last journey, it would be for our children, a thrill beyond anything that we had known. Those in the group were business men, a trifle hard-boiled. They were certainly not sentimentalists. Were they absurd? Only those are absurd who affirm a negative. "The fool hath said in his heart, 'There is no God.'" Agnosticism may be logical, reasonable—the absolute negative not. I like to think that the commerce of saints is a reality, that we are surrounded by a crowd of witnesses, father, mother, etc., and that my mother who always found a way, by selling a painting or otherwise, to come to the rescue of her beloved first-born—has been and is still working seeming miracles for him. Many times my deliverance from a desperate situation did seem like a miracle.

When I returned from Germany and was tramping the streets of New York without a job, I looked from the bridge down to the railway tracks, and they suggested this only—suicide. But I struggled on and help came. I got a position as tutor to the children of a wealthy family and finally a job at the Johns Hopkins. Many times when the situation seemed desperate, help came from unexpected quarters.

One of the greatest thrills of my life was a substantial gift from a gentleman, entirely unknown to me, but whom my friend W. S. Kies interested in my work. When I met him with Mr. Kies, he made a pledge and when I began to thank him, he said it was a privilege. How this enriched my life! Another thrill came in March, 1938. It was an appointment from the trustees of Columbia University with the title, "Honorary Associate in Economics." This was due in some measure to Professor Allan Nevins, to whom I am indebted for many generous acts; but above all it was due to the man I am proud to call chief—President Nicholas Murray Butler. What daring to give me this call, like the daring of the only president I would like to compare him with, President D. C. Gilman!

I am not going to tell about my plans for the remote future, but I want to tell you something about what I am now working on. I want to complete my work on a biographical history of

American economic thought, on which I have been working for many years. The aim of this work is to explain how we think as we do in our economic affairs and relationships. This means something far more than a history of academic economics. Surely no professor of economics can have had the influence on our thinking of old Ben Franklin. Probably no professor of economics can have had the effect on our thoughts of my boyish hero, Horace Greeley. So I might continue mentioning statesmen and writers. But I cannot omit the influence on our thought of revolutionary inventions like mowing, reaping and harvesting machines. And will anyone presume to think he can understand our thought if he neglects Henry Ford and the motor-car. The acceleration in pace has been mental as well as physical. I also want to complete the research necessary to bring my work on monopoly up to date. I would like to gather a small group of about fifteen students to work with me and help me finish these projects.

THE FORWARD LOOK KEEPS ONE YOUNG IN SPIRIT

Almost from the beginning I have been a teacher of graduate students—only to a slight extent an undergraduate teacher. I have found that with undergraduate students it is hard to maintain the relation of association of equals. In most cases the youth of the teacher is too far away from the undergraduate mind for perfect understanding. But when it comes to teaching graduate students, men and women who have long been engaged in serious researches, I have felt that the difference in years melts away. My young friends and associates tell me they do not feel the difference of age. Together we have succeeded in keeping the feeling that we are all engaged in looking ahead. The young had something still to accomplish, the old enough to do to fill their lives. It is the forward look which keeps one young in spirit. About fifty years ago J. B. Clark asked me about my plans for the future. At that time I had mapped out a plan for my entire life which I showed him. I had planned more than any man could do in a hundred years. Today this plan mortifies me. I was embarrassed when my wife recently came across it. In connection with this I think of Professor W. F. Folwell, who at ninety-six had just finished a four volume history of the State of Minnesota, which historians say is a fine piece of work. A newspaper reporter came to see him on his ninety-sixth birthday and asked him, "Now professor—what next?" He said that he wanted to write a history of the regiment of which he was a member during the Civil War, a history of the University of Minnesota, of which he had been first president, and a treatise on economics. He probably realized how remote the possibility of accomplishing this was, but it was the forward look which kept him young in spirit. So, I too, look ahead and make my plans, D.V.

"Life is brief, but art is long, the emergency swift, the test deceptive, and judgment difficult."

* * *

I

Appendix

* * *

SUMMARY OF CATHOLIC ENCYCLICALS
by Right Reverend Msgr. John A. Ryan, D.D.

On May 15, 1891, Pope Leo XIII published an Encyclical which is sometimes designated "On the Condition of Labor," and sometimes *Rerum Novarum*. The first title describes the subject matter; the second is merely the opening words of the Latin version. Just forty years later, May 15, 1931, Pope Pius XI issued the Encyclical which is variously cited as On Reconstructing the Social Order, Forty Years After and *Quadragesimo Anno*. Of these designations, the first specifies the subject matter, the third comprises the first two words of the Encyclical, while the second is a translation of the third . . .

Probably the most significant topics treated in *Rerum Novarum* are: Property, the state, wages, and labor unions. Pope Leo discusses property in two places and from two points of view. Immediately after his introductory paragraphs, he enters upon an argument to prove that the remedy for economic evils offered by the socialists would be ineffective and morally wrong. To abolish private ownership of land and capital and to substitute collective or state ownership would injure instead of helping the working classes and bring about "complete confusion in the community." But this was only the negative aspect of Pope Leo's discussion of private property. More important and more enduring were his positive declarations. He did not content himself with a defense of private property as an institution. To him it was not a matter of indifference whether the actual ownership of capital goods was enjoyed by only a few persons or by many persons. On the contrary, he declared that property should be widely distributed and that the State should "induce as many as possible of the humbler classes to become owners." He emphasized the advantages of a society in which productive goods would be "more equitably divided," and the gulf between vast wealth and sheer poverty bridged over.

The second important subject treated by Pope Leo is the industrial functions of the state. On this matter, he lays down a radical and far-reaching principle. It is this: "Whenever the general interest, or any particular class, suffers or is threatened with injury which can in no other way be met or prevented, it is the duty of the public authority to intervene." This principle should be sufficiently comprehensive to satisfy the most progressive or the most advanced believers in state intervention, unless they happen to be socialists or communists. It would justify, and it does justify, all reasonable measures of protective labor legislation. It sanctions child labor laws, reduced hour laws, minimum wage laws, and legislation for insurance against sickness, old age, and unemployment. Almost as important as its comprehensiveness is the recognition which this principle gives to class legislation. "The richer classes," Pope Leo said, "have many ways of shielding themselves, and stand less in need of help from the State; whereas, the mass of the poor have no resources of their own to fall back upon, and must chiefly depend upon the assistance of the State. And it is for this reason that wage-earners, since they mostly belong to that class, should be specially cared for and protected by the Government."

Undoubtedly, the most important of all the doctrines proclaimed in the Encyclical is that concerning wages. Let us recall that when it appeared, the prevailing opinion, not only among employers but in the professional classes, in the halls of legislatures, and in the theories of economists, was that the wage contract fell under no other regulative principle than supply and demand. Outside of the working classes themselves, it was almost universally held that the wages fixed in the market by the forces of unlimited competition were always fair and just. No matter how low the remuneration of labor descended, it was ethically right if it was determined by a free contract. This immoral doctrine Pope Leo flatly repudiated. "There is," he declared, "a dictate of nature more imperious and more ancient than any bargain between man and man; namely, that the remuneration must be sufficient to support the wage-earner in reasonable and frugal comfort. If through necessity or fear of worse evil, the workman accepts harder conditions because an employer will give him no better, he is made the victim of force and *injustice.*"

Pope Leo had a great deal to say concerning the right to organize and the various kinds of associations. His most significant and important is the following: "We may lay it down as a general and lasting law that workmen's associations should be so organized and governed as to furnish the best and most suitable means for attaining what is aimed at, that is to say, for helping each individual member to better his condition to the utmost in body, mind and property." In other words, the great Pontiff of the Workingman distinguished between effective unions and hypocritical imitations.

After describing briefly the historical conditions which impelled Pope Leo to publish his *Rerum Novarum,* Pope Pius tells us that one of the things which he intends to do in *Quadragesimo Anno* is to vindicate, to develop, and to supplement the teaching of his great predecessor. Hence, the main doctrines of his Encyclical can be helpfully presented by summarizing what he has to say on the four topics dealt with above. It should be noted that both these Popes strongly and explicitly defend that principle that it is the right and the duty of the Church to deal authoritatively with social and economic problems insofar as they involve ethical principles and aspects.

Reaffirming Leo's declaration that the right of ownership comes from God, Pope Pius develops at some length the doctrine that property has two aspects, individual and social. While a person has a full and strict right to the thing that he owns, he may not use it as he pleases. His use of it is limited by obligations to his fellows and to the common good. When the obligations are not defined in detail by the natural law, they may properly be determined by the government, the public authority. Pius XI supplements Pope Leo's teaching on property by his declarations on the rights of capital and labor to the product of industry. He asserts very positively that neither of these agents may claim the whole of their joint product, but that each "must receive its due share."

What is the due share of each? Ever since the rise of modern industrialism, this question has intrigued and baffled the moralists no less than the economists. The answer given by Pope Pius is elementary in its simplicity and overwhelming in its conclusiveness. The product must be divided between capital and labor in such a way, he says, as to satisfy "the demands of the common good and social justice. . . ." Stating some of the implications of this formula in concrete terms, we may say that if an interest rate of two percent on capital is conducive to the common good, the capitalist will not have a right to more than two percent. If the common good will not permit the majority of workers to obtain more than decent living wages, that will be the full measure of their just claims upon the product.

The Holy Father gives specific approval to Leo's description of the authority, scope and functions of the state. Moreover, he applies the Catholic doctrine to certain conditions which have developed since the publication of *Rerum Novarum*. For example, he declares that the rulership of society which has been "usurped by the owners of wealth," belongs in fact to the state; that the state has a right to "specify more accurately what is licit and what is illicit for property owners in the use of their possessions," and that both free competition and economic domination should be "brought under the effective control of the public authority. ... ."

Certain declarations in *Quadragesimo Anno* fall partly under the head of the state and partly under the head of property. Pope Pius points out that since the time of Leo XIII great changes have taken place in the socialist movement. It has become divided into two parts; one even more extreme, if possible, than the socialism which Pope Leo condemned; the other showing various degrees of moderation. The former section is known as communism, and this Pope Pius condemns because it aims at "merciless class warfare and complete abolition of private ownership," even by means of violence. "The more moderate section" retains the name of socialism and mitigates both its advocacy of class warfare and its demand for the abolition of private property. If these changes are continued, says the Pope, it may well come about that the tenets of mitigated socialism will not differ from the Christian principles of social reform. "It is rightly contended," he says, "that certain forms of property must be reserved to the state, since they carry with them an opportunity of domination too great to be left to private individuals without injury to the community at large."

Just demands and desires of this kind contain nothing opposed to Christian truth, nor are they in any sense peculiar to socialism. Those, therefore, who look for nothing else, have no reason for becoming socialists.

Concerning wages, Pope Pius makes explicit that which is implicit in the teaching of his predecessor. "The wage paid to the working man must be sufficient for the support of himself and of his family." What kind or degree of support? It should amount to "ample sufficiency," says the Holy Father. How much is ample sufficiency? Enough "to meet adequately ordinary domestic needs." The wage should be sufficient to enable the workers "to bear the family burden with greater ease and security . . . to support life's changing fortunes, to acquire a certain moderate ownership . . . to have the reassuring confidence that when their lives are ended, some little provision will remain for those whom they leave behind them." If this measure of wage justice had been universally enforced in the United States during the so-called prosperous years of 1921–29, the depression which began in the latter years would not have been nearly so disastrous.

What Pope Pius has to say about the fourth important topic treated by Pope Leo can be stated very briefly. He quotes and confirms his predecessor's declaration that workingmen's associations should enable the members "to better their condition to the utmost in body, mind and property." Moreover, he condemns "the criminal injustice" of those governments which "denied the innate right of forming associations to those who needed them most for self-protection against oppression by the most powerful." Just as Pope Leo's pronouncement was an implicit rejection of the company union, so the words just quoted from Pope Pius contain an implicit censure of those rulers and legislators who fail to enforce and protect the natural right of the workers to form effective unions.

By far the most important part of *Quadragesimo Anno* is that which sets forth a program for the reorganization of industrial society. In the text of the Encyclical, this part has the same heading as the Encyclical itself; namely, "Reconstruction of the Social Order." "When we speak of the reform of the social order," says Pope Pius, "it is principally the state we have in mind." He calls for "the reestablishment of occupational groups." His choice of the word "reestablishment" instead of "establishment" shows that he is not proposing something entirely new. He is taking as a model that organization of industry known as the guild system. In that system, masters, journeymen and apprentices, were all united in one association. Of course, that arrangement could not be set up without change in our machine system, where the place of the associated master workman is occupied by the employing capitalist and the place of the associate journeyman by the propertyless employee. Nevertheless, the main principle and the spirit of the guilds could be adopted and adapted. Occupational groups could be organized, which in the words of Pope Pius "would bind men together, not according to the position which they occupy in the labor market, but according to the diverse functions which they exercise in society." In the railroad industry, for example, the owners, managers and employees, would be united with reference to the common social function which all these classes perform; namely, that of carrying goods and passengers in cars over steel rails.

Great as is the Holy Father's faith in the social order which he recommends, he declares that it will not succeed without a preliminary reform of ethical conduct and ethical standards. "If we examine matters diligently and thoroughly," he says, "we shall clearly perceive that this longed for social reconstruction must be preceded by a profound renewal of the Christian spirit, from which multitudes engaged in industry in every country have unhappily departed. Otherwise all our endeavors will be futile and our social edifice will be built not upon a rock but upon shifting sand."

* * *

II

Appendix

* * *

The Social Creed of the Churches—Statement adopted by the General Conference of the Methodist Episcopal Church—May, 1908.

The Methodist Episcopal Church stands:

For equal rights and complete justice for all men in all stations of life.

For the principle of conciliation and arbitration in industrial dissensions.

For the protection of the worker from dangerous machinery, occupational disease, injuries, and mortality.

For the abolition of child labor.

For such regulation of the conditions of labor for women as shall safeguard the physical and moral health of the community.

For the suppression of the "sweating system."

For the gradual and reasonable reduction of the hours of labor to the lowest practical point, with work for all; and for that degree of leisure for all which is the condition of the highest human life.

For a release from employment one day in seven.

For a living wage in every industry.

For the highest wage that each industry can afford, and for the most equitable division of the products in industry that can ultimately be devised.

For the recognition of the Golden Rule, and the mind of Christ as the supreme law of society and the sure remedy for all social ills.

* * *

III

Appendix

* * *

THE CONSTITUTION OF THE
SOCIETY FOR THE STUDY OF NATIONAL ECONOMY

It is the purpose of the Society for the Study of National Economy to promote the following ends:

1. To encourage the careful investigation and free discussion of the special problems of our national economy.

2. To secure the publication of economic monographs prepared by men whose special training for the work will ensure such a treatment of the subject as will be worthy of public attention.

3. To combat the widespread view that our economic problems will solve themselves, and that our laws and institutions which at present favor individual instead of collective action can promote the best utilization of our material resources and secure to each individual the highest development of all his faculties.

Believing that an organization of those who favor these objects will assist in promoting their growth and recognizing that a general unity of sentiment is necessary to a hearty cooperation, the Society has adopted the following platform to indicate its general attitude toward our social and economic problems.

I. The state is a positive factor in material production and has legitimate claims to a share of the product. The public interest can be best served by the state's appropriating and applying this share to promote public ends.

II. Sovereignty resides in the people and is one in its nature, whether exercised by a local or general government. The actual economic and social conditions of a country determine whether issues are of a local or national importance and whether, therefore a given function should be assigned to municipality, state, or nation. The constitutional distribution of powers should conform to that distribution most in harmony with the social and economic conditions of the country.

III. True economy in government affairs does not necessarily consist in a reduction of public revenues, but in such a distribution and administration of public expenditures as will in the most efficient manner promote public ends.

Good administration cannot be expected in a society where the people view the state as a merely negative factor in national life, and where, therefore, they attempt to remedy administrative evils by limiting government action instead of purifying and rendering efficient government service. Our own history proves that attempts to secure economy by diminishing public expenditure and to better legislation and administration by narrowing the scope of their action result in a marked deterioration in the character and ability of the men who make and administer our laws.

The true method of obtaining purity and economy in our administration is through the assumption of its proper functions by the state, since the consequent importance and dignity of government service would force public attention, attract the best class of citizens to the consideration of public affairs, and necessitate the greatest economy in administration.

IV. Our present educational system has failed to maintain that standard of intelligence and industrial efficiency below which no community can allow its members to fall without impairing the rights and endangering the welfare of other communities.

Its defects are owing partly to the selfishness and partly to the inability of local authorities. We are therefore compelled to look to the national government to protect the rights and interests of the whole against the shortsightedness and selfishness of the parts, and to supplement by national grants of money the efforts of each locality.

V. The present problems of our economy which arise from the increasing differentiation of the laboring and capitalist classes must be studied and solved with reference to the general interest of the community as opposed to the interest of either or both classes.

Public interest demands that the sanitary and industrial conditions of the laborer shall be such as will enable him to develop in himself and perpetuate in his family the qualities necessary to make him a desirable citizen of a great republic. Such conditions can only be realized when the laborer has an adequate compensation and such limitations of the hours of labor as will leave him opportunity for mental and moral growth and thus prevent him from sinking into a mere mechanism. The utilization of our material resources demands that the qualities upon which the accumulation of the capital depends shall be developed in every class of society. The growth of such qualities is hindered by existing laws, which favor that type of production on a large scale which can flourish only by combining large capital in a few hands with cheap and inefficient labor instead of that system which would naturally grow up in our national economy of smaller industries so distributed as best to utilize our material resources.

It is the duty of the state to enforce those measures which will assist in realizing all the conditions of a sound industrial system against both the greed of the capitalists and the shortsightedness of the laborer.

VI. The arbitrary discrimination of our transportation companies not only violates the acknowledged rights of individuals and communities, but also tends to develop an artificial organization of industry by which labor and capital are diverted from those points having natural advantages to such as are favored by the interest or caprice of great corporations. It is only by government intervention that these rights can be maintained against the encroachment of great corporations actuated only by private interest; and until they have been secured it will be impossible to develop a sound industry.

VII. The best development of our national resources demands that a certain proportion of the surface of the country be covered with forests; that a suitable rotation and variety of crops be observed; that the most approved machinery be applied; and that the best breeds of livestock be utilized. To attain these ends it is necessary that the land of the country shall be in the hands of a class of resident owners who possess capital enough of their own to equip the farms adequately and to develop their resources in the best manner. Our present system of land laws permits individuals and localities, led by motives of private interest, to reduce the amount of forest land below the proportion which it should bear to arable land. They favor the acquisition of the land either by a class of farmers so inadequately supplied with capital that the pressure of present indebtedness compels them to adopt a system of culture which, looking to present gains, exhausts the soil; or by a class of non-resident owners in whose interest that type of tenants is developed, who, with a low standard of life, can obtain from the soil the greatest return for the landlords. It is the duty of the state to insist that in every locality there shall be reserved for forests such a proportion of its area as the public welfare demands, and to change our present laws so as to favor the acquisition of the land by those whose interests in management will coincide with those of the public.

VIII. The vast extent of our territory and the great variety of our soil and climate clearly indicate that the prosperity of each section can be best promoted by developing its own peculiar resources and relying on other sections for those commodities in the production of which it is naturally at a disadvantage, while the increasing interdependence of all the parts of our industrial economy upon one another makes it impossible for the industries of one section to be developed to the highest extent except upon the basis of a similar development in those of every other section. It is therefore to the interest of each locality to favor a close economic union with other localities and to lend material aid in developing their resources. Among the most obvious methods of serving the common interests are the following:

1. The collection and dissemination of information in regard to national industries and the best manner of developing them.

2. A careful investigation of our mineral and agricultural resources by means of accurate surveys of the geology, flora, and fauna of our territory, so that we may best economize our mineral wealth, discover injurious animals and plants, prevent their propagation, and preserve and develop those which are likely to prove useful.

3. The establishment of experimental stations where new processes may be discovered and tested, new industries developed, and the relative value of different crops and breeds of animals may be determined.

4. The positive encouragement of the introduction of the best processes and the most suitable crops and livestock by the establishment of expositions and fairs, and by such bounties and exemptions as seem best calculated to secure the desired end.

While individuals and societies may contribute something toward these results, yet, owing to the haphazard character of their effort, no adequate assistance can be expected from them. It is, therefore, not only beneath the dignity of a great nation, but also contrary to its interests, to rely upon the charity of its individual members for the promotion of so necessary an end as the symmetrical development of its material resources.

* * *

IV

Appendix

* * *

QUOTATIONS FROM THE LAST WILL AND TESTAMENT OF WILLIAM FREEMAN VILAS

. . . first in importance among the purposes of this trust, provision shall be made for the maintenance and suitable equipment, one after another as means shall afford until ten such be established, of professorships of a special class to promote the advancement of knowledge.

Each professor of this class shall receive not less than five thousand dollars, nor more than ten thousand dollars, in yearly salary, as the trustees shall provide; and they may fix the salary of each irrespectively of the others, and may, when less than the maximum shall have been originally fixed—as will no doubt be the rule— increase the salary of any such professor, on the recommendation of the regents, at any time, or from time to time, until said limit shall be reached; but no salary, when fixed at any sum originally or by increase, shall be reduced while the same person holds the professorship, except upon his retirement. . . .

At the time of establishing each one of such professorships the trustees shall also provide, in addition to the professor's salary, a further annual sum of allowance, to be expended under his direction, to further proper auxiliaries to enable his due accomplishment of the ends proposed to him, which shall include personal assistants, such as clerks, stenographers, computers, mechanicians, laboratory employes, and whatever others, when requisite, and supplies of appropriate materials, implements, books, apparatus, specimens, and the like. In fixing such sum the trustees will look to the advice of the regents and consider the objects or nature of the line of investigation which such professor is assigned to pursue; but he ought to

300

be so liberally supplied, within reasonable bounds, that no hindrance or interruption of his work will become necessary, and the increase of knowledge may have the best favoring hope possible in the circumstances. And the trustees may increase, or may diminish the sum of allowance so provided, whenever and as often as it is deemed best, upon the request of the regent; or may, on like request, make special and limited appropriation from the available net income to aid any particular research or investigation, or to provide for the cost of any expedition or journey by any such professor, or any assistant, with all needful auxiliaries of persons and things.

Appointments may, if the regents so desire, be made provisionally on probation for one, two, or three years, or for successive years or periods not more than five years in all in probation, but after five years' continuous service, if satisfactory, any such professor shall have final appointment, or otherwise be dismissed from such professorship. And whenever a final appointment shall be given, whether after five years', or less probationary service, or with none, the professor so appointed shall not thereafter be removed, or be deprived of his right to pay after retirement hereinbefore given, except for good and sufficient cause duly proven at a fair hearing by the regents, or with the aid of a committee specially raised therefor, after due notice and opportunity to defend.

These professorships are designed to promote advancement of knowledge rather than to give instruction, and it shall forever be a limitation on the power to require service of any incumbent thereof that not more than three hours in one week, nor more than one hour in one day, shall be exacted of him for teaching, lecturing or other instruction to students, or otherwise, against either his objection or that of the trustees; any such service with assent of both being open. But the regents may determine the reasonable requirement of time to be employed in investigation, prescribe the subjects thereof, and the general line or course to be pursued; and the professorships shall be respectively designated, in summary phrase, accordingly; and they may be assigned to any college, school or department in the university, or stand independently, as the regents shall determine. Any branch of human learning may be selected as the subject of special study; but when the subject and general course of inquiry of any such professorship shall have been once determined and entered upon, they shall not be changed during the active service of any professor by retirement, or otherwise, the regents, when appointing a successor may prescribe any subjects or line of investigation anew; and the trustees may fix upon any sum of annual allowance, or a different salary within the prescribed limits; so that whatever shall then appear most desirable shall be available as upon original establishment.

The qualifications for such professorships being left to the wisdom of the regents, with opportunity for probationary service before a final appointment, and the power of retirement remaining in the regents, it is right and expedient to secure to incumbents with certainty beyond the risk of interruption the means of life in assured comfort, fixing upon their character and liberty the hope of beneficial service in imparting it to others that may serve to aid, rather than retard, the clarification and definition of results attained. Yet although so untrammelled by obligation to teach—which in proper instances the regents may not require at all, or only at convenient periods—and free to pursue his fixed lines of research in his own way, still it may be expected that, in fact, each such professor will gather about him as fellow workers and assistants, so far as may be, students who will both gain learning, and inspiration to promote it, from the participation in his pursuits and the opportunities of such association, which he will both desire and best know how to inculcate in them.

Due provision must be made for publication of the results of investigation by all such professors, either by the regents or the state; or, if found necessary and desirable the trustees may provide therefor from the available net annual income.

Suitable quarters or buildings for the work of such professors should be furnished by the regents; but, in necessity, the trustees possess needful authority, under a later article of this deed.

NOTE ON VILAS WILL

At the time of the Vilas will in 1902, salaries of five thousand dollars to ten thousand dollars seemed very high. At that time my salary at the University of Wisconsin was thirty-five hundred dollars, and few, if any professors received as much. Three thousand dollars was regarded as high and most received less. Twelve thousand dollar salaries, which are now being received by relatively few men at Harvard, Columbia, and the College of the City of New York, were a long way off. The cost of living in Madison was relatively low at the time. Salaries of fifteen thousand dollars to twenty-five thousand dollars now would be about the same as what Colonel Vilas contemplated. So far, no Vilas professorships have been established. I do not understand, however, that there has been any abandonment of the project. I am not in a position to make any authoritative statements, but it is my impression that the Vilas estate was not so large as Vilas anticipated. Also, the provisions made for Vilas' family had to take first place. Many of us figured at the time, that it would take one hundred years to carry out fully the purposes of Colonel Vilas. The trustees of the Vilas estate continue to function, and there has been no abandonment of the significant project.

* * *

Notes

* * *

Page 1

1. The tankard is now in the New York Metropolitan Museum of Art. The Curator is of the opinion that it is not of English origin but was made in America about 1680. However, its origin has never been definitely determined. See *The History of the Ely Reunion held at Lyme, Conn., 1878.* New York, Styles & Cash. pp. 46-50, 80-81.

Page 4

2. *The Ely Ancestry,* Collected by Moses S. Beach and Rev. William Ely, D.C., Edited and enlarged by G. B. Vanderpoel. The Calumet Press. New York, 1902. pp. xiv, xv.

Page 5

3. *Building and Loan Annals,* United States Building and Loan League, Chicago, 1936.

Page 7

4. Ellen E. Adams. *Tales of Early Fredonia.* The Fredonia Censor. Fredonia, 1931. p. 14.

Page 8

5. *Ibid.,* p. 16.

Page 11

6. *New York Times,* editorial.

Page 12

7. Adams, op. cit., pp. 35-37.

Page 13

8. *Ibid.,* p. 14.

Page 69

9. Selig Perlman. *A History of Trade Unionism in the United States.* The Macmillan Co., New York, 1929. p. 93.

Page 73

10. Richard T. Ely. *Social Aspects of Christianity,* new and enlarged edition. T. Y. Crowell. New York, 1889. pp. 147-148.

Page 77
11. *Ibid.,* p. 146.

Page 78
12. Richard T. Ely. "Fundamental Beliefs of My Social Philosophy." *Forum Magazine.* 1894.

Page 88
13. Richard T. Ely. *Social Law of Service.* Eaton & Mains. New York, 1896. pp. 127-128.

Page 91
14. Richard T. Ely. *Social Aspects of Christianity.* pp. 74-77.

Page 95
15. Richard T. Ely. *Socialism and Social Reform.* T. Y. Crowell. New York, 1894. p. 323.

My interest in education has been wide and varied. In 1920, with Professor E. A. Ross and other friends, I established the Washington School for Secretaries. This is somewhat outside the field of my usual activities, but it is one of the events of my life in which I take satisfaction.

Page 97
16. James Albert Woodburn. *A Noteworthy University Seminar in History: Reminiscences and Personalities.* Reprinted from the *Johns Hopkins Alumni Magazine.* Baltimore, 1932, Vol. 22, No. 2.

Page 98
17. Fabian Franklin. Article on Daniel Coit Gilman in *The Nation,* October 22, 1908.

Page 99
18. *Ibid.;* see also Fabian Franklin, *The Life of Daniel Coit Gilman.* Dodd, Mead. New York, 1910.

Page 101
19. *Seen by The Spectator*—Selection of Rambling Papers first printed in *The Outlook.* New York, 1902. p. 86.

Page 103
20. *Ibid.,* p. 96.

Page 109
21. Ray Stannard Baker. *Woodrow Wilson—Life and Letters.* Doubleday, Page. New York, 1927. Vol. I, p. 229.

Page 125
22. Letter from W. F. Folwell, in "American Economic Association, 1885–1909: An Historical Sketch," by Richard T. Ely. In *Proceedings* of the Twenty-Second Annual Meeting of the American Economic Association, 1909.

Page 126

23. Millicent Garett Fawcett. *Political Economy for Beginners.* Macmillan & Co., London, 1876. 4th Edition, p. 125.

24. Mrs. Marcet. *Conversations on Political Economy.* 1817. p. 418.

Page 127

25. Francis A. Walker. Opening Address, Third Annual Meeting of the American Economic Association. *Publications of the American Economic Association.* Vol. 4, pp. 254-255.

Page 128

26. A. L. Perry. *Elements of Political Economy.* Charles Scribners. New York, 1873. p. 202.

27. *Ibid.,* p. 211.

Page 130

28. Daniel Raymond. *Elements of Political Economy.* Baltimore, 1823. 2nd Edition. Vol. 2, p. 13.

Page 137

29. E. R. A. Seligman. "Discussion of the Platform at Saratoga." *Publications of the American Economic Association.* Vol. 1, No. 1.

30. Letter from Simon Patten, July 13, 1885.

Page 139

31. *Publications of the American Economic Association.* Vol. 1, No. 1.

Page 151

32. C. F. Dunbar. "Reaction in Political Economy," in *Economic Essays.* The Macmillan Co. New York, 1904. pp. 44-46.

Page 152

33. *Ibid.,* p. 47.

Page 157

34. John Stuart Mill. *Principles of Political Economy.* Edited by W. J. Ashley. Longmans, Green and Co., London, 1909. p. 300.

Page 179

35. Simon Newcomb. Review of the "Labor Movement in America," in *The Nation.* 1886.

Page 186

36. Richard T. Ely. "The Hoosier Economist: John R. Commons," in *People's Money,* Jan. 1936. p. 63.

Page 198

37. J. F. A. Pyre. *Wisconsin.* Oxford University Press. New York, 1920. p. 228.

Page 199

38. *Ibid.,* p. 230.

Page 201
39. *Ibid.*, p. 332.
Page 202
40. *Ibid.*, p. 253.
Page 252
41. Richard T. Ely. "Fundamental Beliefs of My Social Philosophy."
The Forum. 1894.
Page 256
42. T. R. Malthus. *Inquiry into the Nature of Rent.* London, 1815.
p. 20.
43. Francis A. Walker. *Land and its Rent.* Little, Brown & Co.
Boston, 1883. Preface.
Page 266
44. Richard T. Ely and Ralph H. Hess. *Outlines of Economics.* The
Macmillan Co. New York, 1937. 6th Edition. p. 621.
Page 269
45. F. H. Giddings. "The Modern Distributive Process." Reprinted
from *Political Science Quarterly.* p. 22.
Page 281
46. Richard T. Ely. "The Inheritance of Property." *The North
American Review.* 1891.

* * *

Chronological Bibliography

* * *

1880

"Germany and Russia," in *New York Evening Post*.
"American Colleges and German Universities," in *Harper's Monthly*.
"Emigrations from Germany," in *New York Tribune*.
"Railroads in Germany," in Papers Relating to Foreign Relations of the United States (Washington: Gov't Printing Office).

1881

"Money and Its Functions," in *Bankers Magazine*.
"The Beer Tax, the Assurance of Workmen and the Tobacco Monopoly," in *International Review*.

1882

"Our Common Schools," in *Lippincott's*.
"Bismarck's Plan for Insuring German Laborers," in *International Review*.
"School and Post Office Savings Banks," in *Our Continent*.
"Professional Socialism," in *Christian Union*.
"Johns Hopkins University," in *Christian Union*.

1883

French and German Socialism in Modern Times (New York: Harper).

1884

Recent American Socialism (Baltimore: The Johns Hopkins University).
The Past and Present of Political Economy (Baltimore: The Johns Hopkins University).

"Baltimore & Ohio Relief Association," in *Harper's Monthly*.

"Celebration of Thanksgiving by the Socialists of Chicago," in *Christian Union*.

"Administration," in *Christian Union*.

1885

Methods of Teaching History, with A. D. White, W. F. Allen, C. K. Adams, J. W. Burgess and others (Boston: Ginn, Heath).

1886

The Labor Movement in America (New York: T. Y. Crowell).

Report of the Tax Commission of Baltimore (Baltimore: King Bros.).

Report of the Organization of the American Economic Association (Baltimore: J. Murphy Co.).

"The Economic Discussion in Science," in *Science Economic Discussion* (New York: The Science Co.).

"Commerce and Its Growth in Modern Times," in Gately's *World Progress*, edited by C. E. Beale (Boston: Gately).

Introduction to Barns, W. E., *The Labor Problem* (New York: Harper).

1888

Problems of Today (New York: T. Y. Crowell).

Taxation in American States and Cities, assisted by John H. Finley (New York: T. Y. Crowell).

Report of the Maryland Tax Commission (Baltimore: King Bros.).

"The Tariff and Trusts—Expenditures for Internal Improvements," in *The National Revenues*, ed. by Albert Shaw (Chicago: McClurg).

1889

Social Aspects of Christianity (New York: T. Y. Crowell).

An Introduction to Political Economy (New York: Chautauqua Press).

Natural Monopolies and Local Taxation: reprint of an address delivered before the Boston Merchants Association (New York: Robinson & Stephenson).

The Needs of the City: reprint of an address delivered before the Boston Conference of the Evangelical Alliance, Boston.

1890

"Slums," with Seth Low, in *Century Magazine*.
"Land, Labor and Taxation," in *Independent*.

1891

"Corporations," in *North American Review*.
"Pauperism," in *North American Review*.

1893

Outlines of Economics (New York: Hunt & Eaton).
The Universities and the Churches: reprint of address delivered at
    Thirty-first Convocation, Senate Chamber, Albany.
"Socialism," in *Harper's Monthly*.
Editor of *Repudiation of State Debts in the United States*, by William
    A. Scott (New York: T. Y. Crowell).

1894

*Socialism: An Examination of Its Nature, Its Strength and Its Weak-
    ness* (New York: T. Y. Crowell).
"Fundamental Beliefs of My Social Philosophy," in *Forum*.
"On Natural Monopolies and the Workingman in America," in
    North American Review.
Editor of *American Charities*, by Amos G. Warner (New York:
    T. Y. Crowell).

1895

"Future Organization of Higher Education in the United States," in
    Addresses and Proceedings of National Education Association,
    Denver.
"State Universities," in *Cosmopolitan Magazine*.
"Government Control of the Telegraph," in *Arena*.
Introduction to Fremantle, W., *The World as the Subject of Redemp-
    tion*, 2nd ed. (Oxford: Oxford Univ. Press).
Editor of:
    Punishment and Reformation, by F. H. Wines (New York: T. Y.
        Crowell).
    Social Theory, by John Bascom (New York: T. Y. Crowell).

1896

The Social Law of Service (New York: Eaton & Mains).
Editor of:
  Proportional Representation, by John R. Commons (New York:
    T. Y. Crowell).
  State Railroad Control, by Frank H. Dixon (New York: Crowell).
  Southern Side Lights, by Edward Ingle (New York: Crowell).
  *Taxation and Taxes in the United States Under the International
    Revenue System,* by Frederic C. Howe (New York: Crowell).
  *An Essay on the Present Distribution of Wealth in the United
    States,* by Charles B. Spahr (New York: Crowell).

1897

"Adam Smith" and "John Stuart Mill," in *Library of the World's
  Best Literature* (New York: Peale & Hill).
Religion as a Social Force: reprint of address delivered before Edu-
  cational Congress of World's Fair, St. Louis.
Editor of *Southern Statesmen of the Old Regime,* by William P.
  Trent (New York: Crowell).

1898

"Fraternalism *vs.* Paternalism in Government," in *Century Magazine.*
"Money," in *Progress.*
Editor of:
  *Political Economy, Political Science and Sociology: A Practical and
    Scientific Presentation of Social and Economic Subjects* (Chi-
    cago: The University Assoc.).
  Workingmen's Insurance, by W. F. Willoughby (New York:
    Crowell).
  Congressional Committees, by Lauros S. McConachie (New York:
    Crowell).

1899

The Strength and Weakness of Socialism (New York: Chautauqua
  Press).
Senior's Theory of Monopoly: reprint of paper read before Amer.
  Economic Assoc., Dec. 27, 1899.
"A Decade in Economic Theory," in *Annals of American Academy.*

"The Progress of Socialism Since 1893," in *Chautauquan*.
Editor of *Municipal Monopolies*, by E. W. Bemis (New York: Crowell).

1900

Monopolies and Trusts (New York: Macmillan).
"Competition: Its Nature, Its Permanency and Its Beneficence," in *American Economic Review Supplement*.
"Economics in Secondary Education," in *Educational Review*.
"A Decade of Economic Theory," in *Annals of American Academy*.
"The Nature and Significance of Monopolies and Trusts," in *International Journal of Ethics*.
"Socialistic Propaganda," with Thomas K. Urdahl, in *Chautauquan*.
Editor of:
> *The Economics of Distribution*, by John A. Hobson (New York: Macmillan).
> *World Politics*, by Paul S. Reinsch (New York: Macmillan).
> *Economic Crises*, by Edward D. Jones (New York: Macmillan).
> *Government in Switzerland*, by John M. Vincent (New York: Macmillan).
> *Essays on the Monetary History of the United States*, by Charles J. Bullock (New York: Macmillan).
> *History of Political Parties in the United States, 1846–1861*, by Jesse Macy (New York: Macmillan).

1901

"Public Control of Private Corporations," in *Cosmopolitan Magazine*.
"Reforms in Taxation," in *Cosmopolitan Magazine*.
"Social Progress," in *Cosmopolitan Magazine*.
"Herbert Baxter Adams," in *Review of Reviews*.
"Advantages of Public Ownership and Management of Natural Monopolies," in *Cosmopolitan Magazine*.
"Industrial Liberty," in *American Economic Review Supplement*.
"Municipal Ownership of Natural Monopolies," in *North American Review*.
"Analysis of the Steel Trust," in *Cosmopolitan Magazine*.
"Trusteeship of Literature," in *Library Journal*.

Editor of:
Monopolies Past and Present, by James E. LeRossignol (New York: Crowell).
The French Revolution and Modern French Socialism, by Jessica B. Peixotte (New York: Crowell).

1902

The Coming City (New York: Crowell).
"An American Industrial Experiment," in *Harper's Monthly.*
"Amana: A Study of Religious Communism," in *Harper's Monthly.*
"Ethical Aspects of Ownership," in *Cosmopolitan Magazine.*
A Sketch of the Life and Services of Herbert B. Adams: reprint of an address in *H. B. Adams: Tributes of Friends* (Baltimore: Johns Hopkins Univ. Press).
"The Report of the American Industrial Commission on Labor," in *Yale Review.*
Editor of:
Irrigation in the United States, by F. H. Newell (New York: Crowell).
Economics of Forestry, by E. B. Fernow (New York: Crowell).
Municipal Engineering and Sanitation, by M. N. Baker (New York: Macmillan).
Democracy and Social Ethics, by Jane Addams (New York: Macmillan).
American Municipal Progress, by Charles Zueblin (New York: Macmillan).
Colonial Government, by Paul S. Reinsch (New York: Macmillan).

1903

Studies in the Evolution of Industrial Society (New York: Macmillan).
"A Study of a Decreed Town," in *Harper's Monthly.*
"Economic Aspects of Mormonism," in *Harper's Monthly.*
Editor of:
Irrigation Institutions, by Ellwood Mead (New York: Macmillan).
Railway Legislation in the United States, by B. H. Meyer (New York: Macmillan).

History of American Political Theories, by C. E. Merriam (New York: Macmillan).

1904

Elementary Principles of Economics, with George Ray Wicker (New York: Macmillan).
Editor of *The American City*, by Delos F. Wilcox (New York: Macmillan).

1905

"Psychical Forces of Industry," in *International Magazine*.
Editor of:
  The Foundations of Sociology, by Edward A. Ross (New York: Macmillan).
  The Elements of Sociology, by Frank W. Blackmar (New York: Macmillan).
  Colonial Administration, by Paul S. Reinsch (New York: Macmillan).
  Introduction to the Study of Agricultural Economics, by Henry C. Taylor (New York: Macmillan).
  Some Ethical Gains Through Legislation, by Florence Kelley (New York: Macmillan).

1906

Editor of *Introduction to Business Organization*, by S. E. Sparling (New York: Macmillan).

1907

Editor of:
  Newer Ideals of Peace, by Jane Addams (New York: Macmillan).
  Spirit of American Government, by J. A. Smith (New York: Macmillan).
  International Commercial Policies, by George M. Fisk and Paul S. Pierce (New York: Macmillan).

1908

Outlines of Economics, revised by author and T. S. Adams, M. Lorenz and A. A. Young (New York: Macmillan).

Editor of:

Education and Industrial Evolution, by Frank Tracy Carlton (New York: Macmillan).

Principles of Anthropology and Sociology in Their Relation to Criminal Procedure, by Maurice Parmelee (New York: Macmillan).

1909

The Fundamental Principles of Cooperation (Minneapolis: Right Relations League).

1910

"William Graham Sumner," in *Yale Review.*

Preface to *A Documentary History of American Industrial Society,* edited by John R. Commons and others (Cleveland: A. H. Clark Co.).

Editor of:

Child Problems, by George B. Mangold (New York: Macmillan).

Wage-Earning Women, by Annie M. McLean (New York: Macmillan).

1911

Editor of:

Commission Government in American Cities, by E. S. Bradford (New York: Macmillan).

History of Economic Thought, by Lewis H. Haney (New York: Macmillan).

1912

Editor of *Social Control,* by Edward A. Ross (New York: Macmillan).

1913

"Ulm on the Danube," in *Survey.*

Editor of *Business Organization and Combination,* by Lewis H. Haney (New York: Macmillan).

1914

Property and Contract in Their Relations to the Distribution of Wealth (New York: Macmillan).

Editor of *Problems of Child Welfare,* by George B. Mangold (New York: Macmillan).

1915

"Progressivism True and False," in *Review of Reviews.*

Introduction to Ingram, John K., *History of Political Economy,* revised ed. (London: A. & C. Black).

Editor of:

The Progressive Movement, by Benjamin P. De Witt (New York: Macmillan).

The Wealth and Income of the People of the United States, by W. I. King (New York: Macmillan).

Outlines of Sociology, by John Lewis Gillin and F. W. Blackmar (New York: Macmillan).

The New American Government and Its Work, by James T. Young (New York: Macmillan).

Comparative Free Government, by Jesse Macy and John W. Gannaway (New York: Macmillan).

1916

Outlines of Economics, 3rd rev. ed. (New York: Macmillan).

"Russian Land Reforms," in *American Economic Review.*

Editor of *Social Problems,* by Ezra T. Towne (New York: Macmillan).

1917

The Foundations of National Prosperity: Studies in the Conservation of Permanent National Resources, with Ralph H. Hess, Charles K. Leith and Thomas Nixon Carver (New York: Macmillan).

"Landed Property as an Economic Concept and as a Field of Research," in *Economic Review Supplement.*

"Conservation and Economic Theory," in *Pan American Scientific Congress 3d* (Washington).

1918

The World War and Leadership in a Democracy (New York: Macmillan).

Elementary Principles of Economics (revised), with George Ray Wicker (New York: Macmillan).

"Private Colonization of the Land," in *American Economic Review.*
Editor of:
   Budget Making in a Democracy, by Major Edward C. Fitzpatrick
   (New York: Macmillan).
   Applied Eugenics, by Paul Popenoe and Roswell H. Johnson
   (New York: Macmillan).

1919

"Tenancy in an Ideal System of Land Ownership," with Charles J.
   Galpin, in *American Economic Review Supplement.*
Editor of:
   The Vision for Which We Fought, by A. M. Simons (New York:
   Macmillan).
   City Manager in Dayton, by Chester E. Rightor (New York:
   Macmillan).
   Outlines of Agricultural Economics, by Henry C. Taylor (New
   York: Macmillan).
   The Labor Market, by D. D. Lescohier (New York: Macmillan).

1920

"What is Bolshevism?" in *Review of Reviews.*
"An American Land Policy," in *America and the New Era,* by E. M.
   Friedman (New York: Dutton).
Editor of *The Social Problem,* by Charles A. Ellwood (New York:
   Macmillan).

1921

Editor of:
   International Commercial Policies, by G. M. Fisk (New York:
   Macmillan).
   The Marketing of Whole Milk, by Henry E. Erdman (New York:
   Macmillan).
   Popular Government, by Arnold Bennett Hall (New York: Mac-
   millan).
   The Non-Partisan League, by Andrew A. Bruce (New York:
   Macmillan).

1922

Outlines of Land Economics, assisted by Mary L. Shine and George
   S. Wehrwein—4 vols. (Ann Arbor, Mich.: Edwards Bros.).

"The Price of Progress," in *Journal of Business Analysis and Control.*
Editor of:
The Law of City Planning and Zoning, by Frank B. Williams
(New York: Macmillan).
Efficient Marketing for Agriculture, by Theodore Macklin (New York: Macmillan).
The Little Country Theatre, by A. S. Arnold (New York: Macmillan).
History of Trade Unionism in the United States, by Selig Perlman (New York: Macmillan).

1923

Elementary Principles of Economics, 3rd ed. rev., with Samuel J. Brandenburg (New York: Macmillan).
Outlines of Economics, 4th rev. ed., with Thomas S. Adams, Max O. Lorenz and Allyn A. Young (New York: Macmillan).
"Building and Loan Associations," in *Review of Reviews.*
"Recollections of the Life and Work of Simon N. Patten," in *American Economic Review.*
Editor of *Principles of Real Estate Practice,* by Ernest M. Fisher (New York: Macmillan).

1924

Elements of Land Economics, with Edward W. Morehouse (New York: Macmillan).
Taxation of Farm Lands: reprint of address before Tri-State Development Congress in Duluth, Minn., Jan., 1924.
"A Vision of Real Estate Education in the Future," in *School Life.*
Editor of:
The Appraisal of Real Estate, by Frederick M. Babcock (New York: Macmillan).
A History of Public Land Policies, by Benjamin H. Hibbard (New York: Macmillan).
Workmen's Compensation, by E. H. Downey (New York: Macmillan).
Introduction to Agricultural Economics, by L. C. Gray (New York: Macmillan).

The American Judge, by Andrew A. Bruce (New York: Macmillan).
The Economy of Human Energy, by Thomas N. Carver (New York: Macmillan).

1925

Editor of:
Elements of the Modern Building and Loan Association, by Horace F. Clark and Frank Chase (New York: Macmillan).
Real Estate Advertising, by Ward C. Gifford (New York: Macmillan).
The Administration of Real Estate Boards, by Herbert U. Nelson (New York: Macmillan).

1926

Elementary Principles of Economics, 4th rev. ed. (New York: Macmillan).
"Farm Relief and Flood Control," in *Review of Reviews.*
"Land Economics," in *American Economic Review.*
"America the Land of Joy," in *Review of Reviews.*
Editor of:
Land Planning in the United States for City, State and Nation, by Harlean James (New York: Macmillan).
General Social Science, by Ross L. Finney (New York: Macmillan).

1927

"The Place of Research in Graduate Training," in *Proceedings of the Northwestern University Conference on Business Education.*
"Economics," in *Teaching of the Social Studies,* by E. Dawson (New York: Macmillan).
Editor of *The Principles of Real Estate Law,* by Nathan William MacChesney (New York: Macmillan).

1928

Land Economics, with G. S. Wehrwein (Ann Arbor: Edwards Bros.).
Die Wirtschafts-Theorie der Gegenwart: Kosten und Einkommen bei der Bodenverwertung (Vienna: Julius Springer).

"Land Income," in *Political Science Quarterly*.
Editor of *Urban Land Economics*, by Herbert B. Dorau and Albert S. Hinman (New York: Macmillan).

1929

"The Practical Approach to the World," in *The World Man Lives In*, by Bertrand Russell, M. C. Otto, D. T. Howard and others (New York: Van Nostrand).
"The New Economic World and the New Economics," in *Journal of Land and Public Utility Economics*.
"Distribution as an Economic Problem," in *Supplementary Readings in Economics*, by R. C. Epstein (New York: Harper).
Editor of:
  Roadside Development, by J. M. Bennett (New York: Macmillan).
  The Tax Situation in Illinois, by Herbert D. Simpson (Chicago: Institute for Economic Research).
  The Changing Character and Extent of Municipal Ownership in the Electric Light and Power Industry, by Herbert B. Dorau (Chicago: Institute for Economic Research).
  The Philadelphia Plan of Home Financing, by William N. Loucks (Chicago: Institute for Economic Research).

1930

Outlines of Economics, 5th rev. ed. (New York: Macmillan).
"Taxing Land Value and Taxing Building Value," in *Annals of American Academy*.
Scientific Research in Public Finance and Taxation and the Practical Application of Its Results, with H. D. Simpson: reprint of discussion before a meeting of Northwestern University Associates, Union League Club, Chicago.
"Land Planning and Education," in *Journal of Educational Sociology*.
Editor of:
  Advanced Principles of Real Estate Practice, by Ernest M. Fisher (New York: Macmillan).
  Tax Racket and Tax Reform in Chicago, by Herbert D. Simpson (Chicago: Institute for Economic Research).
  Forces Affecting Municipally Owned Electric Plants in Wisconsin, by E. O. Mallott (Chicago: Institute for Economic Research).

Economic Factors in Paved Track Design and Construction, by
Paul J. Raver (Chicago: Institute for Economic Research).
Financial Aspects of Subdivision Development, by Adrian D.
Theobald (Chicago: Institute for Economic Research).
Outlines of Public Utility Economics, by Martin Glaeser (New
York: Macmillan).
Materials for the Study of Public Utility Economics, by Herbert
Dorau (New York: Macmillan).

1931

Hard Times: The Way In and the Way Out (New York: Mac-
millan).
"Government in Business and the General Welfare," in *Review of
Reviews.*
Editor of:
   Valuation of Vacant Land in Suburban Areas, by Herbert D.
   Simpson (New York: Institute for Economic Research).
   *State, Constitutional and Statutory Law Affecting Municipal Own-
   ership of Public Utilities:* A Wall Chart (New York: Institute
   for Economic Research).
   *Apartment House Increases and Attitudes Toward Home Owner-
   ship,* by Coleman Woodbury (New York: Institute for Eco-
   nomic Research).
   *Population Growth and Its Demand Upon Land for Housing in
   Evanston, Illinois,* by Albert S. Hinman (New York: Institute
   for Economic Research).

1932

"Depression and the 150 Year Plan," in *American Economic Review.*
"Is Prosperity Returning?" in *Town Crier.*
"Our Foreign Debts," in *Town Crier.*
"Economic Factors Underlying Housing and Experience of Limited
   Dividend Companies," Report of President's Conference on
   Home Building and Home Ownership, Vol. III (Washington,
   D.C.).
Editor of:
   Rent Liens and Public Welfare, by Clarence J. Foreman (New
   York: Macmillan).

Effects of Property Tax Offset Under an Income Tax, by Herbert
D. Simpson (New York: Institute for Economic Research).
Municipally Owned Electric Utilities in Nebraska, by Paul J.
Raver and Marion R. Sumner (New York: Institute for Eco-
nomic Research).

1933
"Increasing Public Expenditures," in *Town Crier.*
"Karl Marx and Technocracy," in *Town Crier.*
"In the Short Run," in *Town Crier.*
"World Trade and World Peace," in *Town Crier.*
Editor of *An Outline of Advertising,* by G. B. Hotchkiss (New
York: Macmillan).

1934
"Recovery Program for a State," in *Review of Reviews.*
Editor of *Foreclosures of Property in Manhattan, 1928–1934,* by
John Burton (New York: Institute for Economic Research).

1935
The Great Change, with Frank Bohn (New York: Nelson).

1936
"The Founding and Early History of the American Economic Asso-
ciation," in *American Economic Review Supplement.*
"Land Underlies All," in *Christian Science Monitor.*

1937
Outlines of Economics, with Ralph H. Hess, 6th rev. ed. (New
York: Macmillan).

* * *

Index

* * *

325

The Academic Profession

An Arno Press Collection

Annan, Noel Gilroy. **Leslie Stephen: His Thought and Character in Relation to His Time.** 1952

Armytage, W. H. G. **Civic Universities: Aspects of a British Tradition.** 1955

Berdahl, Robert O. **British Universities and the State.** 1959

Bleuel, Hans Peter. **Deutschlands Bekenner** (German Men of Knowledge). 1968

Bowman, Claude Charleton. **The College Professor in America.** 1938

Busch, Alexander. **Die Geschichte des Privatdozenten** (History of Privat-Docentens). 1959

Caplow, Theodore and Reece J. McGee. **The Academic Marketplace.** 1958

Carnegie Foundation for the Advancement of Teaching. **The Financial Status of the Professor in America and in Germany.** 1908

Cattell, J. McKeen. **University Control.** 1913

Cheyney, Edward Potts. **History of the University of Pennsylvania: 1740-1940.** 1940

Elliott, Orrin Leslie. **Stanford University: The First Twenty-Five Years.** 1937

Ely, Richard T. **Ground Under Our Feet:** An Autobiography. 1938

Flach, Johannes. **Der Deutsche Professor der Gegenwart** (The German Professor Today). 1886

Hall, G. Stanley. **Life and Confessions of a Psychologist.** 1924

Hardy, G[odfrey] H[arold]. **Bertrand Russell & Trinity:** A College Controversy of the Last War. 1942

Kluge, Alexander. **Die Universitäts-Selbstverwaltung** (University Self-Government). 1958

Kotschnig, Walter M. **Unemployment in the Learned Professions.** 1937

Lazarsfeld, Paul F. and Wagner Thielens, Jr. **The Academic Mind:** Social Scientists in a Time of Crisis. 1958

McLaughlin, Mary Martin. **Intellectual Freedom and Its Limitations in the University of Paris in the Thirteenth and Fourteenth Centuries.** 1977

Metzger, Walter P., editor. **The American Concept of Academic Freedom in Formation:** A Collection of Essays and Reports. 1977

Metzger, Walter P., editor. **The Constitutional Status of Academic Freedom.** 1977

Metzger, Walter P., editor. **The Constitutional Status of Academic Tenure.** 1977

Metzger, Walter P., editor. **Professors on Guard:** The First AAUP Investigations. 1977

Metzger, Walter P., editor. **Reader on the Sociology of the Academic Profession.** 1977

Mims, Edwin. **History of Vanderbilt University.** 1946

Neumann, Franz L., et al. **The Cultural Migration:** The European Scholar in America. 1953

Nitsch, Wolfgang, et al. **Hochschule in der Demokratie** (The University in a Democracy). 1965

Pattison, Mark. **Suggestions on Academical Organization with Especial Reference to Oxford.** 1868

Pollard, Lucille Addison. **Women on College and University Faculties:** A Historical Survey and a Study of Their Present Academic Status. 1977

Proctor, Mortimer R. **The English University Novel.** 1957

Quincy, Josiah. **The History of Harvard University.** Two vols. 1840

Ross, Edward Alsworth. **Seventy Years of It:** An Autobiography. 1936

Rudy, S. Willis. **The College of the City of New York:** A History, 1847-1947. 1949

Slosson, Edwin E. **Great American Universities.** 1910

Smith, Goldwin. **A Plea for the Abolition of Tests in the University of Oxford.** 1864

Willey, Malcolm W. **Depression, Recovery and Higher Education:** A Report by Committee Y of the American Association of University Professors. 1937

Winstanley, D. A. **Early Victorian Cambridge.** 1940

Winstanley, D. A. **Later Victorian Cambridge.** 1947

Winstanley, D. A. **Unreformed Cambridge.** 1935

Yeomans, Henry Aaron. **Abbott Lawrence Lowell:** 1856-1943. 1948